A History of British Motorways

A History of
British Motorways

GEORGE CHARLESWORTH

Thomas Telford Limited
London 1984

Published by Thomas Telford Ltd
Telford House, 26–34 Old Street, London EC1

© George Charlesworth, 1984

The publisher wishes to acknowledge the generous financial support of the Rees Jeffreys Road Fund.

British Library Cataloguing in Publication Data

Charlesworth, George
A history of British motorways.
1. Express highways—Great Britain—
History
I. Title
388.1'22'0941   HE363.G7

ISBN 978-0-7277-0159-6

Preface

This book had its origin in the Road Engineering Board of the Institution of Civil Engineers. I had suggested that it was timely to hold a conference to review progress with motorways over their first 20 years and in accepting this suggestion (the conference took place in February 1980) I was asked if I would be willing to write a 'history' of motorways in Britain. The preparation of the book became possible through the generous financial support of the Rees Jeffreys Road Fund.

In the book, in addition to giving an indication of the nature of engineering and other technical issues arising from the construction of the motorways, I have tried to give an idea of the way attitudes and policies towards the provisions of roads suitable for motor traffic have evolved with particular reference to motorways up to the end of 1981. The account, however, is inevitably incomplete as I have not been able to have access to the policy files of the Ministry of Transport covering the important decisions made about motorways. Nevertheless, there can be little doubt that three former Ministers of Transport, the late Lord Boyd, Lord Boyd-Carpenter and Lord Watkinson, all made significant contributions to the decision to start the motorway programme in the latter half of the 1950s. Engineers in the Ministry were also active in preparing the way for a motorway programme after World War II by drawing up standards of layout and design and by carrying out planning studies. Two Chief Engineers, the late Major H.E. Aldington and J.F. Allan Baker (later Director of Highway Engineering), were prominent in this work and Baker was responsible for overseeing the early motorway programme; he was followed by Sir William Harris who had this responsibility, as Director General of Highways, during the most intensive period of motorway building in Britain.

The County Surveyors' Society has also played an important part in the evolution of the motorways. Their early proposals for a strategic motorway network were largely adopted by the Ministry of Transport and several of their members, in particular Sir James Drake in Lancashire and Colonel S.M. Lovell in the West Riding of Yorkshire, were prominent in getting the motorway programme under way. The partnership between the Ministry and the Counties by the creation of the Road Construction Units (RCU) was a crucial factor in the execution of the programme. Consulting engineers have also contributed in no small measure to the planning, design and supervision of construction of motorways.

A substantial number of contractors have gained experience of motorway construction. It is interesting that with some notable exceptions contracts seem to have been completed reasonably expeditiously and with few labour disputes.

Particularly during the 1970s concern was expressed about the impact of motorways on the environment. To meet objections, changes were made in the procedures followed in deciding on the need for and location of motorways by allowing greater public participation in the decision-making process. These slowed down the building programme; however, other factors leading to a reduced programme were the oil crisis of 1973/74, the change of policy towards investment in public transport in urban areas and the general turn-down in the economy by 1980.

Techniques have been evolved and applied to assessing the forecasts of economic benefits to be derived from building motorways and these forecasts indicate that overall the motorways have provided a sound economic return to the community on the investment in them. However, hardly any attempt appears to have been made to assess the actual economic benefit achieved, e.g. by before-and-after studies. Furthermore, no study appears to have been published on the effects of the changes in the procedures for the approval of particular schemes. Some attempts have been made to assess the environmental impact of individual motorways but this is a complex matter involving subjective judgments.

Motorways have undoubtedly provided a rapid means of travel between many areas in the country and, where they have been adopted, as in Glasgow, within urban areas. They have attracted a high proportion of freight traffic and given relief to many towns and villages by by-passing through-traffic. Accident rates are lower although when an accident does occur it tends to be more serious.

Research and development have contributed to the evolution of standards of layout and design but there is reason to believe that a more extensive research programme put in hand earlier, particularly as regards pavement design, could have paid dividends by providing a better basis for designers. With the construction of the M25 the opportunity still exists for a comprehensive study to be undertaken of many aspects of motorway planning, design, construction and use.

Over the years and despite the continual growth in vehicle ownership and in road traffic, successive Governments seem to have been reluctant to support major strategic road building programmes, with almost the sole exception of the 1,000 mile motorway programme which was launched at the end of the 1950s. Perhaps there is a case for setting up a body outside Government charged with the responsibility for looking ahead beyond the normal life-time of a Government and advising on the transport needs of the country, particularly for highways, and on various alternative policies and programmes for meeting those needs.

Acknowledgments

It is a pleasure to acknowledge the help and advice I have received in the preparation of this book. I have had encouragement throughout from the Trustees of the Rees Jeffreys Road Fund, particularly from Ken Summerfield, Maurice Milne and Stephen Glaister.

I have been helped with literature by Paddy Mongar, Head of Technical Information and Library Services, and her staff at the Transport and Road Research Laboratory; by Doreen Lang and Sheila Bates of the British Road Federation; by library staff at the Institutions of Civil Engineers and Municipal Engineers; and by J. McClean of the Department of the Environment map library.

Statistical information about motorway contracts in England was provided by General Policy Highways Division (Assistant Secretary, Irvine Yass) of the Department of Transport and by the Directors (Transport) in the Regional Offices of the Department (Directors B.F. Edbrooke, J. Tiplady, A.N. Brant, N. Dean, D.D. Gate and J.W. Blows). Data about motorway offences were supplied by H. Edwards of the Statistics Division of the Home Office. Information about motorways in Scotland was provided by J.A.M. Mackenzie (Chief Road Engineer), J.R. Lake and F. Robinson of the Scottish Development Department and by John Cullen of Scott Wilson Kirkpatrick and Co. (Scotland); and I had a considerable amount of help over the M4 in Wales from Dennis Hall (Director of Transport and Highways), of the Welsh Office.

I was greatly helped by information about the County Surveyors' Society from Fred Johnson, who, at the time, was Honorary Secretary to the Society.

The photographs are reproduced by kind permission of the Director of the Transport and Road Research Laboratory. Figure 2.1 is reproduced by kind permission of the Institution of Highway Engineers. Figures 2.2 and 3.1 are reproduced by kind permission of the British Road Tar Association. Figures 7.1, 8.1 and 8.2 are reproduced by kind permission of the Controller of Her Majesty's Stationery Office. Figure 8.3 is reproduced by kind permission of Scott Wilson Kirkpatrick and Partners (Scotland).

Ron Bridle and research staff at the Transport and Road Research Laboratory have readily given me help and advice on many matters. I have also benefitted considerably from comments and information from Allan Baker, John Bastable, David Bayliss, John Cox, Fred Crouch, Sir James Drake, R.A. Fryars, Tony Gaffney, Henry Grace, Ken Gwilliam, Sir William Harris, K.C.W. James, John Leach, Ken Ledson, Colonel S.M. Lovell, Haydn Nicholas, Robert Phillipson, O.T. Williams and John Wootton.

I have a special word of thanks to Eileen Bolton for the care she has taken in deciphering and typing my original manuscript.

Contents

List of figures

List of plates

1
Introduction

Definitions

The *British Standard glossary of highway engineering terms*[1] defines a motorway as being "a limited access dual-carriageway road with grade separation, completely fenced in, normally with hard shoulders. It is for the exclusive use of prescribed classes of motor vehicles." Before 1958 there were no such roads in Britain as it was not until December of that year that the first length of road constructed as a motorway was opened to the public by the Prime Minister the Rt Hon. Harold Macmillan. This was the 8 mile long Preston by-pass, part of the M6 in Lancashire. It was highly appropriate that the first section of motorway should have been opened in Lancashire as the then County Surveyor Sir James Drake, CBE, was a protagonist for motorways in this country.

The idea of motorways in Britain is, however, much older: there is a proposal on record in a Parliamentary Bill in 1906[2] for a road to be constructed between London and Brighton, the specification for which was equivalent to that of the British Standard definition of a motorway. The Bill was not proceeded with and neither was another private member's motorways Bill in 1923.[3] This was promoted by a company, The Northern and Western Motorway, under the Chairmanship of the late Lord Montagu of Beaulieu. It was for a toll motorway 226 miles long to be built in sections between London, starting near Uxbridge, and Liverpool. The first section proposed for construction was 110 miles between Coventry and Salford. Powers for the works were to be sought under legislation concerned with light railways and it was claimed in the draft Bill that the motorway would provide work for unemployed persons, help with the production of materials and plant, and reduce maintenance and improvement costs on existing highways. The sponsors thought that users would be willing to pay tolls sufficient to ensure the prosperity of the undertaking. H.E. Aldington, later to be Chief Engineer in the Ministry of Transport, appears to have been associated with the company. Local authorities along the line of the route supported the proposal but the Commercial Motor Users' Association were opposed. Ministers were clearly unhappy about the proposed use of light railway legislation and even when this was changed in a new draft bill in 1924 the Government were not prepared to give it support, mainly on "business" grounds. The proposal was in part revived in 1929 but again found no support from Government. Also at that time a private member's Bill for a 37 mile toll motorway between London and Brighton was not supported by Government and dropped.

The concept of motorways is of course a great deal more than is revealed by the British Standard definition or indeed by the short length of the Preston by-pass. As Leeming[4] pointed out, motorways are to be seen as constituting a system or network of roads restricted exclusively to motor traffic and designed for the needs of the country as a whole. Their purpose is to provide safe, economical and reasonably fast communication between important centres. The motorway system should supplement the existing road system with connections at reasonable intervals, but otherwise should be entirely separate from it.

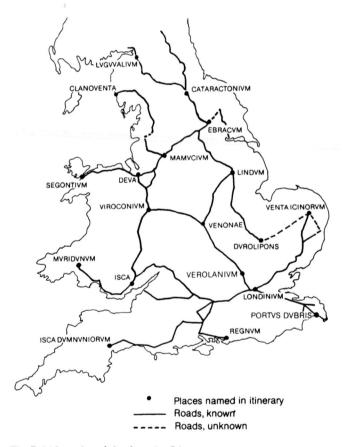

Fig. 1.1 The British section of the Antonine Itinerary

2

Fig. 1.2   The motorway network in Britain, 1980

The idea of a national road system was introduced into Britain by the Romans, who needed a network of roads first for military purposes of conquest and the maintenance of Roman authority and second, as Romanisation spread, for purposes of trade and general communication. It is interesting to compare a map (Fig. 1.1) of main roads in Roman Britain probably around AD 200 derived from the Antonine Itinerary (the road book giving routes throughout the Roman Empire) with the motorway network of 1980 (Fig. 1.2).

Early road policy and the motor vehicle

For several centuries before the invention of the motor vehicle the condition of the roads and responsibility for them had been matters of increasing public concern. A major step forward in administration of roads was taken by the passage of the Local Government Act of 1888 which made County Councils responsible for maintaining all main roads in the country. In 1894 the maintenance and repair of other roads in rural areas became the responsibility of Rural District Councils. There was, however, no administrative machinery for co-ordinating policies and activities of the various authorities in road matters.

With the arrival of the motor vehicle, pressure soon began to develop for better roads to cater for the rapidly growing motor traffic. Motoring organisations were formed and campaigns were launched to try to persuade the Government to act in this matter. Thus the Roads Improvement Association in 1901 put forward proposals for a supreme Road Authority inside or outside Central Government to advise and supervise local authorities in all matters relating to roads and their maintenance, with powers to take action where local authorities failed to do so. It was not until 1909 that legislation was passed for the creation of a central roads authority, the Road Board, which formally came into being in 1910. The story of the Road Board has been told by Rees Jeffreys[5] who was its Secretary from 1910 until shortly before its demise in 1919.

The Road Board

Finance for the Road Board was provided from a Road Improvement Fund created out of taxes on motor vehicles and on petrol. In introducing the Bill setting up the Board, Lloyd George for the Government indicated that

"The Board are given power to act either directly or by themselves constructing new roads, or indirectly, through the existing highway authorities whom the Board will be able to stimulate by means of grants and loans made in consideration of the authorities undertaking either to construct such new roads or effect such improvements in existing roads as will facilitate motor traffic.

"A new road constructed by the Road Board will be primarily a road confined to motor traffic, and the speed limit will not apply on such a road. The Road Board will, however, have power to allow the road to be used for other kinds of traffic if it sees fit and may impose charges for the use of the road on traffic other than motor traffic."

It appears, therefore, that the Board had the resources and the powers necessary to build motorways if it had so wished. However, the Board failed to live up to the expectations of its supporters and in the 9 years of its existence built no new arterial roads or bridges of importance. Rees Jeffreys was of the opinion that the principal cause of the failure of the Board was that the men appointed to it "were not of a type to combine to make a Road Board a success." In particular he blamed the Chairman, a former railway official and appointed by the Treasury, for not having the mentality nor the temperament nor the experience to enable him to build up a new organisation which demanded initiative, imagination and expert knowledge of roads and road traffic. Other contributory causes identified by Rees Jeffreys were: absence of representation of the Board in the House of Commons; the character of Treasury control; and failure to instruct and interest the Associations of Local Authorities, road users, the Press and the general public in the Board's activities.

Formation of the Ministry of Transport

The outbreak of war in 1914 clearly affected the activities of the Road Board, and its programme of road works was inevitably curtailed in the national interest. No doubt this contributed to some of the dissatisfaction with the Board's performance. At any rate with the end of hostilities in 1918 it was clear that an energetic policy was needed to catch up on the arrears of road maintenance and reconstruction, and a Special Fund of about £10.5 million was created by the Government to assist highway authorities to carry out this work.

The Government evidently thought that change was needed in the administration of "ways and communications" and in 1919 an Act was passed creating a new Ministry of Transport by which Act the powers of the Road Board were passed to the new Ministry in September 1919. Roads were a separate department of the new Ministry with a Director General, Sir Henry Maybury, GBE, KCMG, at its head. This post was discontinued after Maybury retired in 1928 and the Roads Department was integrated with the rest of the Ministry under the Permanent Secretary.

References

1. BRITISH STANDARDS INSTITUTION. *British Standard glossary of highway engineering terms.* BS 892. British Standards Institution, London, 1967.
2. GOLDSTEIN A. Discussion of Paper 1. *Proceedings of the conference on 20 years of British motorways.* Institution of Civil Engineers, London, 1980.
3. PUBLIC RECORDS OFFICE. Document Class MT 39. Piece No. 38.
4. LEEMING J.J. What is a motorway? *Highways and bridges,* 1943, **9**, No. 461, 1-3.
5. JEFFREYS R. *The King's highway.* Batchworth Press, London, 1949.

2

Road policies between the wars

The Road Fund

In 1920, changes were made in the taxation of motor fuel and vehicles. The Finance Act repealed customs duties on imported motor spirit and brought into force new excise duties in respect of road vehicles. The Road Act of 1920 provided for the creation of a Road Fund, the revenue of which was derived from the new vehicle excise duties and duties on licences of horse-drawn carriages and drivers' licences. Money standing to the credit of the Road Improvement Fund was transferred to the new Road Fund. In administering the Road Fund the Ministry of Transport was subject to the control of the Treasury.

The existence of the Fund meant that the users of road transport were contributing substantially and directly to the improvement and maintenance of the roads. However, changes began to take place as the size of the Fund grew with the growth in the number of vehicles in use. In 1926 "raids" on the Fund began; the Finance Act that year provided that a substantial proportion of duties on vehicles should be retained in the Exchequer and not paid into the Fund. In 1927 and in 1928 several million pounds were additionally transferred from the Fund to the Exchequer. All this was objectionable to the road interests. The House of Commons did not like the Fund and in the second report of the Select Committee of Public Accounts 1932[1] the Committee noted that

> "under existing arrangements, the House of Commons has no control either over the total commitments which may be incurred by the Fund or over the particular purposes towards which grants may be made from it. Your Committee consider that a system under which it is possible for the Ministry of Transport and the Treasury to incur heavy liabilities in excess of the resources of the Fund without prior authority of Parliament is open to serious objection. For this reason they strongly recommend that in future the annual expenditure from the Road Fund should be submitted for the approval of the House of Commons."

This came about in the Finance Act of 1936, which provided that as from 1 April 1937 moneys for the Road Fund should be provided from sums voted by

Parliament. The Road Fund was finally wound up on 1 April 1956 under the Miscellaneous Financial Provision Act of 1955.

Classification of roads

One of the first tasks undertaken by the new Ministry of Transport was to classify roads. This was done in consultation with the local authorities and the purpose of the classification was to provide a basis for allocating grants from the Road Fund towards the maintenance and improvement of the road system. Classification was based on the relative traffic importance of roads: Class I included the main traffic arteries and trunk routes and Class II other traffic routes of less importance; the two classes together comprised the principal highways in the country, a total in 1921 of some 36,600 miles.

The creation of the Ministry meant that a means existed for the central direction of roads policy in the national interest. The Ministry's authority was further strengthened by the Road Traffic Acts of 1930 and 1934, and especially by the Trunk Roads Act of 1936 when the Minister became the Highway Authority for some 4,500 miles of particularly important routes outside London and county boroughs and large burghs. Legislation passed in the Local Government Act 1929 gave greater powers to counties in England and Wales: all main roads, all roads in rural districts and all classified roads in urban districts and boroughs other than county boroughs became "county roads"; the rural districts ceased to be highway authorities although they could apply to counties to have certain responsibilities, notably maintenance, to be delegated to them. The Local Government Scotland Act 1929 made County Councils the sole highway authorities in counties and also the highway authority for classified roads in small burghs. The counties could delegate certain of their functions as in England and Wales.

Grants for roads

On its formation, the Ministry of Transport continued the programme of grants for road works put in hand at the end of World War I to repair the damage and deterioration suffered by the roads of the country during the war. Road improvements were becoming increasingly necessary to keep pace with the growth of traffic. At the same time the Government was faced with serious problems of unemployment, and road works were seen in those days as a means of providing unemployment relief. Programmes were initiated by the Ministry of Transport between 1920 and 1925 and again in 1929/30 with this object in view. At this time the Minister was not the highway authority for trunk roads; this came later in Trunk Road Acts.

As from April 1921 grants were made towards the approved cost of maintenance of Class I and Class II roads and bridges, originally at the rates of 50% for Class I and 25% for Class II; these rates were increased to 60% and 50% respectively in 1929. For road improvements, the normal rate of grant was the same as for maintenance, but in many cases contributions from the Road Fund were on a higher scale, e.g. where roads were up-graded as a result of improvement. In addition funds were contributed towards the cost of construction of new roads and works which were undertaken sooner than normally for the relief of unemployment.

Unemployment schemes in the 1929/30 programme[2] covered the following.

(1) Sections of trunk road were selected in collaboration with the County Councils concerned. Grants were offered at a rate of 75% and upwards depending on the financial position of the authority in relation to the volume of work to be undertaken. In suitable cases the grant was offered subject to conditions as to the recruitment of labour, sometimes by transfer from depressed areas and adjacent areas, or by restriction of employment to men with dependants.

(2) County Councils and other councils were invited to submit comprehensive programmes for the improvement of classified roads and bridges and the construction of new roads and bridges which could be carried out during 5 years.

(3) Grants in excess of normal rate were offered in cases where the local authority was prepared to accept special conditions as to recruitment of labour; an additional 15% to the normal grant was offered where the local authority was prepared to undertake that a percentage of the men employed upon the works would be drawn from the depressed areas. In depressed and adjacent areas the requirement was that all labour should be taken from Employment Exchanges and that preference should be given to men with dependants.

(4) It was made a condition of grants towards the cost of works expedited for the relief of unemployment that, as far as practicable, plant and machinery should be of UK manufacture and all materials of UK origin and that otherwise products of the Empire should be used wherever possible.

The economic crisis which occurred shortly after this programme was initiated resulted in a severe cut-back in resources allocated to it and although a substantial number of schemes was completed, e.g. some 500 miles of by-pass had been built by 1935, less than half the work contemplated initially was completed.

Royal Commission on Transport

It is of interest to record the views of the Royal Commission on Transport[3] in 1931 on the construction of new roads. Based on traffic censuses published by the Ministry of Transport they concluded that the highway system as a whole was not congested and that traffic congestion existed in practice only in towns and other urban areas. They noted that a considerable mileage of new arterial roads had been constructed and remarked

"we do not propose—nor do we wish—to criticise those which have already been constructed or are in course of construction. . . . But looking at the network of highways which spreads over the country, and considering the mileage of new construction which has been completed during the last ten years and that which is either now in hand or about to be commenced, we have come to the conclusion that we cannot support any scheme which would involve the expenditure of very large additional sums of public money on the provision of new arterial roads.

"A suggestion in this sense was made to us by Mr Rees Jeffreys who proposed that a number of new roads for long-distance motor traffic should be constructed at the entire cost of the Road Fund. . . . We feel that new roads of this type are not required."

The Commission did, however, consider that the provision of new by-pass roads was very desirable and "in many cases absolutely essential". These apart, their view was that the best way to proceed was by the improvement of existing roads.

The Commission's views were even more emphatic on the question of motorways, particularly if built as toll roads. They commented

"We are strongly opposed to any suggestion of this nature . . . and we are not prepared to support any proposal which would have the effect of creating new tolls or prolonging the life of existing tolls. But apart from this objection in principle and apart, too, from the unsightly features which these roads would produce—for they would have to be carried over existing highways by means of viaducts—we see practical objections. Roads of this type if constructed, would be either financially successful or unsuccessful. If the former, there would be a danger in the possibility of public highways in the vicinity being neglected. A highway authority might be tempted to rely unduly on the capacity of the 'motorway' to carry traffic and to neglect to maintain the public highways in a proper condition. This would inflict inconvenience and even hardship on those road users who were unwilling—or could not afford—to use the toll road. If, on the other hand, one of these roads was financially unsuccessful we feel that there would be a considerable risk of its abandonment by the owners and of pressure being subsequently brought to bear on the highway authority to take over the road."

The financial climate and views of this kind meant that construction of new roads was held back in the early 1930s. By the middle of the decade the economy was reviving and the Ministry of Transport began to prepare a 5 year programme covering the period 1935/40. Highway authorities were invited to put forward proposals for inclusion in this programme and it was during this period that pressures mounted for the construction of a national system of motorways.

Restriction of Ribbon Development Act

The authority of the Ministry of Transport had been steadily increasing since its formation, e.g. through the London Traffic Act 1924, the Road Traffic Acts of 1930 and 1934 and the Trunk Road Act of 1936, and the responsibility and opportunity for the Ministry to formulate and implement national policies for roads and road traffic were considerably greater. One important step in this direction was afforded by the Restriction of Ribbon Development Act 1935[4] which, among other things, included a section on standard widths for roads. In a circular letter to local authorities in March 1936, the Permanent Secretary to the Ministry of Transport remarked that the Act for the first time enabled roads of the country to be planned on principles of uniformity related to the present and future requirements of traffic. The Act gave powers of control over land ultimately required for a proposed new road and over new means of access. Councils were told to look well ahead when considering for submission to the Minister the appropriate standard widths for their roads and it was suggested that the rate of increase of traffic up to the traffic census of 1935 would serve as a useful indication in estimating future requirements.

The layout of roads in relation to standard widths was considered by a committee drawn from Ministry staff, the County Surveyors' Society and the Institution of Municipal and County Engineers. Based on this committee's recommendations, the Minister concluded as follows.

(1) The unit width of each traffic lane should be 10 ft. For two-lane carriageways carrying a large proportion of heavy vehicles the width should be 11 ft.
(2) Dual carriageways were desirable where traffic in the peak hours was expected to reach 400 vehicles/h. Where more than two lanes were necessary, dual carriageways were to be preferred to widening single carriageways. Dual carriageways were often justified solely on grounds of public safety.
(3) The standard widths adopted should provide for future widenings of the carriageways with cycle tracks and footpaths as might be necessary. For this purpose there should be ample central reservations, margins and verges. Dual carriageways should be separated by a central reservation of the maximum width consistent with the layout of the road.

A list of minimum standard widths was drawn up ranging from 60 ft for single carriageways not exceeding 30 ft, with footpaths, to 140 ft for dual (more than two-lane) carriageways with footpaths, cycle tracks and wide verges. It is perhaps significant that, whereas prior to the 1935 Act trunk road improvement schemes commonly involved widening 30 ft carriageways, the Report on the Road Fund for 1935/36 included several dual carriageway schemes, e.g. Crawley by-pass, Winchester by-pass, A59 Liverpool–Preston.

The attention of highway authorities was drawn to the requirement under the Act to consult with any planning authorities concerned with the exercise of their powers in relation to planning schemes. The Permanent Secretary pointed out that it was essential that planning authorities should be informed as quickly as possible of standard widths proposed to be adopted for roads in the area covered by the planning scheme as this could have a considerable bearing on the planning of lands adjacent to the roads.

This Act enabled highway authorities with the approval of the Minister of

Transport to control development along main highways and by 1939 the Act applied to some 72,000 miles of road including Class I and Class II roads.

Motorway developments abroad

Early in the century, the idea of providing roads exclusively for the use of motor vehicles began to be advanced. Mention has been made earlier of the private members' Bills in 1906 and 1923/24 in Britain. Similar moves were taking place in Europe and in the USA[5]. The first road constructed solely for the use of motor vehicles appears to have been built in 1914 in the USA on Long Island. This road was some 65 km long with a single carriageway 10 m wide with limited access. In Germany in 1909 a society was formed for the study of roads and motor vehicles and which opened an experimental road to the west of Berlin in 1921. The road was 9.8 km long with dual 6 m wide carriageways having a central reservation of 1.50 m and no access except at the ends.

Italian autostrade

The most significant steps at about this time occurred in Italy. An engineer, Piero Puricelli, founded a company *Strade e Cave* (Roads and Tunnels)[6] for the promotion of roads exclusively for the use of motor vehicles; the company was later named *Autostrade*. A scheme originated by the company was supported by the Italian Touring Club and received official approval in 1923. The scheme envisaged roads reserved exclusively for motor vehicles, linking important centres and other places of special interest. The route, while being as direct as possible, was to avoid built-up areas and consist of long straight sections connected by curves of large radius. Single carriageways were to be provided with at least three traffic lanes and design was to be such as to permit motor vehicles to travel safely at high speed (100 km/h). No crossings on the level were to be permitted and traffic was subject to police control. At suitable points facilities for fuel, repairs etc. were to be provided.

Construction began on the first roads in the scheme in 1924 in the neighbourhood of Milan (Milan-Varese) and some 80 km of road were opened to traffic in 1925. Branch roads connecting this road with Lakes Como and Maggiore followed, creating in all some 130 km of the so-called Milan–Italian lakes route. In subsequent years seven other motorways were constructed: Bergamo–Milan in 1927 (48 km); Naples–Pompeii in 1929 (21 km); Brescia–Bergamo in 1931 (45 km); Florence–coast in 1932 (opening section 80 km); Turin–Milan in 1932 (130 km); Venice–Padua in 1933 (25 km); and Genoa–Serravalle in 1935 (50 km). All but one of these roads were constructed by State-subsidised companies with reversion to the state after a definite period. By 1939 several of the roads were controlled by the *Azienda Autonoma Statale della Strada* (the State Highway Administration).

German Autobahnen

The concept of the Italian *autostrada* had an influence on ideas for roads adapted to the needs of motor traffic, but a much more important impact on ideas for motorways in Britain developed from German experience in the 1930s. One of the early actions taken in 1933 by the Nazi Government[7] was to prepare a plan to construct a network of modern motorways "to meet the needs of traffic for several decades to come". The roads were to have dual carriageways each 7.5 m in width with a central reservation 3.5 to 5 m wide planted with hedges to reduce dazzle. Level crossings with other roads were to be avoided and speeds of well over 100 km/h were contemplated. Construction was to make use of locally available

Fig. 2.1 Institution of Highway Engineers proposed system of motorways, May 1936 (copyright Institution of Highway Engineers)

material as far as possible. The initial plan was to build some 5,000 km of these motorways over a 5 year period. As in Britain, it was claimed that these road works gave benefits through the reduction of unemployment; it was estimated that it would take 200 men 1 year to construct 1 km of road. The previous lack of a central authority over road building was to be overcome by the appointment of an Inspector-General of German Road Construction with duties of deciding the location of the new motorways and superintending their construction. By the outbreak of World War II in September 1939 some 3,200 km of motorway were in use, with 2,000 km under construction and a further 3,300 km planned[5].

In a report of an inspection of the German motorway system in 1946[8] the following comments are made on the purpose of these roads.

"It has been stated by the German authorities that the network of motor roads was designed on an industrial and peacetime traffic basis. This has often been questioned abroad where it was suggested that the roads had been built primarily for military purposes. Although a high-speed road system would have obvious uses in wartime it would clearly be of the greatest benefit in speeding up the general life of the country in peacetime and there is no real evidence to show whether military needs were seriously considered or not. If the roads had been built for military purposes it is difficult to understand why some quite important links in the system were left unfinished and why some of the roads appeared to have been almost unused during the war. It is probable that the shortage of petrol played an even more serious part in curtailing German long-distance road traffic than it did in Britain."

Motorways in the USA

In parallel with the developments in Italy and Germany in the 1920s and 1930s a number of roads of motorway type were being built in the USA, for instance the systems of parkways (roads reserved exclusively for motor cars) in and around New York City. One of the most significant motorway developments was the Pennsylvania Turnpike, a toll motorway which was opened to traffic in 1940. However, at the time, these developments in the USA seemed to have less impact on ideas about motorways in Britain than those in Europe, particularly Germany.

Proposals for motorways in Britain

From the mid 1930s pressure for the construction of a system of motorways in Britain mounted. In 1936 the Institution of Highway Engineers[9] put forward proposals for a system of motorways consisting of 51 lengths of road totalling about 2,800 miles (see Fig. 2.1). In November 1936 the Rt Hon. Leslie Hore-Belisha, then Minister of Transport, in reply to a Parliamentary Question about motorways said [10]"I have often given consideration to this matter but in a thickly populated and thickly roaded country such as ours, I am not prepared to recommend embarking on the construction of an entirely new road system. I think our task is to improve the system we now have."

In 1937 the AA and RAC were invited by the German Government to form a party to inspect the German motorways and as a result these motoring organisations together with the British Road Federation arranged for a delegation of 57 members of both Houses of Parliament, 88 County Surveyors and members of County Councils, 18 members of professional societies associated with roads and road transport, and 61 members of organisations representing road users, vehicle manufacturers, road transport and road construction. It was presumably by deliberate policy of the Ministry of Transport that no one from that Ministry took part in the visit although the Minister was interested to see the conclusions reached by the delegation.

The main purpose of the visit was to see at first hand what the German motorway system was like and to assess what relevance motorways might have in Britain in relieving "the incapacity of British roads to accommodate efficiently and safely the traffic now existing and the rapidity with which this traffic continues to increase."

The unanimous conclusions reached by the delegation[11] concerning main highways in Britain were that the need was urgent for certain special highways to be constructed and designed for exclusive use by motor vehicles. These motorways should be planned on a national basis with careful regard to cost, preservation of amenities and the future growth of traffic.

The delegation considered that works of this character, designed to definite standards and with appropriate treatment, sited on lines away from centres of population, would best conserve the amenities of the countryside. They thought such an augmented road system would improve traffic conditions upon existing highways and so relieve congestion as to reduce appreciably the toll of road accidents.

The delegation's visit and report was followed in 1938 by a visit to Germany by the Minister of Transport, the Rt Hon. Leslie Burgin. As a result of his visit he recommended that, as an experiment, approval should be given to a scheme put forward by Lancashire County Council for some 60 miles of a north–south toll-free motorway through the county between Carnforth and Warrington. This was not proceeded with at the time because money was not available for it.

County Surveyors' Society's plan

In October 1937 the County Surveyors' Society held a meeting to consider the views of their members who had formed part of the German Road Delegation. They concluded

"that the Society, having considered the views of the members who formed part of the German Roads Delegation, are of opinion that an adequate study of traffic movement information would indicate that a certain number of entirely new roads is a necessity and further that the number of such new roads would not be large.

"that completely new through roads with adequate connections to existing centres of population may, in the opinion of the Society, prove more economical in construction

Fig. 2.2   County Surveyors' Society proposed national motorway plan, 1938 (copyright British Road Tar Association)

and use than the widening of existing main arteries to the same standard, and that the segregation of motor vehicle traffic from all other forms of traffic would tend towards a substantial reduction in the number of road accidents; further that the construction of motorways for motor vehicle traffic would be substantially cheaper than their construction for all forms of traffic.

"that the new motorways should be constructed as complete units and not in short lengths.

"that the new motorways together with the other arteries of trunk road value should form a co-ordinated system for through traffic and that the whole of the construction and improvement work thereon should be controlled by a time programme.

"that existing methods of administration should be improved in the direction of speedier execution of works and the elimination of irritating delays.

"that, in the Society's opinion, new roads and motorways carefully designed in relation to the landscape and its preservation, whilst not causing injury to amenities are likely in time even to improve them. On the other hand the widening of existing roads, with the attendant demolition of property will in many cases offend against amenities."

Following upon this, the Society set up a committee to prepare a plan for a national system of motorways for the whole country, and in May 1938 the

Society[12] came forward with a national plan for a less ambitious motorway system than that which the Institution of Highway Engineers had suggested in 1936.

The plan, which is shown in Fig. 2.2, was for 1,000 miles of motorway linking the main industrial centres in the country. Although this plan was discussed with the Parliamentary Roads Group and submitted to the Minister of Transport it did not at that time find favour with the Minister. The official attitude towards motorways in Britain was no doubt contained in the address[13] by the Chief Engineer in the Ministry, the late F.C. (later Sir Frederick) Cook, to the British Association at Cambridge in 1938 in which he said

> "The opinion is frequently expressed that the solution of the road problem lies in the provision of motorways on the lines of the German *Autobahnen*. The extent to which motorways would relieve traffic on existing routes and their effect on accident causation is dependent upon their mileage in relation to the highway system as a whole. In a densely roaded country such as ours, conditions would not permit the construction of a system of motorways which would be more than a small fraction of our 180,000 miles of public highways. Investigation on certain important routes has shown that through traffic, apart from that which is primarily local in character, varies from 17 to 25 per cent of the whole. It may therefore be expected that at least three-fourths of the traffic on those routes which motorways are designed to supplement would continue to use the existing roads including public service vehicles (excepting perhaps long distance motor coaches) and all local traffic whether private or commercial. From a technical aspect the use of what is in reality the permanent way at one and the same time by motor and horse-drawn vehicles, cyclists and pedestrians is quite unsound; but the problem is not one of engineering only and the construction of motorways on the scale which is sometimes urged involves economic and other factors which must be considered not in relation to any one section of the community but to the country as a whole."

Cook clearly recognised the need for factual information on which to base road plans and in his paper to the British Association he stated that a survey of the 4,500 miles of trunk road for which the Minister was then the highway authority was in hand to ascertain the extent to which existing trunk roads could be widened to the desired dimensions and the location of diversions where a new alignment was desirable. Standard widths and forms of layout based on potential traffic requirements were being determined to which future construction or improvement would conform.

The Alness Committee

In 1939 a report by the Select Committee of the House of Lords on the Prevention of Road Accidents[14] was published. The Committee under the chairmanship of Lord Alness was appointed "to consider what steps should be taken to reduce the number of casualties on the roads." In commenting on the Ministry of Transport, the Committee recorded that they were not impressed by the evidence which they heard from its representatives regarding the organisation and working of the Department so far as road accidents and road construction were concerned. The Committee formed an impression that there was in these matters "a lack of vision, of initiative and of driving force in the Department". They went on to note, however, that the Ministry often had difficulties over securing agreement of a large number of local authorities to projected road improvements.

The Committee considered that definite recommendations about new roads were outside their terms of reference but pointed out that "the more new roads on modern lines which are constructed, the more congestion will be relieved and the number of accidents it is hoped will diminish". They thought that the road system was inadequate and out of date. Only 280 miles of important new roads had been built in the previous 7 years and since the Trunk Road Act of 1936 less work had been done on trunk roads than during the preceding 5 years; but the Ministry hoped to have a 20 year programme worked out by the end of 1938.

The Committee, after discussing some of the problems of introducing a German-type motorway system in Britain, were of the opinion that the construction of such roads was not impossible and they did not wish to discourage the building of motorways. What they suggested was that an experimental motorway should first be built (London–Birmingham was a possibility) and that the effect of that experimental motorway on road safety and on road transport generally throughout the whole area served should be the subject of careful statistical and scientific examination. They also proposed that a study should be made of road construction machinery in use abroad to see if costs of constructing motorways in Britain could be reduced by the use of the latest methods.

Any action on the Alness report or other recommendations and proposals for road improvements was brought to a halt by the outbreak of war in September 1939.

References

1. SELECT COMMITTEE OF PUBLIC ACCOUNTS. *Second report of the Select Committee.* House of Commons report no. 42. HMSO, London, 1932.
2. HMSO. *Report on the Road Fund 1929–30.* HMSO, London, 1930.
3. ROYAL COMMISSION ON TRANSPORT *The co-ordination and development of transport, final report.* HMSO, London, 1931.
4. MINISTRY OF TRANSPORT. *Restriction of Ribbon Development Act 1935 Section I—Standard widths for roads.* Circular 454 (Roads). Ministry of Transport, London, 1936.
5. BONNET A.G. Outline of the history of motorways throughout the world, in Europe and in France. *Rev. Gen. des Routes et des Aerodromes,* 1959.
6. BOLIS B. The Italian motor roads from 1924 to 1939. *Strade,* 1939, **21**, No. 11, 575–584; No. 12, 614–623.
7. SEIDEL H. The German State motor roads. *Quarry,* 1934, **39**, No. 450, 119–120.
8. ROAD RESEARCH LABORATORY. *German motor roads 1946.* Road research technical paper no. 8, DSIR, RRL. HMSO, London, 1948.

9. INSTITUTION OF HIGHWAY ENGINEERS. *The post war development of highways,* appendix A. Institution of Highway Engineers, London, 1943.
10. BAKER J.F.A. The London–Birmingham motorway. The general motorway plan. *Proc. Instn Civ. Engrs,* 1960, **15**, 317–332.
11. GERMAN ROADS DELEGATION. *Report upon the visit and its conclusions.* German Roads Delegation, London, 1938.
12. COUNTY SURVEYORS' SOCIETY. *A scheme for motorways.* County Surveyors' Society, London, 1938.
13. COOK F.C. *Road development in Great Britain.* British Association, Cambridge, 1938.
14. SELECT COMMITTEE OF THE HOUSE OF LORDS. *Report on the prevention of road accidents.* HMSO, London, 1939.

3

1939–1950: the years of restrictions

Diversion of resources

The outbreak of war in 1939 meant that a radical appraisal of road programmes was necessary. Those road works which were considered to have a strategic value or which were in an advanced state of completion were allowed to continue and a few others were taken to the stage where they could be safely left. Civil engineering resources had to be deployed in many other ways, for instance in the massive programme of airfield construction, but some new road works were required to provide access to military establishments and war factories, and to provide routes and bridges of adequate capacity and strength required for operational purposes, notably for access to ports to be used for the invasion of Europe. One important result of the wartime airfield construction programme in Britain and work on temporary landing grounds and roads in campaigns overseas was the wider understanding which engineers developed of soil mechanics and of the machinery which could be used when road building started again in peace time.

Planning in war-time

Although prosecution of the war was of first importance some thought was also being given throughout the war to the future. In 1942 the Institution of Civil Engineers[1] recommended that the plan put forward in 1938 by the County Surveyors' Society for 1,000 miles of motorway should be implemented when hostilities ceased. A year later the Institution of Municipal and County Engineers[2], in a memorandum to the Minister of Works and Planning, pointed out that motorways were one of the most important elements in national and regional planning.

Early in 1943 the Institution of Highway Engineers[3], which in 1936 had put forward a plan for 2,800 miles of motorway, prepared a report on post-war highways. The Institution considered that little real progress had been made towards a solution of the highway problem in Britain. They drew attention to comments in the report of the Committee on Land Utilization in Rural Areas[4] issued in 1942 which advocated the provision of roads for fast traffic preferably by means of a number of new trunk roads rather than by the piecemeal widening of existing roads. The Institution put forward the main requirements of a replanned road system as

(1) a skeleton network of high-speed roads to accommodate long distance mechanical transport
(2) a secondary system of mixed traffic roads connecting neighbouring industrial areas and serving as feeder roads to the main high-speed routes and as link roads connecting such routes and existing trunk roads on the outer ring of centres of industry and population
(3) local parkways accommodating all classes of road users from industrial areas to recreational centres
(4) minor roads to serve mainly local requirements.

It was considered that (1) should be motorways. The Institution's report included some suggestions concerning the layout and design of motorways, the facilities such as refreshment rooms and petrol supplies required by travellers, and facilities required by highway departments, for example for maintenance.

The Institution was in no doubt that the planning of motorways should be done by a national planning authority in consultation with the various interests to whom the construction and maintenance of an efficient road system were of vital importance. They considered that there was insufficient collaboration between the multiplicity of highway authorities and that uniformity could only be obtained by administration on a national basis. Motorways should be administered by the State and other roads by local authorities.

Perhaps the pressures coming from these various bodies were having effect in the Ministry of War Transport since in May 1943 P.J. Noel-Baker, the joint Parliamentary Secretary, announced that while the Government did not think there was sufficient justification for a widespread system of motorways, they were satisfied that "it will be expedient and economical to construct suitable lengths of road of this type where engineering and traffic considerations make this course preferable to the extensive remodelling of existing roads in an attempt to make them more suitable and safer for mixed traffic." In this the Government would be guided by the development of the transport system as a whole. Noel-Baker said there was a strong case for motorways to enable traffic to by-pass built-up areas. He stated that proposals to give the necessary legislation for this would be sought from Parliament in due course. Drafting a Bill for this purpose started in 1945 but the Bill did not finally get on to the statute books until 1949.

Proposals by the British Road Federation

In 1944 the British Road Federation[5] published a report *Roads and road transport* which had been prepared by its Post-war Reconstruction Committee. The Federation endorsed the proposals for the construction of a limited number of new motorways such as those formulated by the County Surveyors' Society in 1938 and urged that the Government should immediately prepare plans and make the necessary arrangements for the acquisition of land so that work could proceed as soon as conditions permitted. They suggested that in deciding on the location of new roads regard should be had to the needs of industry and agriculture and to the necessity of linking the road system with other transport modes. The requirements of military security and of providing access from town to country for leisure should also be considered. The Federation was of the opinion that a strong case existed on purely economic grounds for improving the road system, particularly by constructing motorways. There would be an immediate return from reduced transport and motoring costs through savings in time, fuel and tyres. The Federation also noted that there had been a very great development of constructional work in connection with airfields and that machinery and labour would be available to be transferred at short notice to the modernisation of the road system.

In the Federation's view, the ultimate control of road policy lay with Government but they thought that the detailed administration and operation of the road system might be organised on a regional basis, with authority at a regional level to co-ordinate and direct the work of the local authorities subject to over-riding control by Central Government. They suggested that there was a considerable body of opinion in favour of the establishment of a National Road Board to advise the Government on road policy.

In an Appendix to the Federation's report, the late Sir Charles Bressey, CB, a former Chief Engineer of the Roads Department of the Ministry of Transport, remarked that the attitude toward motorways adopted up to that time by British highway authorities had been marked by hesitation and inaction which he thought was due, in part at least, to an impression that motorways were usually associated with tolls. (Bressey possibly had in mind examples in Italy and the USA and his involvement with the Northern and Western motorway project in 1923/24 at the Ministry of Transport; his view was that tolls were not acceptable in Britain.) He pointed out that up to that time no motorways had been built in Britain and that highway authorities had put their trust in the widening and realignment of existing roads, "most of them dating from centuries when pack-horses and lumbering state-wagons were the characteristic means of travel". He thought it remarkable that any measure of success should have followed this policy; there had been no fundamental change in road engineering that in any way corresponded to the complete transformation of vehicle design.

Some technical aspects of motorways

In June 1945, just after the end of hostilities in Europe, several professional bodies arranged a joint meeting at the Institution of Civil Engineers on the post-war development of road motor transport. Three papers[6] were presented, one on roads, one on vehicle design and construction, and one on traffic.

The paper on roads was given by the late Major H.E. Aldington, CB, then Chief Engineer in the Ministry of War Transport; he devoted most of it to the design of motorways. He thought that existing roads could never be adapted to be entirely satisfactory and he set out a number of main principles to be followed as far as possible in the design of new roads for through traffic, principles which he considered could be followed more readily in the case of motorways than all-purpose roads. These principles were

(1)   the fullest practicable measure of segregation of the various classes of road users
(2)   dual carriageways for up and down traffic
(3)   the elimination of vehicular traffic cuts at road intersections
(4)   the elimination of the crossing of vehicular, pedestrian and cycle traffic on the same level
(5)   the elimination of standing traffic
(6)   the gradual feeding-in of one traffic stream to another at points where two flows join, in order to reduce longitudinal traffic disturbances
(7)   an accurate alignment with regular longitudinal curves eased into the tangents by transition curves
(8)   curves suitably superelevated for the designed speed
(9)   careful and regular grading with vertical curves to give proper sight lines
(10) a simple system of direction and warning signs
(11) a uniform running surface
(12) the provision of lay-bys every few miles to permit vehicles to stand off the carriageway
(13) strict limitation of frontage access.

He also stated that new roads to meet the needs of a particular area should be considered in relation to the highway system as a whole and that in deciding where roads were needed and of what traffic capacity a comprehensive traffic survey should be made.

Some of his proposals for standards of design for motorways are given in appendix 3.1.

Aldington pointed out that in the economic interest of the country it was necessary to be able to show "complete justification" for expenditure on new roads and that decisions must be based on "a realistic appreciation of the facts". He added, however, that a constructional programme with some assurance of continuity of work would justify the acquisition of the most up-to-date plant and that the demand for plant would help British manufacturers.

There was, perhaps surprisingly, little of relevance to motorways in the second paper at this meeting dealing with vehicle design and construction; heavy goods vehicles were still limited to a speed of 20 mile/h. However, in the third paper, on traffic, J.S. Nicholl, CBE, remarked "There are those who seem to imagine that a network of motorways will solve all our traffic problems. Nothing could be more misleading. Motorways clearly can only cater for a limited, if an important, portion of the use, even of motor vehicles." Nicholl seemed to believe that to achieve maximum flow on a motorway speeds would have to be low, somewhere between 18 and 25 mile/h, and consequently high speeds would involve high costs as more lanes would be required to accommodate the same volume of traffic. He also believed that high speeds, when maintained over a period of time, involved a greater strain on man and machine. He suggested that "even on motorways a maximum speed of 50 or 55 miles/h might prove to be for the ultimate good of the majority." Speculation of this kind revealed a need for factual information about actual traffic and driving behaviour on motorways under British conditions, but it was going to be about 14 years before a motorway was built in Britain on which to obtain such information.

Post-war policies

With the end of hostilities in 1945 the various ideas and proposals made during the war were hoped to be given more definite form and the new Labour Government was not long in issuing its policy for highways, although in the event this turned out to be more a pious hope that real achievement. The Minister of Transport, the Rt Hon. Alfred Barnes, made a statement in the House of Commons on 6 May 1946 in which he said that in view of the various competing claims on labour and other resources the road plan for the next few years would have to be very flexible but that special attention would be directed to: the promotion of road safety; the provision of improved access to ports, markets and areas where developing industries were located; better through connections; improvements in both urban and country roads; reconstruction and development of devastated areas; improved access to and return from work; greater facilities for agriculture; and reduction of traffic congestion. A 10 year programme was contemplated in three stages. In the first 2 years arrears of maintenance would be overtaken, damage by enemy action or by military vehicles repaired and improvements carried out on sections shown by accident records to be specially dangerous. Certain road schemes interrupted by the war would be resumed and construction begun on works of high importance to national development, e.g. the Severn Bridge and the Jarrow Tunnel. In the next 3 years safety and maintenance work would continue and new construction would include a limited number of motorways and other improvements in development areas. The final 5 years would see a comprehensive improvement on the principal national routes. Where reconstruction to modern standards was impracticable owing to existing frontage development, certain of these roads would be supplemented by new roads reserved for motor traffic. The plan included the reconstruction of an orbital road round London. It was intended that preparatory work should be undertaken to permit other major schemes to be put in hand as soon as resources permitted. The proposals are shown in Fig. 3.1.

As part of this policy a motorways section was set up in the Chief Engineer's Department (Chief Engineer, H.E. Aldington) in the Ministry Headquarters under J.F.A. Baker (later to become Director of Highway Engineering). This section was charged with looking into plans and standards for motorways and Baker was a member of the team, mentioned in chapter 2, which inspected the German *Autobahnen* in 1946. However, work on the section was halted by the economic

Fig. 3.1 Future pattern of principal national routes, 1946 (from Milne & Westhorpe, Proc. Inst. Road Tar Conf. London, 1971) (copyright British Road Tar Association)

situation in 1946/47 and Baker was sent to be Divisional Road Engineer in Wales. During his time there, he accompanied the Minister on a tour of the German *Autobahnen* in 1950. He returned to Ministry Headquarters a few years later as Chief Engineer and was eventually responsible in that capacity for overseeing the planning, design and construction of the early motorways until his retirement in 1965. On his retirement the Rt Hon. Tom Fraser, then Minister of Transport, wrote "the creation of our motorway system in particular will always be associated with your period of office", and 2 years later the Worshipful Company of Carmen awarded Baker their Viva Shield and Gold Medal inscribed "For pioneering the British motorway system".

The Trunk Roads Act 1946

As part of a policy of increased central control of main roads, the responsibility of the Ministry of Transport for roads of through traffic importance was increased by the passage of the Trunk Roads Act 1946. This Act increased the mileage of roads for which the Ministry was the highway authority from the 3,685 miles of the Trunk Roads Act 1936 to 8,190 miles—in England 5,308 miles, in Wales 934 miles and in Scotland 1,948 miles. The new Act required the Minister to keep the national system of through routes under review and gave the Minister powers to extend or otherwise improve the system as circumstances might demand, for example as required by the needs of agriculture, changes in the location of industry and the redistribution of the population. The Act also included provisions for overcoming certain obstacles to the application of modern developments in highway construction, e.g. the Minister could henceforth depart from the conventional layout of dual carriageways and construct the two carriageways on different alignments, leaving between them land not forming part of the highway. There were also powers relating to junctions of trunk roads with side roads, including the stopping-up of junctions, powers to transfer privately owned bridges on trunk roads to the Minister, and powers to construct bridges or tunnels carrying trunk roads across navigable waterways. The Minister's powers under the two Trunk Roads Acts now became exercisable in county boroughs and large burghs and in the County (but not the City) of London.

Surveys

Following the Minister's statement in the House of Commons in 1946, the Ministry began to carry out preliminary survey and road location work on trunk roads and principal national routes. Air survey methods were brought into use early in this work (in 1947/48 the Director-General of the Ordnance Survey completed two such surveys covering 80 miles of principal routes) and by 1949/50 preliminary surveys were completed for almost the whole of the trunk road system, and detailed surveys either from the air or on the ground of some 5,000 miles had been completed.

Economic issues

These early post-war years were remarkable for the amount of planning which took place affecting the whole community. The Central Government at that time was committed to taking an active role in planning the economy, particularly through the nationalisation of primary industries and transport. Local government was having to tackle problems resulting from the war, such as rebuilding bomb-damaged cities and meeting the demand for housing. Private industry was having to change from a war-time to a peace-time economy still subject to many controls. Selection from among the many plans put forward for investment was not easy and almost certainly the necessary data and techniques for appraising proposals on economic grounds did not exist or were at an early stage of development. In the case of roads, C.T. Brunner, CBE[7], in 1946 attempted to determine the extent to which increased expenditure on the improvement of the road system would be economically justified. Taking into account possible savings in time, fuel, tyres, repairs to vehicles and accidents (insurance) which might be expected from modernisation of the road system, and making an estimate of the cost of a minimum programme of road modernisation (including 1,000 miles of motorway), he concluded that the cost of such a programme, spread over 10 years would be well within the expected economies in vehicle operating costs, even on the low basis of 1946 volumes of traffic. Brunner later, in 1949[8], put forward a case, argued on these lines, for the development of the road system of South Wales.

In 1948 a report[9] by a joint committee of the British Road Federation, the Institution of Highway Engineers and the Society of Motor Manufacturers and Traders on the *Economics of motorways* was presented to the Minister of Transport. In this report the committee included an estimate of the savings to commercial traffic travelling between London and Coventry which might accrue from use of motorway instead of the A5 and A45 roads, and assessed the return on constructing the motorway in benefits to commercial traffic alone to be 9.7%. The committee concluded that motorways should rank with other capital projects contemplated in the next few years and added that the construction of an adequate system of motorways would provide the greatest return to be obtained from the expenditure of national effort and resources.

The Government seems to have been unmoved by these analyses. Indeed, the road programme of 1948/49 suffered heavily from the restriction of capital investment. The Road Fund report for that year recorded that over the whole country the labour force of 95,000 engaged on highways was reduced in the course of the year by some 20,000. Major improvements were confined to those needed to maintain essential communications or to remedy dangerous situations and to those assisting exports or reducing imports. Exceptionally other works were permitted where there was pronounced unemployment, a familiar story from the 1920s and 1930s.

Planning activities

In spite of financial restrictions, planning of new roads continued. Mention has been made of the surveys being carried out by the Ministry and they were also carrying out traffic censuses and acquiring land for future road schemes. The Ministry engineers were also working on the design of motorways and Aldington[10] followed his earlier paper in 1945[6] by one on design and layout of motorways to the Institution of Highway Engineers in 1948. In this paper he discussed the importance of locating motorways where they would attract traffic to them by siting them as close to sources of traffic as possible, including using them to act as relief roads or by-passes of local areas. He thought the idea of planning motorways to avoid built-up areas to be unsound. He laid particular emphasis on the aesthetics of motorways and discussed the importance of visualising the road alignment in perspective and fitting the alignment into the general topography of the ground. He pointed out the importance of soil surveys in revealing economies that might be made by minor alterations in location to avoid unstable subsoil and by enabling better decisions to be made regarding type and thickness of foundation required.

Of the road plans which were being evolved by local government, the most significant in relation to the evolution of motorways in Britain was that prepared by James Drake for Lancashire in 1949[11]. He envisaged his roads scheme as being part of the plan for the economic development of the county. He carried out extensive studies of traffic and accidents on the existing road system so as to provide a factual basis for planning an improved system. His plan for a new system included: twelve express routes totalling 217 miles, of which all were dual carriageways and 94 miles of them motorways; 410 miles of roads for the use of important traffic within the county, of which 190 miles were to be dual carriageways and 17 miles of them motorways; and 280 miles of linking roads.

Special Roads Act 1949

To allow the construction of roads such as motorways which are restricted to specific types of traffic, new legislation was required and this was brought about by the passage of the Special Roads Act 1949. This Act provided for the construction of roads reserved for special classes of traffic. Under this Act any highway authority might be authorised by means of a scheme to provide a Special Road for the use of traffic of any class prescribed. Where the Minister was to provide the Special Road, the scheme had to be made by the Minister and in the case of a local authority it had to be made by that authority and confirmed by the Minister. Before making or confirming a scheme, the Minister had to give "due consideration to the requirements of local and national planning". Special Roads provided by the Minister were to become trunk roads. The Act specified nine classes of traffic for the purposes of Special Roads, four covering various groupings of motor vehicles and the other five relating to vehicles drawn by animals or

27

pedestrians, to pedal cycles, to animals and to pedestrians. The Act thus went wider than providing just for motorway traffic. Only authorised traffic could use a Special Road and the Minister was given authority to make regulations with respect to the use of such roads.

Under the Act, restrictions were placed on statutory undertakers, except for the Post Office, on laying mains etc. in Special Roads. Powers were provided to control access to a Special Road, including stopping up and diversion of roads which would otherwise cross the Special Road. Requirements concerning the publication of proposed schemes and the holding of inquiries into objections to schemes were set out. In some circumstances (except where objections were made by local councils and certain other bodies) the Minister could dispense with the holding of an inquiry. When an inquiry was held the Minister could make or confirm the scheme either without modification or subject to such modifications as he thought fit.

Costs of Special Roads were to be borne wholly or in part by moneys provided by Parliament and powers with certain limitations were provided to acquire land in connection with a Special Road scheme.

The Act included a schedule of four orders under the Trunk Roads Act 1946, to be treated as schemes under the new Act. These were the Stevenage by-pass in Hertfordshire, the Newport by-pass in Monmouthshire and roads near the approaches to the proposed Severn Bridge in Gloucestershire and Monmouthshire; they were presumably the first schemes to be identifiable as motorway schemes in Britain under the new legislation. It is interesting that in March 1945 the Ministry had invited consulting engineers Sir Owen Williams and Partners to make preliminary investigations into a motorway to by-pass Newport. Surveys for motorways for the Ross spur and the Lune Valley route were also in progress. Orders covering two further motorway schemes, the north of Twyning–North Lydiate Ash trunk road in Gloucestershire and Worcestershire and the Port Talbot by-pass in Glamorgan, were made shortly after the passage of the Act.

Fifty years of motor traffic

By the end of 1949 legislation was available to permit the construction of motorways. A considerable amount of preliminary survey of main routes in the country had been completed, local highway authorities had prepared plans for new or improved roads, the motor manufacturers were rapidly increasing production of new vehicles and the end of petrol rationing, still in force after the war, was now in sight. Even so capital expenditure on new roads was still severely limited and was to remain so for several years to come.

Thus, just over 50 years after the motor car was legally permitted to use the roads in 1896, Britain still had no roads specifically designed and dedicated to their use although there had been a considerable amount of legislation affecting roads and traffic. Motorways had already been in use for many years in Europe and the USA and their superiority in moving people and goods by road seems generally to have been accepted by those who had studied them. Although the first proposal for a motorway probably was put forward in Britain in 1906 and although Britain had originated the concept of a dedicated track for specific vehicles by the invention of railways, the idea of extending this concept to road vehicles was left for other countries to develop. The multiplicity of highway authorities at the start of the century no doubt acted against the evolution of a national road system in the early days, but this difficulty was recognised by Lloyd George who set up the Road Board with the object of providing a central body, with funds drawn from road users, to create an improved road system in the country. As has been indicated, the Board failed to live up to expectations.

Replacement of the Board by the Ministry of Transport in 1919 meant that Central Government took over the role of co-ordinating transport policy. As has been seen, they had not been particularly successful up to 1950 in securing funds for new and improved roads. Investment in roads was largely linked to programmes for the relief of unemployment rather than as a positive policy to reduce congestion and road accidents. As mentioned previously the Alness Committee report[12] in 1939 was, indeed, openly critical of the officials in the Ministry for their lack of vision, of initiative and of driving force in the Department. With the high turnover of Ministers of Transport the Committee possibly thought that policy failures should be ascribed to permanent staff in the Ministry. It is perhaps relevant to note that in 1938 only 27 miles of the 4,450 miles of trunk road were dual carriageway.

Writing in 1949, Rees Jeffreys[13] asked whether the Ministry had succeeded as the central road authority and concluded that it had failed to provide an adequate and safe road system. He had several reasons: roads policy was governed by political considerations with no consistent aim to provide the roads and bridges needed; large programmes were initiated only to relieve unemployment and none was carried to completion; no Minister was given long enough to develop a co-ordinated transport policy; powerful railway interests strongly opposed any action by Government which would assist road transport in general and road hauliers in particular; the Minister of Transport in matters of finance was subject to the dictates of the Chancellor of the Exchequer; a long-term plan for roads was needed involving the provision and planned expenditure of large capital funds.

Rees Jeffreys was writing 30 years after the creation of the Ministry of Transport. It would be interesting to know what views he would have held after a further 30 years, years which saw the creation of a motorway system in Britain.

References

1. INSTITUTION OF CIVIL ENGINEERS. *Post-war National Development Panel no. 2*—Roads. Institution of Civil Engineers, London, 1942.

2. INSTITUTION OF MUNICIPAL AND COUNTY ENGINEERS. *Memorandum to the Minister of Works and Planning.* Institution of Municipal and County Engineers, London, 1943.
3. INSTITUTION OF HIGHWAY ENGINEERS. *The post-war development of highways.* Institution of Highway Engineers, London, 1943.
4. COMMITTEE ON LAND UTILIZATION IN RURAL AREAS (The Lord Justice Scott Committee). *Report.* Command 6378. HMSO, London, 1942.
5. BRITISH ROAD FEDERATION. *Roads and road transport.* British Road Federation, London, 1944.
6. INSTITUTION OF AUTOMOBILE ENGINEERS. *The post-war development of road motor transport.* Section I, roads; Section II, progress of motor vehicle design and construction; Section III, traffic. Institution of Automobile Engineers, London, 1945.
7. BRUNNER C.T. *The ideal road system and its economy.* Institution of Highway Engineers, London, 1947.
8. BRUNNER C.T. *Traffic problems with particular relation to South Wales.* Institution of Highway Engineers, London, 1949.
9. BRITISH ROAD FEDERATION. *Economics of motorways.* British Road Federation, London, 1948.
10. ALDINGTON H.E. Design and layout of motorways. *J. Instn Highway Engrs,* 1948, **1**, No. 2.
11. DRAKE J. *Road plan for Lancashire.* Lancs CC, Preston, 1949.
12. SELECT COMMITTEE OF THE HOUSE OF LORDS. *Report on the prevention of road accidents.* HMSO, London, 1939.
13. JEFFREYS R. *The King's highway.* Batchworth Press, London, 1959.

Appendix 3.1. Motorway standards proposed by Aldington in 1945[6]

Design speed	75 mile/h (interestingly, Aldington thought it was doubtful whether a driver should expect to travel continuously on a motorway faster than 60 mile/h).
Formation width	For two-lane dual—93 ft.
	For three-lane dual—109 ft.
Marginal strip	1 ft wide at each side of the carriageway, flush with it and of a contrasting colour.
Carriageway	Dual two-lane—22 ft excluding marginal strip.
	Dual three-lane—30 ft excluding marginal strip.
	(Aldington thought two-lane would normally be adequate.)
Verge	Normally 15 ft wide and clear of obstructions (but some planting of shrubs or small trees permitted); may be reduced to 5 ft at bridges.
Central reservation	Not less than 15 ft. Width to be maintained at bridges.
Curves	Radius not less than 3,000 ft.
Gradients	Normal maximum 1 in 30 but up to 1 in 20 may be permitted in some hilly country.
Lay-bys	To be provided at intervals to enable drivers to draw off the carriageway to rest or make minor repairs.

Roadside facilities	No frontage access allowed but places to be provided for the supply of petrol and refreshment and for police purposes. Parking places off the highway, particularly at view points.
Bridges	Modern designs, types of construction and materials should be used appropriate to the circumstances.
Pavement design and surfacing	Attention to foundations essential. All road surfaces should, as far as practicable, be non-skid.

4

1950–1960: motorway construction begins

Introduction

The decade opened with legislation permitting the construction of motorways but, as so often has been the case, there was an "economic crisis" with a cut-back in capital expenditure, which meant there was little money available for the construction of new roads. Expenditure was concentrated on the upkeep of existing roads, with new works limited either to those necessary to deal with danger spots or those which were required as part of the development of other parts of the national economic programme. Some increase in expenditure on the maintenance of trunk and classified roads was permitted in 1951/52 because of the importance of these roads from the defence point of view. Planning was, however, continuing and surveys and censuses of trunk roads were being carried out and investigations were begun of schemes under the Special Roads Act. Various orders relating to side roads which crossed or entered the routes of trunk roads were also being made together with other orders relating to trunk roads.

Select Committee on Roads 1952/53[1]

In January 1953 a Select Committee of the House of Commons began an examination of the estimates concerning roads. Because of the restrictions on capital expenditure on roads, the Committee were precluded from commenting fully on new road construction. Even so, several interesting general matters which could have had a bearing on capital investment in roads emerged from the enquiry.

Financing the road programme

The Committee spent a fair amount of time trying to elucidate from a Treasury official, F.E. Figgures, an understanding of the arcane-sounding procedure by which funds were made available to the Ministry of Transport. It emerged that the Ministry had first to make a bid for a programme to the Government's Investment Programmes Committee; the Ministry's Chief Engineer would be a member of the Ministry's team which would be examined by that Committee.

The Ministry then prepared its estimates for submission to the Treasury in the light of that Committee's decision on the total physical road expenditure. At this stage, according to Figgures, the Treasury would try to squeeze the Ministry's estimate "in order to try to save money on it, in order to give less public money than the investment programme or that the Government has considered could be made available in terms of the national resources to the roads". He did not wish to disclose the amount of the moneys which had been squeezed from the Ministry but remarked that the extent to which this happened was a matter which was agreed between the Minister and the Chancellor of the Exchequer. However, it was also clear that the final level of the Ministry's estimates depended very much on the arguments between officials in the Ministry and in the Treasury. Figgures doubted if that sort of argument could ever be a scientific one, but research in later years has shown that the areas of uncertainty affecting investment issues could be reduced below those obtaining in 1953.

It was very clear that the size of the road programme depended heavily on the ability of the Minister of Transport to persuade his colleagues in Government, and in particular the Chancellor, of the need for investment in roads. It was also clear that Treasury officials played a significant role in the decisions taken on the roads vote and indeed it was made clear to the Estimates Committee that the exercise of all the Ministry's grant-making powers and expenditure on trunk roads were subject by statute to Treasury approval. Treasury rules included a requirement that their specific approval had to be obtained before entering into any commitment in respect of a scheme of major improvement or new construction where the estimated total cost exceeded £100,000 or where the scheme involved construction of a new road or bridge the total cost of which was estimated to be more than £25,000. Another requirement was that prior Treasury approval had to be obtained to the appointment of consulting engineers or architects.

Research on road construction

The Select Committee examined witnesses from the Road Research Laboratory about savings in road expenditure which might be achieved through research. Evidence was given of substantial savings on maintenance as a result of the application of the work of the Laboratory, but research on the road structure was held up for lack of full-scale experimental sites. In written evidence the Laboratory pointed out that large sums of money would be needed when new roads were to be constructed and that costs, excluding the cost of land, might be £200,000 per mile (at 1953 prices). Research on the road structure had reached a stage when full-scale experiments were required, particularly on a road built over clay, and that in the absence of new road construction these could not be made. A small experiment in Yorkshire in 1949 had demonstrated that savings of £20,000 to £30,000 per mile through more economical forms of construction were possible there and that greater savings would be expected in the construction of roads over clay soils. The Ministry of Transport had located a possible site for an experiment at Alconbury Hill, Huntingdonshire, where a major road improvement was planned. The Laboratory estimated that construction work and collection of necessary data whilst the road was in use would take 4 to 5 years at least. The experiment did not begin until 1957 although the site had been chosen in 1945 and the results from it were later incorporated into standards of construction for roads adopted by the Ministry of Transport, but not before construction and some failures with early motorways had occurred.

The Select Committee asked the then Permanent Secretary to the Ministry of Transport, the late Sir Gilmour Jenkins, whether he thought that more money spent on research might lead to economies. Whilst he thought that research "properly directed" could over a long period show economies and improvement in efficiency, he thought that the best kind of research for road construction was experience on the job. He did not regard it as fruitful to spend a lot more on research at that time.

It is also significant to note Jenkins's view of motorways, which he expressed to the Committee. He said that he personally was not in favour of a system of roads on the lines of the German *Autobahnen* although he did think that there was a considerable amount of major improvement work, such as building by-passes, the improvement of bridges and a new Severn Bridge, which would improve the flow of traffic.

Change in Government policy

From 1953 there were signs of change in the Government's attitude towards capital investment in trunk roads. Plans and pious hopes were beginning to have a greater air of reality. There was possibly no single reason for this, but some of the factors at work could have included: improvements in the UK economy (food rationing, the last remnant of war-time restrictions, ended in 1953); the build-up of car ownership across the community leading to a broad-based demand for better roads; pressures from county and municipal councils; and pressures from commercial road interests. On the political level, three successive Ministers of Transport, the late Alan Lennox Boyd (later Lord Boyd), John Boyd-Carpenter (now Lord Boyd-Carpenter) and Harold Watkinson (now Lord Watkinson), must have all played significant roles in persuading their colleagues in Government that a substantial programme of capital investment in roads should be started.

It is also possible that road building programmes in Europe and the USA played a part in influencing opinion. In 1954/55 in the USA recommendations were made to Congress by President Eisenhower for the construction of a national system of interstate highways consisting of some 37,600 miles of controlled access highways to be built during the next 10 years. It was argued that an adequate highway system was vital to the continued expansion of the economy and that projected figures for gross national product would not be realised if the highways were allowed to continue to deteriorate. It was pointed out that the increased weight of vehicles, higher average speeds and heavier axle loads had caused a serious deterioration of "inadequately designed highways". The need for modernisation of the road system to reduce the accident toll and to reduce vehicle operating costs was stressed and an important reason advanced for the proposals was for civil defence. Large-scale evacuation of cities was envisaged in the event of A-bomb or H-bomb attack and the capacity provided by the proposed interstate system including the necessary urban connections thereto was regarded as a vital civil-defence measure.

In February 1955 John Boyd-Carpenter made a statement to the House of Commons about the first instalment of an expanded road programme, commenting that there had been few major improvements and very little new construction in the road system since 1939, with the result that the problems now to be faced were immense. Items selected for an early place in the programme were those which the Government judged to be of the greatest urgency for relieving congestion of traffic, particularly industrial traffic, and for promoting road safety. An important factor in the selection was the state of preparedness of schemes and the availability of land. The programme was to include motorways and the Minister referred to the London–Yorkshire motorway and the north–south motorway through Lancashire. The Minister's statement referred to "certain major projects of national importance" which should be ready for commitment towards the end of the 3 year period 1956/59 and that because of their high cost "the Government have in mind that tolls should be charged in suitable cases".

It was pointed out that responsibility of the Minister of Transport for roads in Scotland was to be transferred to the Secretary of State for Scotland on 1 April 1956 and that it was hoped that a crossing of the Firth of Forth could be started within the next 4 years. Responsibilities for roads in Wales were similarly transferred to the Secretary of State for Wales on 1 April 1965 (see chapter 8).

A start on motorway schemes in Lancashire

Lancashire County Council, through its enterprising and energetic County Surveyor and Bridgemaster, Sir James Drake, had been pressing for several years for a start to motorway construction in the county as part of its plan for roads. These pressures were reinforced at a conference on roads in Lancashire in 1953[2] organised jointly by the British Road Federation, the Lancashire and Merseyside Industrial Development Association and the Lancashire County Council. The Conference agreed that a letter should be sent to the Minister of Transport urging immediate action to remedy the serious loss in productivity with the consequent effect on exports and unnecessarily high accident rate caused by the inadequate and dangerous roads in and adjoining Lancashire.

The first positive steps forward were taken by the Minister of Transport in 1953/54, who served notice of his intention[3] to make two Special Road schemes in

Lancashire under the 1949 Act. These schemes were the Bamber Bridge–Broughton (Preston by-pass) and the Hampson Green–north of Carnforth (Lancaster by-pass) schemes. After a period for objections these schemes were confirmed by the Minister in 1955. Work started on the 8 mile long Preston by-pass in 1956 and when it was completed in 1958 it became the first length of motorway to be open to public use in Britain. Work on the Lancaster by-pass started in 1957.

During 1955/56 the Lancashire County Council submitted a scheme made by them under the 1949 Act to the Minister for a Special Road (the Stretford – Eccles by-pass) just to the west of Manchester. This was later confirmed by the Minister and work started in 1957 with a 75% grant from the Ministry.

Survey work for a motorway between Birmingham and Preston was reported to be 80% complete in March 1956[4].

Other plans and schemes announced

In October 1956, Harold Watkinson, then Minister of Transport and Civil Aviation, in a written answer to a Question in the House of Commons, gave a description of five road projects (not all motorways) to which he attached special importance and to which over-riding priority was to be given in the next few years. These projects were

(1) an improved trunk road from London to the north-east to be based on the existing Great North Road
(2) a new motorway from London to the north-west, the first part of which was to be the motorway from north London to the south-east of Birmingham; this was to be followed by the north of Birmingham–Lancashire motorway linking up with the Preston by-pass
(3) improvements of the two existing trunk roads from London to the south-east by-passing the Medway towns and Maidstone and Ashford
(4) a spur from the Midlands to South Wales including the Ross spur motorway between Upton-on-Severn and Ross and substantial reconstruction of the Heads of the Valleys road; also a new motorway from Upton-on-Severn to the outskirts of Birmingham
(5) a road from London westwards to London airport, the West of England and South Wales.

Survey work and administrative processes concerning some of these motorway schemes were well in hand at the time of the Minister's statement. The Ross spur Special Road scheme which had been announced by the Minister in 1949 was confirmed by him in 1954/55 and construction work began there in 1958.

In 1954 H.E. Aldington,[5] who had retired a few years early from his position as Chief Engineer at the Ministry of Transport, gave an outline of the proposals put forward by the Ministry for improving the road connections from South Wales to the Midlands and to the West of England and for improvements in the South

Wales road system. Motorways formed a substantial part of these proposals and included: the construction of a 76 mile motorway from Almondsbury just north of Bristol to Birmingham; a motorway from Almondsbury across the Severn estuary, requiring a 3,240 ft suspension bridge and another bridge over the Wye, and by-passing Newport with a tunnel some 1,050 ft long to join trunk road A48 west of Newport; and the Ross spur motorway. It is a measure of the post-war delay in road construction that in March 1945 consulting engineers Sir Owen Williams and Partners had been invited by the Ministry of Transport to undertake preliminary investigations into the possibility of constructing a by-pass of the A48 at Newport to motorway standards. A Public Inquiry was held in 1947 and the scheme was scheduled under the Special Roads Act 1949. Although design work had progressed to near tender stage, it was deferred in 1952 and not started up again until 1960.

In 1955/56 the Minister announced his intention to make two schemes: the south of Luton–Watford Gap–Dunchurch Special Road scheme (the London–Yorkshire motorway first section) and the Watford and south of St Albans–Redbourn–Kidney Wood, Luton Special Road scheme (St Albans by-pass); the schemes were confirmed in October 1956. Construction began in March 1958 and the 75 miles or so comprising the schemes were opened to traffic in November 1959.

There was now a new sense of purpose about road building and nowhere was a lead more clearly given than by Harold Watkinson, then the Minister of Transport and Civil Aviation, at the opening of the conference on highway needs of Great Britain held at the Institution of Civil Engineers in 1957[6]. In answering his own question as to how he and his Ministry looked at the highway needs of Great Britain he said "Above all things we consider that our duty lies in deeds and not words. If we can have less verbiage and more mileage of road construction completed we shall at least be making a real contribution to . . . the cause of better roads in fact and not in projection or plan." By the end of the decade 400 miles of motorway schemes were under construction or in preparation. These included extension of the London–Yorkshire motorway from Crick to Leeds, work on the Birmingham–Preston motorway, the new route from Birmingham to South Wales, parts of a new route from London to South Wales and the 25 mile Medway motorway. Preliminary planning had also started on an extension of the Birmingham–Preston route northwards from the Preston by-pass to Penrith. The motorway framework in 1959 is shown in Fig. 4.1.

Lancashire had been the first county to open a motorway but several other County Surveyors and consultants were also pressing ahead energetically with work on the various schemes announced by the Minister. Experience in the planning and design of motorways was being gained by these engineers and by engineers in the Ministry of Transport and contractors were also gaining knowledge and experience in building motorways.

Urban motorways

During this decade, and indeed in the late war and early post-war years, plans were made and published for redevelopment of many towns and cities, e.g. Greater London, the City of London, Birmingham, Manchester, Edinburgh, Glasgow, Cardiff. These plans included proposals for new and improved roads, some of which were being thought of in terms of urban motorways.

In 1956 the British Road Federation convened a conference on urban motorways[7] at which papers were presented by speakers not only from Britain but also from countries abroad where, as distinct from in Britain, motorways had been built in towns. At the end of the conference it was formally resolved that "the economic needs and traffic problems of large cities demand the construction of urban motorways" and the British Government were urged to take steps to carry

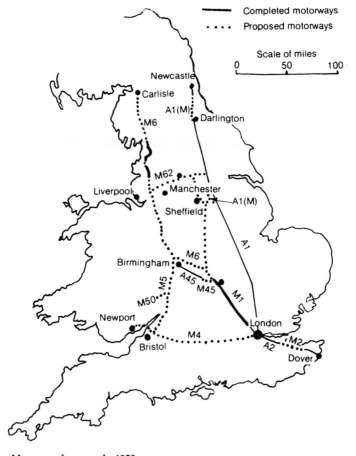

Fig. 4.1 Motorway framework, 1959

those motorways which had already been planned and authorised into the cities they were designed to serve.

The complex problems of planning roads in urban areas were also discussed by the conference on highway needs of Great Britain at the Institution of Civil Engineers in 1957,[6] where the Minister of Transport and Civil Aviation, after referring to his programme for inter-urban motorways and trunk roads, said that next came the task of eliminating bottle necks in urban areas by schemes both within and at the approaches to large towns and cities; he made reference to the Stretford–Eccles by-pass which was being built as an urban motorway.

The development of ideas and policies concerning urban motorways are discussed more fully in chapter 9.

London – Birmingham motorway study

In 1946 the scope of the activities of the Road Research Laboratory was widened to include research on road traffic and safety. Hitherto it had been largely confined to work on road materials and construction. As part of a programme of traffic research an investigation[8] was begun in 1955 in collaboration with the University of Birmingham into the traffic and economic aspects of the construction of the London–Birmingham motorway. Some financial support for the project was provided by the American Conditional Aid scheme and parts of the work were supported by the Rees Jeffreys Road Fund and the European Productivity Agency.

The project was in no way concerned with the decision already reached by the Ministry of Transport to construct the road, but the Ministry co-operated in the project as did several local authorities and the police. The object of the study was to develop methods of making traffic and economic assessments of the results of large-scale road construction.

Road-side origin and destination surveys were made of traffic likely to be affected by the proposed motorway and journey time surveys were carried out along many routes taken by traffic. An analysis was made of the amounts of traffic likely to transfer to the motorway from existing routes on the basis of the time drivers were likely to save by transferring. To do this, information was needed about likely speeds on the motorway, and since no motorways then existed in Britain from which to draw this information, investigations were carried out on motorways in Europe. Economic assessments were made of savings in time, operating costs and accidents and related to the cost of construction and maintenance of the motorway: as a result it was estimated that the motorway would produce a return of about 10% on the capital cost of construction.

Shortly after the motorway was opened to traffic, some studies were made to compare forecast traffic volumes and speeds with those actually observed. Averaged over the whole motorway, traffic volumes appeared to be some 4% less in 1960 than those predicted (but during the second year of operation volumes were 23% higher than in 1960). Speeds were about 5 mile/h (8 km/h) higher than those assumed in the calculations[9,10]. Some of the speeds observed on this motorway, on the Preston by-pass and on European motorways are shown in Table 4.1.

Accident studies during the first year of operation of the motorway indicated that for each casualty on the motorway, about 3½ were saved on other roads as a result of transference of traffic; the savings were generally in line with those predicted[9].

There was, understandably, a considerable public and professional interest in this, the first substantial length of motorway in Britain, and a conference on it was held at the Institution of Civil Engineers in the spring of 1960; papers were included on the general plan for motorways, on the economic and traffic studies just mentioned and on the design and the construction of both the Luton–Dunchurch section and the St Albans by-pass.

Standards and regulations

Once it was decided to design and build motorways the Ministry of Transport had to decide on the standards of layout and construction to be used and also on regulations governing motorway usage.

A considerable amount of attention had been given in earlier years to the layout and design to be adopted when motorways were to be permitted (see chapter 3 and reference 11). Before the Preston by-pass and London–Birmingham motorways were designed the earlier proposals for 11 ft wide lanes were changed to 12 ft and proposals for 4 ft 6 in wide hard shoulders with wider lay-bys at 1 mile intervals were dropped in favour of 8 ft wide continuous hard shoulders. The main layout features adopted at this time[12] were:

Carriageways	Dual 24 ft (two-lane) or 36 ft (three-lane) with 1 ft marginal strips of contrasting colour on both sides of each carriageway
Central reserve	13 ft wide
Hard shoulders	8 ft wide (later increased to 10 ft)
Verges	3 ft 6 in
Design speed	70 mile/h
Horizontal curvature	Minimum radius 2,865 ft (2° curvature)
Gradients	Normal maximum 3%; 4% in hilly country
Speed change lanes	12 ft wide, 400–800 ft long
Vertical clearance	16 ft 6 in

Several junction layouts were devised by the Ministry covering motorway junctions and intersections of motorway and all-purpose road. In rural areas it was thought that junctions every 10 or 12 miles might prove sufficient, but in developed areas junctions would need to be more frequent and a minimum spacing of 3 miles was generally required.

Bridges were to be designed to Ministry of Transport standard loadings and

Table 4.1. Motorway speeds on straight, level sections: km/h

Class of vehicle	London–Birmingham, June 1960	Preston by-pass, May 1960	European motorways, June 1957			
			Germany	Netherlands	Belgium	France
Car	95	85	87	85	83	83
Heavy goods (over 30 cwt. multi-axled)	61	53	61	64	56	56

these were specified for bridges carrying a motorway, for bridges carrying public highways over a motorway, for accommodation bridges and for footbridges.

Pavements were to be designed to Ministry of Transport standard specifications which covered both rigid and flexible construction. In 1960 the Road Research Laboratory issued their road note 29 *A guide to the structural design of flexible and rigid pavements for new roads*[13] drawn up in the light of available knowledge from research and of experience of road engineers in the Ministry of Transport, the County Surveyors' Society and elsewhere. It has served to help unify standards of construction throughout the country. The note has been updated from time to time since then.

Landscaping

The Ministry attached great importance to the landscape treatment of motorways and for the London–Birmingham motorway had the expert advice of the Advisory Committee on the Landscape Treatment of Trunk Roads under the chairmanship of the Hon. Sir David Bowes-Lyon. Detailed planting proposals, based on recommendations of this committee, were prepared by the landscaping staff of the consulting engineers Sir Owen Williams and Partners.

Planting took the form of groups of forest trees indigenous to the surrounding countryside and one of the areas treated in this way was near Luton. This area did, however, come in for some criticism from Sylvia Crowe,[14] the landscape architect who thought the bridges and embankments formed clumsy shapes.

Service areas and emergency facilities

Because frontage development was not permitted on a motorway, service facilities were to be provided in areas set back from the motorway with access at the rear to the ordinary road system for staff and supplies to those areas. Parking space was to be provided and the services were to include fuel supplies and refreshments. The areas were to be let to private developers and in the case of the London–Birmingham motorway the first two areas were at Newport Pagnell, leasedto Motorway Services Ltd, and at Watford Gap, leased to Blue Boar (Motorway) Ltd.

Motorways were to be equipped with an emergency telephone system with telephone points located on the hard shoulder at about 1 mile intervals, the phones being connected directly to a police station.

The police force in the area through which a motorway passed was responsible for organising suitable patrols and supervision of the motorway traffic there.

Responsibility for maintenance, and in particular for clearance of snow and ice, was in the case of trunk road motorways passed to the County Councils as agent authorities for the Ministry of Transport. In designing the London–Birmingham motorway provision was made for depots adjacent to the motorway for storage of dumps of grit and salt and for housing snow-clearing and gritting vehicles at 12 mile intervals.

Motorway signs

In 1957 the Minister of Transport appointed a committee under the chairman-ship of Sir Colin Anderson to advise him on suitable traffic signs for use on motor-ways[15]. The committee identified the need to give motorway users clear and sim-ple directions which could be read and understood at the higher speeds for which motorways were designed, and they decided that the standard type of direction sign then in use by the Ministry for signing all-purpose roads was inadequate for motorways; much larger signs were needed.

In the process of framing their recommendations the Committee inspected signs on motorways abroad and were helped in a number of experimental investigations by the Road Research Laboratory. Detailed design work on signs was carried out for the committee by Jock Kinneir. The signing system evolved was tried out experimentally on the Preston by-pass and a few modifications were made in the light of experience there before adopting the system used on the Lon-don–Birmingham motorway, which is essentially that in use today on all motor-ways. Some principal design features of the signs were

—lower case lettering with initial capitals on all motorway signs
—all informatory signs relating to the motorway in white lettering on a blue background (whether or not on the motorway itself)
—signs legible to drivers travelling at 70 mile/h without them diverting their gaze more than 10° to 15°
—height of lower case letters like x at least 12 in
—lower edge of each sign not less than 5 ft above road level
—all direction signs at junctions electrically lit.

The system recommended by the committee covers signs for use on joining a motorway, on the motorway itself including emergency signs, on leaving a motor-way, at forks in a motorway, and at the end of a motorway.

Regulations

The main legislation on highways including the Trunk Roads Acts of 1936 and 1946 and the Special Roads Act 1949 was consolidated in the Highways Act 1959.

Motorway rules restricted their use to motor vehicles of specific classes, which included cars, vans, goods vehicles and motorcycles over 50 cc capacity. Invalid carriages, motorcycles under 50 cc capacity, mopeds of all kinds, heavy tractors and self-propelled plant over 7½ tons unladen weight, farm tractors and similar vehicles were all excluded. Vehicles carrying abnormal, indivisible loads wider than 14 ft were not permitted unless individually authorised by order of the Minister of Transport. At that time there was no speed limit on any class of vehicle permitted to use the motorway, except that vehicles towing a caravan or other trailer with fewer than four wheels (or with four close-coupled wheels) not being articulated vehicles were restricted to 40 mile/h. No more than one trailer could be towed behind any vehicle.

Other main rules specifically applying to motorways were as follows.

—One-way driving must be observed at all times on the dual carriageway.

—There must be no U-turning.

—Vehicles must not stop or remain at rest on the carriageway unless compelled to do so by the presence of any other vehicle, person or object.

—If a vehicle breaks down or has to be stopped in an emergency, it must as soon as practicable be moved on to the verge and, even there, not stop longer than necessary.

—Vehicles on the carriageway must not be reversed except in special circumstances.

—Vehicles normally must not be driven on to the verge nor on to the central reservation.

—Vehicles must not be driven by learner drivers.

—Persons getting out of vehicles in emergency must stay on the verge unless they are giving help or recovering something dropped on the carriageway.

—Animals carried in vehicles must be kept on board or, if they have to be removed, they must be kept under proper control on the verge.

The *Motorway code*

To give special guidance on the use of motorways, the Ministry of Transport and Civil Aviation and the Central Office of Information published a *Motorway code* in 1958. This was incorporated into the *Highway code* issued by the Ministry with the authority of Parliament in 1959.

In addition to covering the main regulations concerning the use of motorways, the code gave guidance on motorway driving, some of which was as follows (a section on motorway driving is included in the current *Highway code*).

—Make sure your vehicle is in good condition.

—Driving for long spells at an even speed may cause drowsiness. To prevent this, drive with adequate ventilation and stretch your legs at the parking or service areas.

—When joining a motorway at an intermediate access point . . . watch for a safe gap between vehicles in the nearside traffic lane on the motorway and increase your speed in the acceleration lane to the speed of traffic in the nearside lane before joining it. Give way to traffic already on the motorway.

—Drive at a steady cruising speed comfortably within your capacity and that of your vehicle.

—Keep within the carriageway markings and cross them only when changing from one lane to another . . . . Do not wander from lane to lane.

—On a two-lane carriageway keep to the left-hand lane except when overtaking.

—On a three-lane carriageway, you may keep to the centre lane when the left-lane is occupied by slower moving vehicles. The outer (right-hand) lane is for over-taking only . . . .

—Do not drive too close to the vehicle ahead of you in your lane . . . .

—Overtake only on the right . . . . Never overtake on the left.

—Before pulling out to your right into a traffic lane carrying faster moving traffic, watch out for and give way to traffic in lanes to your right. Use your mirror . . . Give a clear signal of your intention well before you change from one lane to another.

—If you see a knot of vehicles in the distance, which may mean that there has been an accident, reduce speed at once and be prepared to stop.

—When you leave the motorway, remember to adjust your driving to the different conditions of the ordinary road system.

Numbering of motorways

In 1959 the Minister of Transport announced his intention with regard to the route numbers to be given to motorways in England and Wales. These were to be allocated on similar lines to those on all-purpose roads. For those roads, England and Wales had been divided into six sectors by the six great routes radiating clockwise from London (A1 to Edinburgh, A2 to Dover, A3 to Portsmouth, A4 to Avonmouth, A5 to Holyhead and A6 to Carlisle), section 1 lying between the A1 and A2, section 2 between the A2 and A3 and so on. All other Class A roads in England and Wales had two, three or four figure numbers, the first figure of which was the same as the number of the sector in which it lay. In the same way Class B roads had three or four figure numbers, the first figure being the same as the appropriate sector number.

For numbering motorways, England and Wales was to be quartered by the Lon-don–Yorkshire motorway, a possible Channel Ports motorway, a future Exeter radial motorway and the London–South Wales radial motorway. These roads were to be numbered M1 to M4 respectively. M5 was to be reserved for the

Bristol–Birmingham motorway, and M6 for the Penrith–Birmingham motorway (and its eventual extension to join the London–Yorkshire motorway north of Crick). Two figure numbers were to be reserved for spurs and for motorways lying within the sectors bounded by the single number motorways.

This system was to apply to long-distance motorways. Where a motorway was merely a by-pass along an existing route, such as the Doncaster by-pass along route A1, it was not to be given a separate 'M' number but the letter M was to be added in brackets after the existing route number, e.g. A1(M).

Select Committee on Trunk Roads 1958/59

Six years after a Select Committee had examined estimates on roads in 1952/53 another Committee of the House of Commons[16] was appointed to examine estimates for trunk roads, giving particular attention to new construction and major improvements. Perhaps inevitably the Committee went over some of the ground covered earlier. One such item was research.

Road Research Laboratory

In its report the Select Committee said that, if the trunk road programme were to be planned efficiently and priorities properly allocated, there must be adequate research into traffic needs before plans were drawn up. If trunk roads were to be built to the most satisfactory standards, research into materials and methods should be well advanced before actual construction got under way. The Committee were not satisfied that the programme had been adequately prepared. They referred to the work of the Road Research Laboratory and to the delay in starting the Alconbury Hill experiment mentioned in 1952/53 and the lack of research on earth-moving machinery. They considered that, despite the recommendation in 1952/53 for an increase in work at the Road Research Laboratory, expenditure on research was not significantly increased until after the beginning of the trunk road programme instead of in anticipation of it; they went on to say that "despite widespread recognition for several years past of the need for more research, Britain's first motorways are in the nature of experimental roads."

The same considerations applied to research into traffic needs as to constructional research and the Committee was of the opinion that the Minister, in deciding whether to give priority to rural motorways or to urban road construction, "should have been armed with adequate information about behaviour of the nation's traffic".

The Committee, whilst noting that there were lively contacts between the Road Research Laboratory and the Ministry of Transport and Civil Aviation, recommended that attention should be given to improving the relationship between the two organisations. This was the subject of recommendations by a Select Committee in 1957/58 on the Department of Scientific and Industrial Research[17]. As a result of both these recommendations arrangements were made for consultation between the Ministry and the Laboratory on the designs and specifications for all trunk road and motorway schemes costing over £500,000. Details of tenders for work done to new specifications prepared in consultation were also to be seen by the Laboratory. In their Annual Report for 1959, the Road Research Board noted that this required a regular transfer from the Ministry to the Laboratory of certain items of information and that suitable arrangements had been made.

Planning

The Select Committee were clearly unhappy about the basis of the trunk road programme and thought that no adequate scheme of priorities related to the nation's needs existed. They had the impression that one result of the lack of a national plan had been the overemphasis on "motorways through fields" to the neglect of the problem of urban bottle-necks.

The concept of a national through-route system implied central direction and the Committee considered that no special organisation existed to administer a programme for the system directly. The Ministry made use of the pre-existing local authority system but the Committee thought that this was not suited to the implementation of large motorway schemes which straddled several counties. They noted, however, that the Ministry was fully aware of the need to by-pass the existing machinery for major motorway schemes and had on several occasions successfully employed consulting engineers and put work out to direct tender. Local authorities clearly thought there was a case for more delegation to them as agent authorities. The Committee recommended that possible reform of the national trunk road organisation should be considered by the Ministry and local authorities concerned and the Ministry agreed to do this to see whether suggestions by the Committee were practicable and would lead to economies and greater efficiency.

Land acquisition

The problems associated with the acquisition of land for trunk road schemes and especially those concerning the disposal of such land if eventually not required were discussed at some length, as they had been in 1952/53. The Committee concluded that the quantity of land acquired for trunk roads, including motorways, was not excessive in relation to foreseeable needs. They did raise queries concerning the machinery of acquisition and it appeared that the Ministry was aware of problems and attempting to make improvements.

On the question of land required for motorways it is of interest to note views expressed by C.T. Brunner[18] at the Institution of Civil Engineers' conference on the highway needs of Great Britain. He pointed out that, including flyovers and junctions, motorways required some 14 acres of land per mile (3.5 hectares/km) and he estimated that the value of that land was negligible in relation to the value of a motorway to the economy. Further, the motorway would benefit agriculture by enabling produce to be moved to market more rapidly. He was supported in his views at the conference by Colin Clark, then the Director of the Agricultural Economics Research Institute.

During construction land is required for temporary use such as stacking top soil and compounds. At Preston this cost only £15 per acre, but current costs can run into thousands of pounds.

Lighting motorways

The Select Committee recommended that the Minister should make an early decision on whether to light motorways or not, but the Minister replied that there was not at that time sufficient evidence to show that they should be lighted and that he had decided not to light the London–Birmingham motorway. He would decide further policy after further experience. This was a matter which was to be raised again at another Select Committee in 10 years' time.

It is interesting to note that the interchanges on the Preston by-pass had high column lighting which was installed during construction. However, the Ministry required this to be removed before the motorway was opened.

The Ministry of Transport and Civil Aviation

There was some satisfaction for the Ministry on this occasion at the end of the examination by the Select Committee. The Committee recorded that they were impressed with the amount and quality of the construction they saw in progress. They thought that the Ministry had shown themselves willing to adapt their procedures to cope with the rapid expansion of the programme of work and that the agent authorities were co-operating enthusiastically with the Ministry. Although the Committee believed that the trunk road programme had been inadequately prepared they were satisfied that there was a growing awareness of this by the Minister and the Secretary of State for Scotland.

Problems

The decade ended with a substantial programme of motorway construction and planning in hand, but a number of problems had emerged. Writing in the *Financial Times* on 10 November 1958, Baker referred to the problem of deciding on priorities and to the lengthy procedures which had to be gone through before motorway construction could begin. While noting that the statutory processes were designed to protect the rights of private individuals they were, in the case of large schemes, taking 3 years or more. This had meant a relatively slow early growth of the new road programme. It was essential to plan well ahead in order to maintain the tempo of the programme and he reported that some 850 miles of new or improved trunk roads (including motorways) were in hand at the end of 1958. Some constructional problems revealed in the first roads to be completed could with hindsight be ascribed to inadequacies of design. The first problem occurred on the Preston by-pass when frost damage occurred shortly after the road was opened. This was not an isolated case and the County Surveyor, Sir James Drake, said[16] that "We have had a terrific amount of frost damage at the same time as this [damage to the by-pass] happened. I think it is general thoughout the country." He recorded that conditions when the verges were built were very wet and there appears to have been a drainage problem. Concrete haunches had been laid on a shale sub-base which tended to trap water which penetrated the fine cold asphalt temporary surfacing; water in the road structure could lead to frost heave. A two-stage process had been adopted for the surfacing in that a temporary surface was laid with the intention of allowing settlement to take place before the final surfacing was placed. When the frost occurred the ultimate full strength of the surface had thus not been achieved. The problem was cured by providing extra drainage and by the addition of the final surfacing. Drake said that the practice of starting with a temporary surface was changed with the London–Birmingham motorway where a more permanent surface was provided at the start.

A more serious problem arose with the design of the hard shoulders specified by the Ministry of Transport for both the Preston by-pass and the London–Birmingham motorway. The specification at Preston was for 4½ in of gravel overlaid with 4¾ in thickness of mixed stone, sand and loam on which was sown grass seed. On the London–Birmingham motorway difficulties arose with grass and one half the length of shoulders was amended to have a stone-based surface treated with hot tar and chippings. The shoulders were 8 ft wide[19].

Experience on these motorways soon showed that neither the width nor the strength of the shoulders was adequate, particularly for the heavier vehicles. The Ministry asked the Road Research Board to advise on the problem and subsequently shoulders 10 ft wide and fully paved were adopted by the Ministry. Coburn[10] reported that the number of emergency stops recorded by the police on the Preston by-pass in 1959 was about one for each 23,000 vehicle-miles and breakdowns in 1960 on the London–Birmingham motorway averaged about one in 17,000 vehicle-miles. He showed that these rates were in line with expectation.

Writing about 5 years later in 1965, H.N. Ginns[20] who was Deputy Chief Engineer at the Ministry of Transport at the time remarked "It is generally accepted that the earliest motorways were under-designed and under-specified due to the desire to keep costs low and to lack of experience of some of the materials used and of the punishing effects of high-speed heavy traffic." This comment seems amply to have borne out the fears of the 1958/59 Select Committee that "Britain's first motorways are in the nature of experimental roads".

References

1. SELECT COMMITTEE ON ESTIMATES. *Fifth report. Roads 1952–53.* HMSO, London, 1953.

2. BRITISH ROAD FEDERATION. Lancashire Roads Conference. *British Road Federation Mon. Bull.*, 1953, 201–220.
3. MINISTRY OF TRANSPORT AND CIVIL AVIATION. *Report on the administration of the Road Fund 1953–1954.* HMSO, London, 1955.
4. MINISTRY OF TRANSPORT AND CIVIL AVIATION. *Report on the administration of the Road Fund 1955–1956.* HMSO, London, 1957.
5. ALDINGTON H.E. New road developments in South Wales. *Surveyor*, 1954, **113**, No. 3238, 244–246.
6. INSTITUTION OF CIVIL ENGINEERS. *Proceedings of the conference on the highway needs of Great Britain.* Institution of Civil Engineers, London, 1958.
7. BRITISH ROAD FEDERATION. *Urban motorways.* British Road Federation, London, 1956.
8. COBURN T.M., REYNOLDS D.J. and BEESLEY M.E. *The London–Birmingham motorway; traffic and economics.* Road research technical paper no. 46. HMSO, London, 1960.
9. GLANVILLE W.H. The London–Birmingham motorway. Economic and traffic studies. *Proc. Instn Civ. Engrs*, 1960, **15**, 333–352.
10. COBURN T.M. *Rural motorways.* Road Research Laboratory Harmondsworth, Laboratory note LN/787/TMC, 1965. Unpublished.
11. HUTTON T.E. *Design of motorways.* Road paper 42. Institution of Civil Engineers, London, 1953.
12. BAKER J.F.A. The London–Birmingham motorway. The general motorway plan. *Proc. Instn Civ. Engrs*, 1960, **15**, 317–332.
13. ROAD RESEARCH LABORATORY. *A guide to the structural design of flexible and rigid pavements for new roads.* Road note 29. HMSO, London, 1960.
14. CROWE S. The London–York motorway: a landscape architect's view. *Archit. J.*, 1959, **30**, No. 3360.
15. MINISTRY OF TRANSPORT ADVISORY COMMITTEE ON TRAFFIC SIGNS FOR MOTORWAYS. *Motorway signs.* HMSO, London, 1962.
16. SELECT COMMITTEE ON ESTIMATES. *First report. Trunk roads 1958–59.* HMSO, London, 1959.
17. SELECT COMMITTEE ON ESTIMATES. *Fifth report. Department of Scientific and Industrial Research 1957–58.* HMSO, London, 1958.
18. BRUNNER C.T. An assessment of the economic loss to the country due to inadequate highways: a consideration of some of the factors involved. *Proceedings of the conference on the highway needs of Great Britain.* Institution of Civil Engineers, London, 1958.
19. WILLIAMS S.O. and WILLIAMS O.T. The London–Birmingham motorway. Luton–Dunchurch: design and execution. *Proc. Instn Civ. Engrs*, 1960, **15**, 353–386.
20. GINNS H.N. *English motorways—development and progress.* Final Report of the Public Works and Municipal Services Congress and Exhibition Council, London, 1966.

5

1960–1970: a decade of growth

Introduction

By 31 March 1960 there was a total of 95 miles of motorway in use in Britain[1] and work was in hand on the Ross spur (21 miles), the Lancaster by-pass (11 miles), the Maidenhead by-pass (5 miles) and on three major viaducts on the future M6 in Cheshire and Lancashire. In addition the Maidstone by-pass (7 miles) and the Doncaster by-pass (15 miles), which did not form part of the national motorway network but which were designed as full motorways, were under construction.

Writing in the *Financial Times* on 16 November 1964, Baker reported that 300 miles of the inter-urban motorway system were open to traffic with 150 more miles under construction. By 1970[2] there were 660 miles of trunk road motorway open to traffic in Britain (567 miles in England, 23 miles in Wales and 70 miles in Scotland) with well over 350 miles under construction. There were, however, only about 10 miles of urban motorway in use with a similar mileage under construction. Averaged over the decade there was thus just over 1 mile of motorway being opened per week. By way of comparison, in March 1968, some 12 years after the start of the interstate system of motorways in the USA, about 2,400 miles were open to traffic, an average completion rate of around 40 miles per week.

At the start of the decade, the Ministry of Transport were working on the programme of the five major projects mentioned in the last chapter. These were: reconstruction of much of the Great North Road (A1); completion of the London to Birmingham to Lancashire motorway and Midlands connecting links; London to the Channel ports including the Medway motorway; Birmingham to South Wales and Bristol motorway; London to Heathrow Airport and on to Maidenhead, the Severn Bridge and Newport by-pass. In August 1962 the Minister, the late the Rt Hon. Ernest (later Lord) Marples, announced the Government's intention to complete 1,000 miles of motorway in the early 1970s. He did not give many details at that time of actual schemes and this was a matter of some concern to the local authorities in planning their own road programmes.

Ministry projects might well make local authority road improvements unnecessary or involve new requirements.

County Surveyors' Society plan

In 1961 the County Surveyors' Society set up a committee to consider the Ministry of Transport plan comprising the five major projects. The committee were concerned with two main questions: first, the adequacy of the plan as a national network; and second, the mixing of all-purpose sections of road and sections of Special Road on major through routes such as the A1. A report was prepared containing proposals for an additional 1,700 miles of motorway. This report was considered by the Association of County Councils and forwarded to the Ministry early in 1962. Evidently existence of the proposals became public knowledge before the Minister had had time to reply. Perhaps because the Minister was formulating his 1,000 mile plan at the time and did not want to be pre-empted, he took exception to the County Surveyors' actions although they pointed out that they were not responsible for the publicity given to their report. The Minister wrote "I can find little sign of the exhaustive study which I would have expected to see precede the publication of such proposals". The County Councils' Association pointed out that the report was concerned with principles upon which a national network should be planned. The Minister had not published his plans and the County Surveyors wanted to find out what they were. The County Surveyors' Society also took the view that the Minister was responsible for carrying out the studies required.

The Ministry replied in October 1963 saying that the Department was engaged on a thorough study of many fundamental factors related to the assessment of forward planning and that much data had to be collected for cost/benefit purposes. This would take time but the Ministry did not think the Society could usefully assist in these long-term studies.

In January 1964 the President of the County Surveyors' Society, J.H.H. Wilkes, wrote to J.F.A. Baker, the Director of Highway Engineering at the Ministry, pointing out that the Surveyors had noticed cases where the results of surveys and traffic assignments by the Ministry's consultants in some areas were not consistent with each other and did not agree with results obtained by the Surveyors. It was suggested that there was a need for a uniform method of presenting data so that results obtained by one engineer could be readily assimilated by another and the method should lend itself to computerisation. The Society recognised that trunk road motorways were the Minister's roads but argued that they did not "exist as an entity entirely separate from County roads". Planning road systems was of such complexity that all possible measures should be brought to bear and Wilkes invited Baker to meet the Surveyors.

A meeting took place a week or so later and it was agreed that the Surveyors could help in the analysis and interpretation of planning data. The Ministry were reviewing "facts" collected in the early 1950s in the light of the existing motorway system, bringing in more up-to-date information. It was accepted by the Ministry that an extended national motorway system should be thought of and planned at once without waiting for the final data to emerge.

Another meeting about this time took place between the County Councils' Association and the Ministry at which it was agreed that further co-operation between the Ministry and County Councils was desirable and that informal and unpublished consultations in the early stages of planning were the best ways of getting things done. Some degree of harmony between the counties and the Ministry seems to have been restored by these meetings.

Although their proposals for a national motorway plan had in effect been rejected by the Ministry, the County Surveyors' Society engaged its members in a revision of the 1962 plan and by 1968 had prepared a revised version (Fig. 5.1) which represented "the consensus of views of the County Surveyors of England, Scotland and Wales." Several advantages were claimed for the plan.

(1) It would provide a framework for future developments in the location of population and industry.

(2) It would provide a foundation for forward planning of individual motorway projects and thus avoid uncertainties and delays inherent in the present procedure.

(3) It would make it possible to integrate proposed new regional and local routes into the national network.

(4) It would provide a target against which progress could be measured.

The Society's proposals were considered by the County Councils' Association early in August 1968 but the Association were not in favour of publication of the plan. They did agree that it might be used as a basis for obtaining very early publication of the Ministry's own programme of motorway and other major road works. This was evidently taken up with the Ministry and towards the end of August W.G. (later Sir William) Harris, who had succeeded Baker as Director of Highway Engineering and was later made Director General of Highways at the Ministry, wrote to both the County Councils' Association and the Association of Municipal Corporations inviting them to a meeting to explain on a confidential basis what the Ministry had in mind. He said that the Ministry was anxious to ensure that as much information as possible was in the hands of local authorities. The Ministry was working towards a national road plan which he believed would meet the needs of the local authorities. The proposals for a national road plan were put forward in a Green Paper[3] in 1969 and in final form in a White Paper[4] the following year and are referred to at the end of the chapter.

Consultants and the counties

The Ministry of Transport has over the years employed County Councils as its

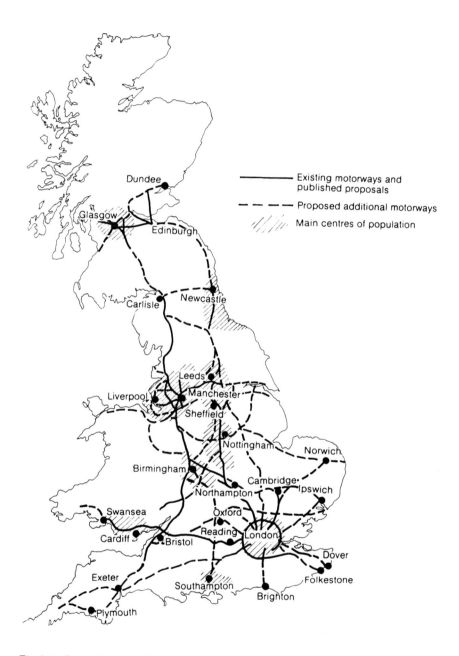

Existing motorways and published proposals

Proposed additional motorways

Main centres of population

Fig. 5.1   County Surveyors' Society proposed national motorway plan, 1968

agents for the maintenance of trunk roads. When proposals for motorways began to be considered in the early years after World War II the Ministry turned to consultants to carry out preliminary feasibility studies rather than to the counties concerned. In 1954, in 1955 and again in 1959 the Ministry had written to the counties informing them of its decision to appoint consulting engineers for certain motorway schemes. The County Councils' Association had taken exception to this on the grounds of the Minister's failure to fulfil an undertaken given in the first report of the Local Government Manpower Committee to approach agent authorities to find out whether they could undertake trunk road surveys or works before they were put in hand by the Ministry. In 1955, John Boyd-Carpenter, then Minister of Transport, had given an assurance that in regard to the vast bulk of schemes it was intended to use "the tied method" of appointing local authorities.

At a meeting in 1960 with Minister of Transport, Ernest Marples, the Association was told that the general policy of the Minister was that work on large motorway schemes involving more than one County Council should not normally be placed in the hand of one county but should go to consultants.

Discussions took place between the County Councils' Association and the Ministry on these issues and in June 1963 R.N. Heaton, a Deputy Secretary at the Ministry, wrote to the Association about the role of local highway authorities in the carrying out of motorway and trunk road major improvement programmes. He reiterated the right of the Ministry to carry out such programmes otherwise than through the agency of a local highway authority but said that their policy had been to use them for most of this work. Because of the continuing expansion of the road programme this policy had been reviewed and no drastic change was intended. It was believed, however, that some extension of the use of consultants was necessary, particularly for larger schemes; the ability of a local highway authority to undertake work would depend on its resources.

The Association in reply strongly deplored any extension of the use of consulting engineers on motorway and trunk road schemes where the County Councils concerned were willing and able to undertake the preparation and supervision of such work and urged that prior consultation should take place with the council involved.

The concern of the County Surveyors about the Ministry's policy was expressed by a former Honorary Secretary of their Society who wrote that "the effect could be gradually to filch away from the County Highway Authorities all the major schemes on trunk roads and the end result of such a policy would be that experience in the construction of major projects would be gained by consultants only, leaving County Councils no opportunity of such works which alone will enable them to recruit and retain staff for similar work on county roads."

In written evidence to the Select Committee on Motorways and Trunk Roads in 1969[5] the Ministry of Transport stated that consulting engineers had been employed to design and supervise the construction of a considerable proportion of the first 1,000 miles of motorway although parts had been carried out by County Councils under agency agreements.

Road Construction Units

As the motorway programme gathered momentum, the Ministry of Transport was faced with the problem of carrying out its responsibilities for the programme in the face of limited engineering resources and the concern of local highway authorities and of consultants for their roles in the programme. In the first half of the 1960s the Ministry of Transport employed about 50 local authorities (mostly County Councils) as agents; and it also employed some 30 firms of consulting engineers on schemes which were regarded as inappropriate to local authority design staff. At the end of March 1965, these teams had been invited to prepare between them 150 motorway and trunk road projects of over £250,000; in addition, there were in preparation about 75 programmes of other classified road schemes within the counties. On average each county was preparing only about three major road schemes at a time; some had a dozen or more and others none at all. Some rationalisation of this state of affairs seemed desirable and the Lofthouse Committee report[6] recommended in the interests of efficiency a reduction in the number of design and construction organisations involved in the trunk road and motorway programme.

In 1966, impressed by this argument, the Minister of Transport, the Rt Hon. Barbara Castle, considered the possibility of setting up a National Road Board mainly with a view to obtaining more funds for roads but also to improve their administration. In July 1966 a symposium on road administration and finance[7] was organised by the British Road Federation and this matter was discussed. The Federation at that time supported the concept of a self-financing national roads board "independent in the broad sense but publicly accountable and with well defined responsibilities to Parliament". There were objections within the Ministry[8] to the creation of such a board on the grounds that the Central Government had to retain control over the extent of the national investment in the road programme, its place in national and regional planning and the determination of priorities. From the point of view of the counties there was a feeling that the Board would virtually eliminate the role of County Councils as agents of the Ministry for trunk road construction and progressively reduce their function as highway authorities for major roads.

When W.G. (later Sir William) Harris was appointed to succeed Baker at the Ministry of Transport in 1965 he was asked particularly to look into the possibility of a unit being created in the Ministry to undertake a substantial part of the design and supervision of trunk road, especially trunk road motorway schemes. He found that with the continued expansion of the road programme and the general shortage of experienced highway engineers the engineering resources of the counties were showing signs of strain and the setting up of a Ministry unit in competition would cause still further disruption. He was also aware that difficulties would inevitably follow from any major reorganisation which did not allow active participation of County Councils, a limited number of whom, e.g. Lancashire, Yorkshire West Riding and Durham, were then involved in the motorway programme.

The Minister announced her intention to issue a White Paper on transport policy towards the end of 1966 and is understood to have insisted that any alternative to her first option of a Road Board had to be defined in acceptable terms in time for the White Paper.

As a matter of urgency, Harris began discussions with the then President of the County Surveyors' Society, Col. S.M. Lovell, and his successor Basil Cotton, and with the Secretary of the County Councils' Association, A.C. Hetherington, about a new organisation for handling motorway and other trunk road schemes. During these discussions it became clear that a new form of partnership with the counties was required in creating the new organisation. There would be an obvious advantage to delegate as much authority as possible to the new organisation in the interest of speedy action while ensuring proper accountability, which was only possible under the rules of Government Departments if the new bodies were parts of the Ministry of Transport.

The scheme put forward envisaged the setting up of six large-scale Road Construction Units (RCUs) covering the whole of England (none was considered necessary in Wales and in Scotland) which would concentrate the processes of design and supervision of major road schemes into a relatively small number of joint teams[9]. Whilst welcoming the proposal for closer co-operation with the Ministry, and accepting the need to improve existing arrangements, some doubts were expressed within counties as to whether the RCU scheme was the best way of proceeding. It was felt that the first priority was the preparation of a carefully phased programme of major works to deal with the national network of motorways and feeder routes. Continuity of design and construction work would follow as a natural sequence. There was also an urgent need for an agreed set of standards for design and constructional methods. Worries were also expressed about the arrangements for staffing RCUs, particularly as they affected careers of local authority staff. There was a feeling that the introduction of RCUs was simply an expansion of the Civil Service at the expense of counties and that since there were so few experienced engineers in the Ministry, the RCUs would be largely staffed by County Council personnel.

Agreement on a scheme was, however, eventually reached between the Ministry and the County Councils' Association in the autumn of 1966; the Association accepted the arrangement as a compromise between the Minister's original idea of a National Road Board which they disliked and the agency arrangements which they preferred[5].

Colonel S.M. Lovell, CBE, then County Surveyor of the West Riding of Yorkshire, was invited to become "general manager" nationally for the RCUs by secondment to HQ Ministry of Transport under the general title of Chief Engineer, later to be called Deputy Director General. Lovell eventually declined the post but before doing so carried out all the negotiations with the County Councils and spent some months at the Ministry Headquarters. He also assisted in the negotiations for the appointment of Directors of the RCUs.

Each Road Construction Unit consisted of a relatively small headquarters and from two to four Sub-Units. The first Unit was set up in the North West on 3 April 1967 and all six Units were in being by April 1968, the areas they covered being shown in Table 5.1. Units and Sub-Units were staffed for the most part by staff on loan from the County Councils in whose areas they were located, and the minimum period of participation in the formal agreement between the Ministry and Council was normally 7 years. Altogether 17 counties were participating in

Table 5.1. Road Construction Unit areas

Area	Counties	Area	Counties
North Western (Regional office: Preston)	Cumberland Westmorland Lancashire Cheshire	Eastern (Regional office: Bedford)	Kesteven Holland Norfolk Rutland
North Eastern (Regional office: Harrogate)	Northumberland Durham North Riding West Riding East Riding Lindsey		Huntingdonshire Cambridgeshire West Suffolk East Suffolk Northamptonshire Bedfordshire Oxfordshire
Midland (Regional office: Leamington Spa)	Derbyshire Nottinghamshire Staffordshire Salop Leicestershire Warwickshire Worcestershire Herefordshire		Buckinghamshire Hertfordshire Essex
		South Eastern (Regional office: Dorking)	Berkshire Surrey Kent Hampshire West Sussex East Sussex
South Western Regional office: Taunton)	Gloucestershire Wiltshire Somerset Dorset Devon Cornwall	Greater London	Special arrangements apply in London which is the responsibility of London Highways Division in Headquarters

Table 5.2. Participating counties

RCU	Participating counties
North Western	Lancashire, Cheshire
North Eastern	Durham, Yorkshire (West Riding)
Midland	Derbyshire, Staffordshire, Warwickshire
South Western	Devon, Gloucestershire, Somerset
South Eastern	Hampshire, Kent, Surrey
Eastern	Bedfordshire, Buckinghamshire, Essex, Hertfordshire

the scheme (Table 5.2) and it was envisaged that counties would move in and out as the pattern of work changed.

Directors of the Units were on the staff of the Ministry and Chief Engineers of the Sub-Units were the County Surveyors of the participating counties acting as part-time officials of the Unit of which they were a part.

The first Directors of RCUs and their deputies were drawn equally from local authorities and the Ministry of Transport. Only the post of Director of the Midland RCU was advertised and Ron Bridle was the successful applicant. Sir James Drake, previously County Surveyor and Bridgemaster in Lancashire, became Director of the North Western RCU and Maurice Milne, previously County Surveyor of West Sussex, was appointed Director of the South Eastern RCU. The civil servants who were appointed Directors were Pat Lyth (South Western), Gilbert Norris (North Eastern) and Bill Spencer (Eastern). Where the Director was from a local authority the deputies appointed were civil servants. In the other three Units they were selected from local authorities by advertisement. All the Controllers of Administration were civil servants except in the North Western RCU.

The role of the Directors of Units was to co-ordinate the work of the Sub-Units, to maintain general control of programming and progress, and to arrange for the allocation of work to Sub-Units, including arranging for participating county Sub-Units to carry out work in counties which were non-participating. The RCUs did not determine the schemes on which they worked; these were decided by the Ministry Headquarters following discussions between all the County Councils affected by the schemes and the Divisional Road Engineering organisation of the Ministry. The RCU was responsible for the detailed planning and design of schemes put to them.

The Ministry hoped that this new organisation would have several advantages.

—Scarce engineering manpower resources would be concentrated into larger units for which a stable long-term programme of work could be foreseen.
—Continuity of work and experience for design and on-site supervision teams would be provided, thus improving efficiency and productivity.

—Greater uniformity of standards and practice would be achieved.

—Closer co-operation in the development of new techniques and procedures would be possible.

—Maximum delegation could be given to those in immediate control of the work, streamlining administrative procedures.

—The Ministry would be enabled to enter into direct contractual relations with the industry and thus develop the best tendering and contract control procedures.

—Ministry staff would be provided with the opportunities to participate in the design and supervision of road schemes with a consequent improvement in feedback on the overall issues involved.

It is evident that the setting up of the RCUs could have had serious consequences for work which had hitherto been handled by consultants. Indeed the intention was that a greater proportion of the motorway and trunk road programme in rural areas would be carried out by the RCU Sub-Units. The Ministry stated[5] however that consulting engineers would "continue to be employed at about the present level—particularly when highly specialised problems arise and to meet peaks in the workload." It was anticipated that consultants would be employed more on urban schemes, particularly where special structural engineering problems were involved.

One problem in setting up the RCU organisation was to determine the level of staffing required to carry out the programme of work concerned. There were only limited data available for this; some obtained in the West Riding of Yorkshire on the Sheffield–Leeds motorway indicated an output of some £250,000 per road-man year and £125,000 per bridge-man year and these values were adopted by the Ministry in assessing Sub-Unit proposals. The shortage of experienced engineers was a major difficulty and meant that programmes could not proceed as quickly as they otherwise would. The growing use of computers in planning and design work, whilst on the one hand helping to reduce staff shortages, on the other expanded the number of possible schemes which could be investigated. Development in the use of computers in highway engineering have been briefly discussed by Bridle.[10]

As time went on increasing amounts of time were taken up in preparing for possible questions at Public Inquiries, in investigating more alternative schemes and through the introduction of more sophisticated methods of analysis, both economic and technical. Another development was the amount of engineers' time taken up in supervising contracts, a matter discussed by Kerensky.[11]

Research organisation

The Road Research Laboratory, which had been part of the Department of Scientific and Industrial Research (DSIR), was transferred to the control of the

Ministry of Transport when DSIR was disbanded on 1 April 1965. As there had always been close collaboration between the Laboratory and the Ministry, particularly with the engineers, the change of control made little immediate difference to their relationships.

The Road Research Laboratory was the principal centre for research within the Ministry on matters relating to the design and construction of motorways and their use. Related programmes of development, e.g. on specifications and traffic control devices, were carried out under the Chief Highway Engineer.

In 1966 the Minister appointed Professor Christopher Foster as Director-General of Economic Planning in the Ministry Headquarters to strengthen the resources for research, development and long-term planning for transport. This new Directorate began by studying methods of forecasting and assessing costs of transport on trunk routes, and an important part of its work was concerned with the development of computer-based economic models.

During this decade a growing amount of research began to be carried out in universities into various aspects of motorway design and usage. As an example, the Ministry commissioned a research study by Leeds University into the economic effects of the construction of the M62.

Motorways and all-purpose dual-carriageway trunk roads

The Ministry of Transport's approach to the planning of a national trunk route network has, over the years, consistently been uncommitted to one particular type of road. The 1,000-mile motorway network has been the nearest approach to a uniform system, but at the same time as motorways were being built other important trunk roads such as the A1 were being improved in part as motorways and in part as all-purpose dual carriageways. This approach is one about which County Surveyors expressed reservations.

This was also a matter raised by the British Road Federation in evidence to the Select Committee on Motorways and Trunk Roads[5]. The then Director of the Federation, Robert Phillipson, said "the Ministry is building roads which are very nearly motorways but they are not getting the best advantages out of them and not the advantages they would get if they built motorways". The Federation considered that all significant new inter-urban trunk roads should be built as motorways. The view of the Ministry, expressed by Sir William Harris, the Director-General Highways, was that until new schemes were examined in detail "from the point of view of other traffic use and the economic return and their physical location we are not prepared to commit ourselves" as to whether they were motorways or not. The Ministry were not saying the new roads would not all be motorways but they were not committing themselves until each scheme had been studied.

The precise nature of the technical assessments and political judgments entering into decisions about particular schemes are not easily available but it is of

Table 5.3. *Mean journey speeds: mile/h*

Vehicle type	M1	A1
Cars	58.5	51
Light goods	48	43.5
Medium goods	41	36.5
Heavy goods	37	32.5
All vehicles	49	43

Table 5.4. *Accidents per mile (1960/62)*

Accident severity	M1	A1
Fatal	0.44	0.62
Serious	2.54	3.97

some interest to record the results of a comparison in 1960/62 of some 70 to 75 miles of the southern section of M1 with an aggregation of about the same length in total of sections of dual carriageway on the A1, some of which were to motorway standard. A comparison of journey speeds and of accidents gave the results shown in Tables 5.3 and 5.4.

Interpretation of these data has to be made with care because the A1 sections were not continuous and not all were dual three-lane like the M1. However, all classes of vehicle were able to travel faster on the M1 motorway than on the A1. Accidents per mile were less on the motorway and probably accidents per vehicle-mile were also less, but relevant traffic data on which to base the calculation were not immediately available.

In 1963 Maxwell Boyd, then the motoring correspondent of the *Sunday Times*, described a drive along the A1 from London to Newcastle.[12] At that time just over half the 287 miles were dual carriageway and he observed that "Today the road is reasonably fast . . . and a drive that once took 8 or 9 hours can be done in 7". He then went on to comment on the nature of the road when dualling would be completed. "A1 will be a patchwork quilt. Parts of it will be like a newly-built motorway. The rest will be converted to all-purpose dual carriageway, but to three different specifications. Some sections will have flyovers instead of intersections, others will have ordinary road junctions where traffic can thrust out into the fast-moving stream without warning."

Planning and programming

The preparation of a motorway or other major trunk road scheme can be a lengthy process. In 1957 Colonel S.M. Lovell,[13] then County Surveyor of Yorkshire West Riding, identified 31 items which might have to be observed, starting with a Ministry request to the local authority to prepare Order details until the stage where the contractor started work on site. In 1969 the Ministry[5] listed the following stages of scheme preparation

—preliminary surveys and consultations, including investigation of alternative lines for the road
—publication of the proposals for the line

61

—fixing the line by Order or as a scheme under the Highways Act 1959
—development of engineering design work
—publication of proposals for the alteration of side roads and accesses
—fixing these alterations by Order under the Highways Act
—preparation of land plans
—land acquisition
—detailed engineering design and preparation of contract documents
—invitations to tender
—letting of contract.

Because of the complexity of these processes it was taking some 5 to 7 years from initial investigation to the completion of motorway and major trunk road schemes; preparation of schemes had to start several years ahead of actual construction with consequent problems for forward planning.

To start with the Ministry tried to deal with this by announcing the strategic network of 1,000 miles of motorway together with a rolling programme of trunk road schemes expected to start 4 or 5 years ahead. This arrangement did not prove satisfactory, mainly because of the variations in the times taken to prepare different types of scheme, and in February 1967 new arrangements were made in which the programme was divided into two parts, the "preparation pool" and the "firm programme". The intention was to establish a pool of motorway and all-purpose trunk road schemes over and above existing programmes from which selections would be made for inclusion in the programme for the early 1970s. The advantages seen for this arrangement were firstly that it would allow preliminary preparation of a substantial reservoir of potential schemes and secondly that it would enable decisions on priorities to be taken in the light of much fuller information about the costs and benefits of schemes. The arrangement appeared on the whole to be finding favour with County Surveyors after 2 or 3 years' experience.

Selection of schemes

One of the earliest methods used by the Ministry of Transport to judge the need for road improvements in rural areas was to assess the extent to which the existing roads were overloaded, overload being defined by the extent to which a road carried a greater volume of traffic than its "design capacity". These standards of design capacity included: for dual two-lane motorways up to 33,000 passenger car units (pcu) per 16 hour August day; and for dual three-lane motorways over 33,000 pcu per 16 hour August day. Although simple to use, overload was not satisfactory in several respects, e.g. stretches of existing road with the same degree of overload could have widely divergent traffic conditions; and it provided no real measure of the economic benefits which might flow from an improvement.

The Ministry then adopted an assessment based on travel and accident loss (TAL). The loss was the difference between operating costs and accident costs as they actually were on the roads and what those costs would be if the roads were built to the Ministry's modern standards for rural dual carriageways. TAL was calculated from observed speeds and accident records using estimates by the Road Research Laboratory of vehicle operating costs and accident costs.

This method provided a first stage, rough-and-ready guide to priorities but something more was required to provide a cost/benefit analysis of the kind devised by the Road Research Laboratory[14-16] and which was being progressively developed by the Ministry. In 1967 the Ministry set up a Highways Economic Unit staffed by economists, engineers and administrators and supported by mathematicians to carry on this work. This Unit evolved a standardised method of appraisal, COBA (COst/Benefit Analysis), which was applied to schemes in the preparation pool and which is still undergoing development in the 1980s.

In 1968, the Ministry of Transport, jointly with the Scottish Development Department and the Welsh Office, issued a memorandum[17] containing revised guidance on methods to be used to forecast levels of future traffic on roads in rural areas. The memorandum was prepared by the Highway Engineering Divisions, Statistics Division and the Road Research Laboratory of the Ministry of Transport and covered: basic data requirements; traffic growth including a traffic forecast table up to the year 2000; modifications to forecasts such as the effects of traffic generation; and the design period.

Control of schemes

Experience with the rapidly developing programme during the earlier 1960s and the difficulties mentioned of uncertainties about the time taken for preliminary stages of schemes to be completed, with consequent problems of relating "starts" to the proper allocation of funds, led the Ministry to consider the use of critical path analysis techniques for reviewing progress with road schemes. The techniques were applied experimentally to the preconstruction stages of some motorway schemes and in view of the success of this experiment they decided to use the techniques on all major schemes in the programme. A joint Working Party was set up with representatives from the Ministry and from local authority associations to recommend methods and procedures to be adopted, and their recommendations relating to trunk road and motorway schemes were implemented in 1967.

The County Councils' Association in evidence to the Select Committee on Motorways and Trunk Roads in 1969[5] remarked "County Councils pioneered the use of critical path analysis techniques in the road construction field and are gratified that the Ministry are now actively sponsoring their application . . .".

Land purchase

A particular bone of contention with County Councils when acting as agent authorities for the Ministry of Transport was the excessive delay which they believed was occurring over the purchase of land for road schemes. This was a matter which County Surveyors had raised with the Select Committee on Trunk Roads in 1958/59 and which the County Councils' Association brought up with the Select Committee on Motorways and Trunk Roads in 1968/69. This latter committee remarked in their report that they were "disturbed to find the identical points being raised by local authority witnesses ten years later in spite of the review promised by the Ministry."

In reply to this in 1971 the Ministry of Transport[18] said that only the Secretaries of State had power to acquire land for trunk roads and the Departments must, therefore, be equipped to carry out the processes of land acquisition. They pointed out that in many cases a compulsory purchase order needed to be made and the appropriate Secretary of State had to be satisfied that the land proposed to be acquired was no more than was needed for the scheme in question. The Ministry did, however, remark that the recent increased delegation on engineering, contracts and land acquisition from Department Headquarters to Divisional Road Engineers in England would shorten lines of communication in the desired direction. There had also been greater delegation of authority to Directors of Road Construction Units.

Inquiries

Depending on the nature of objections raised to the proposed line of a new motorway after publication by the Minister of a proposal to make a scheme under Section 11 of the Highways Act 1959, a Public Inquiry might have to be held. If after such an Inquiry the Minister proceeded to make a scheme its validity could be challenged. If, as usually was the case, alterations to side roads and private accesses were involved further inquiries might be necessary. All these processes gave rise to delays which varied depending on the number and nature of objections which might be raised.

Until 1967 the main statutory steps were taken consecutively; the line was fixed by scheme before design work was carried out to establish where side road alterations etc. were necessary; side road Orders were made before land plans were settled and draft compulsory purchase orders published. After 1967 more flexibility was introduced by allowing concurrent procedures to be followed in suitable cases. This meant that design work could proceed continuously without artificial gaps and objections could be dealt with in one operation, which it was believed would be more helpful to the public by presenting proposals in a more complete form.

Anyone could lodge an objection to a scheme whether their property was affected or not, but they need not disclose the grounds of their objection in advance of an Public Inquiry. The Minister had discretion as to whether to hold an Inquiry unless objections were lodged by certain public authorities, but once an Inquiry was decided upon there was obvious scope for prolonged dispute, as was to become very evident in later years.

Contractual arrangements

In 1963 the Ministry changed its methods of tendering. Up to that time competitive tenders were sought by public advertisement, and this had led to problems for the Ministry in sometimes having to consider passing over the lowest tender because of doubts about the capabilities of the firm submitting it; and contractors would sometimes submit tenders merely to keep their name before the client, thus leading to a number of abortive tenders.

Under the new procedure, which was agreed in advance with the Federation of Civil Engineering Contractors (FCEC), a limited number of firms of known experience and capacity were invited to submit tenders for works. Contractors interested in undertaking highway work were supplied at intervals through the FCEC with information about schemes likely to start in the next 2 years so that contractors could notify the Ministry of those schemes for which they wished to be invited to tender. When a scheme was to go ahead, a preliminary inquiry was made of about ten firms who had expressed an interest in the scheme, and normally six of these would be actually invited to tender.

Six years later, in 1969, in evidence to the Select Committee on Motorways and Trunk Roads[5] the FCEC representatives expressed their satisfaction with the system; the Director of the Federation said "I think it is the considered view of the Federation that selective tendering is the best way to operate. This is in accordance with the Banwell[19] and Harris[20] reports which have been fully debated and argued." Selective tendering was also endorsed in the Lofthouse report on *Efficiency in road construction*[6] published in 1966 by the Economic Development Committee for Civil Engineering. The Lofthouse Committee saw other aims for future development of the construction industry as: more continuity of work; more specialisation in major highway works; better communications; more collaborative working; a close analysis of costs and benefits; and a clearer appreciation of the price of public accountability.

Some aspects of design and construction

Road layout

In 1966, the standard cross-section for motorways which had measured some 129 ft overall for dual three-lane was reduced by 13 ft to 116 ft overall. This was achieved by a reduction of 5 ft in the width of each verge, a 6 in reduction in the width of each hard shoulder and the omission of a separate 1 ft marginal strip adjoining the central reserve. It was estimated that these changes would reduce cost by some £22,000 per mile, a saving of around 3% on construction costs. A further £10,000 per mile was to be saved by: amendment to the drainage specification; elimination of hard shoulders on slip roads; siting the access to maintenance compounds at interchanges; and setting up a system of parent and satellite maintenance compounds in place of individual stations with full facilities.

The changes to the cross-section were of concern to the local authorities and to the motoring organisations, particularly as regards the effect on safety of the reduced distance between opposing carriageways, and the Select Committee of 1968/69[5] recommended that a detailed study should be made and published by the Road Research Laboratory (RRL) of the likely effect on accident rates of the reductions in motorway standards and that any future decision on this matter by the Ministry should be taken in the light of such a study. In their official reply[18] to this recommendation the Ministry of Transport said that they considered that the effect on safety of the changes would be negligible. 150 miles of motorway built to the new standards would be opened by the end of 1971 but at least 2 years' accident experience would be necessary to assess any significant change in accident rate. The Ministry considered it was too early to make such a special study and that the resources of the RRL could be better employed on other work. In any case, the Ministry were now installing safety barriers on the central reservations of all motorways.

Safety fences

In 1966 a Select Committee of the House of Commons[21] enquired into the work of the Road Research Laboratory and, in commenting on the length of time spent on research, referred specifically to work on the design of crash barriers for motorways and recommended that the Ministry should instruct the Laboratory "to give special priority to bringing their research work on crash barriers for motorways to a speedy conclusion".

In their reply to this recommendation in 1968, the Ministry observed that trials with safety fences on two 9 mile sections of motorway began in 1964 and that in 1966 the RRL had recommended that a tensioned beam fence was best for use on central reservations. A fence of this type was being erected on some 6 miles of the M4 to give protection against lamp standards in the central reservation and along 1 mile of the Hendon urban motorway. In consequence the Ministry saw no need to instruct the RRL further in the matter.

The Ministry went on to discuss the possible value of safety fences on motorways and concluded that on the evidence then available, the installation of safety fences on all motorways would not give good value in terms of casualties saved by comparison with other projects. However, it might be that as traffic volumes increased, the value of safety fences might also increase and further trials on high volume roads would be made.

Some 2 years later in August 1970, the Minister of Transport decided to install safety barriers on the central reserve of motorways with a view to completing the installation on 1,000 miles by 1975.

Weather

An interesting new element in design arose with two motorways in hilly country: the M6 section between Lancaster and Penrith in the neighbourhood of Shap and the M62 where it crossed the Pennines. Detailed meteorological studies were made in each case to assess the effects of choice of route on the likely occurrence on the motorways of fog, frequency of frost, snow and high winds. Descriptions of these investigations were given by J.K.M. Henry[22] for the M6 and by Colonel S.M. Lovell[23] for the M62. (See chapter 7.)

Service areas

By the end of the decade there were 16 service areas on motorways providing refuelling and refreshment facilities, toilets, telephones, parking and a breakdown service and eleven more were under construction. Others were being planned at approximately 25 mile intervals as the motorway network was extended.

Hazard warning signs

The occurrence of unexpected hazards under the fast, free-flowing conditions on motorways led the Ministry of Transport to investigate the possibility of providing remotely controlled signalling systems to warn drivers of those hazards. Trials were started on 26 miles of the M5 south of Birmingham with signs at 2 mile intervals remotely controlled by the police. The signs could show one or more of the legends "Accident", "Fog" and "Skid risk" combined with "Slow" and a pair of alternately flashing amber lights. An alternative system was introduced as a matter of urgency following multiple accidents in fog at the end of 1965 and consisted of simple vertical flashing amber signals, battery operated and individually switched, located at 1 mile intervals. When turned on the signals indicated that drivers should not exceed 30 mile/h.

Following experience with these early systems, the Ministry developed a computer-controlled system which provided for the remote operation and supervision from police force headquarters of a new type of motorway traffic signal and an improved emergency telephone system. The signals told drivers when to change lanes or reduce speed. Usually the signals were mounted on columns in the central reserve, but on very busy motorways they were mounted on gantries one over each lane. By 1970 signal systems were in use on 80 miles and contracts let for systems on a further 400 miles.

Bridges

Bridges and associated structures accounted for some 25 to 30% of total motorway expenditure. With such a large programme of bridge construction there were strong reasons in favour of standardisation of methods of design, choice of materials and methods of construction and this was encouraged by the Ministry of Transport. The evolution of more detailed methods of analysis and the use of computers made possible more efficient designs and the Ministry of Transport and County Surveyors' Society collaborated in the writing of new computer programmes for bridge design. A major development in design was the concept of the streamlined box girder form of construction used on the Severn Bridge.

Among the many remarkable bridges and structures which came into use during the decade some of the more spectacular were: the Barton High Level Bridge carrying the M62, now the M63, over the Manchester Ship Canal which was opened in 1960; the Thelwall Bridge on the M6 over the Manchester Ship Canal and River Mersey which was opened in 1963; the Medway Bridge on the M2 opened in the same year; the Forth Bridge (not strictly a motorway but forming an essential link between the M90 to the north and the M8 and M9 to the south of the Forth) which was opened by HM the Queen in 1964; the Severn Bridge which was opened by HM the Queen in 1966; and the Almondsbury interchange also opened by HM the Queen in 1966.

Specifications

The Ministry of Transport acts as a central co-ordinating body responsible for translating research and practical experience into specifications for road design and construction. The Ministry's *Specification for road and bridge works*[24] was revised during the 1960s, the fourth edition coming into use in April 1969. This revision drew extensively on the experience gained from work on motorways and had a particular objective of defining contractual requirements more clearly and allowing contractors to have greater freedom in the choice of materials and methods of construction. Methods of measurement for road and bridge works were also revised in accordance with the standard drawn up by the Institution of Civil Engineers adapted to suit the needs of highway construction.

Maintenance

As has been mentioned earlier, the standards of construction on the first motorways, which were essentially experimental, proved not to be adequate for the traffic which they had to carry. This necessitated major repairs in some cases. In 1962 a £1.5 million programme of repairs on the M1 was underway. The work included: the reconstruction of hard shoulders; the extension of central reserve drainage throughout the whole length of the motorway; replacement of the telephone system; and repairs to the slow lanes. As a result of experience with the early failures, higher standards of construction were adopted which it was believed would not need other than normal maintenance for at least 10 years.

With the intense traffic on them, some of the concrete motorway surfaces became polished and slippery when wet. Various techniques of grooving and surface dressing were developed to cope with this problem but not without bringing other problems. Grooving gave rise to tyre noise and surface dressing had to be carefully controlled to ensure satisfactory adhesion of chippings to the surface. An unfortunate experience on the M4 led to a large number of shattered windscreens from flying stones.

It is important that the motorway system is kept open at all times and in all weathers. Considerable attention was therefore paid from the start to winter maintenance on motorways; this is carried out on an agency basis by the County Councils. Maintenance depots were built at intervals of about 12 miles at which hoppers for loading salt or grit were installed and where suitable vehicles for loading and spreading these materials were stationed, along with snow-clearing vehicles. The motorways were kept open throughout the severe winter of 1962/63.

In October 1967 the Minister of Transport set up a Committee on Highway Maintenance jointly with the Secretaries of State for Scotland and Wales, the Association of Municipal Corporations, the County Councils' Association and the Urban District Councils' Association, under the chairmanship of Dr A.H. Marshall of the University of Birmingham. The Committee had terms of reference requiring it to consider desirable maintenance standards, productivity and administration; its report was published in 1970[25].

Because of the high speeds of traffic on motorways especial care needed to be taken in carrying out maintenance. To give guidance on this and on dealing with emergencies, the Scottish Development Department and the Ministry of Transport issued a *Traffic safety code*[26] in 1962 "to give advice and guidance to highway authorities, agent authorities, contractors, statutory undertakers and others concerned on the measures needed to be taken when road works or other temporary obstructions and emergencies on motorways make it necessary."

Driving conditions

As the motorway network developed, drivers began to gain experience of driving at high speed along relatively long stretches of uninterrupted highway. The attraction of motorways to drivers was reflected in the growth of traffic on them which was substantially above that on other roads; Ginns[27] in 1966 recorded that traffic growth on four typical motorways was over 20% per annum.

Accident experience on motorways was also proving favourable: e.g. casualties on the London–Birmingham motorway were just over 1.0 per million vehicle-miles in 1964 compared with 2.42 on all rural trunk and Class I roads.[27] Fatality rates were also less but accidents when they happened on motorways tended to be more serious; of the figures quoted above, about 7% of casualties were fatal on the motorway compared with about 3.5% on other important rural roads.

The importance of vehicles being maintained in good condition for driving on motorways soon became apparent. 90% of "emergency" calls by drivers were vehicle breakdowns, of which 30% were due to tyre failures.

Weather conditions could make driving particularly hazardous on motorways if drivers did not adjust their speeds. This was brought home by some dramatic multiple accidents in fog. Wet roads also gave rise (and still do) to visibility problems caused by the spray thrown up by fast-moving traffic. Research showed[27] that for private cars at 60 mile/h the fitting of mudflaps could reduce spray by a quarter, which was about the same as that achieved by reducing speed to 55 mile/h. Heavy vehicles were a much more serious problem and research indicated that the fitting of mudflaps would produce a much greater effect. Unfortunately heavy vehicles are still a problem.

Another way of combatting the spray problem is to make the surface of the road porous so that water does not accumulate on it. Trials of possible surfacings were begun on the High Wycombe by-pass, M40, to assess their practicability.

Because of the concern in many quarters over the effect of speed on accidents on motorways, the Ministry of Transport sought advice from the Road Research Laboratory about the likely effects of introducing speed limits on them. Largely on the basis of the information provided by the Laboratory the Minister, the Rt Hon. Barbara Castle, in 1965 introduced an experimental 70 mile/h speed limit on all roads, including motorways, not already subject to lower limits. The Road Research Laboratory was asked to evaluate the effect and it published its conclusions in June 1967[28]. The report indicated amongst other things that there was an estimated saving of 20% in total motorway casualties following the introduction of the speed limit and it was on the strength of this report that the Minister decided to continue the speed limit indefinitely in September 1967.

Motoring organisations opposed the speed limit and criticised the role of the Road Research Laboratory in the experiment, in evidence to the Select Committee on Road Research in 1967,[21] on the grounds that as the Laboratory had become a part of the Ministry of Transport rather than an independent part of the Government scientific service (as it had been in the former Department of Scientific and Industrial Research) a suspicion of undue influence by the Ministry on the Laboratory could arise.

On dual three-lane motorways, the use by heavy vehicles of the fast lane began to be criticised as causing delay and giving rise to potentially dangerous situations. In May 1966, six months after the 70 mile/h limit was first introduced, the Ministry banned the use of this lane by heavy vehicles and this measure seems to have been welcomed by the motoring organisations and by car drivers generally.

Green and White Papers

As briefly mentioned earlier, in 1969 the Government issued a Green Paper *Roads for the future*[3] putting forward for public discussion proposals for future trunk road development beyond the present programme. In a foreword to the Paper, the Minister referred to the 1,000 miles of motorway to be completed in the early 1970s; he continued "it is no longer sufficient to plan in terms of so many miles of road since the nation is concerned with effective networks rather than with individual roads."

The Green Paper came in for criticism from motoring organisations and from the British Road Federation. The Automobile Association considered it to be a time-consuming procedure which could lead to a gap between the completion of the 1,000 miles of motorway and the Green Paper programme; the Society of

Motor Manufacturers and Traders said it gave no indication of standards to which routes would be developed, apart from them being dual carriageways, nor of priorities; the British Road Federation were disappointed by the level of expenditure proposed.

In May 1970 the Government followed up the Green Paper with a White Paper *Roads for the future: the new inter-urban plan for England*[4] (proposals for roads in Scotland and in Wales were published earlier). It was claimed that the concept of the comprehensive development plan put forward in the Green Paper "was widely welcomed". Existing programmes would provide 1,000 miles of motorway and about the same mileage of all-purpose dual carriageway by the end of 1972. The Government concluded that if the expanded network could be completed in the next 15 to 20 years together with a programme of work on other trunk roads "real congestion on the inter-urban trunk road system as a whole could be virtually eliminated."

The problems of traffic in towns were coming increasingly to the forefront and transport planning surveys were being carried out in the major conurbations. The White Paper envisaged a change in the balance of expenditure between roads in rural and in urban areas in favour of urban road schemes.

Summary

The 1960s saw the largest road building programme ever started in Britain and at the end of the decade the inter-urban network of main routes had been substantially modernised by the construction of motorways and all-purpose dual carriageways. The 1,000 mile motorway programme which had started under a Conservative administration was continued in the second half of the period by a Labour administration which, by 1970, was planning not only further extensions of the inter-urban system but also a growth of expenditure on roads in urban areas.

There were undoubted pressures on Governments to provide for the needs of the increasing number of car owners and of the road transport industry generally and there were pressures then, which are still strong today, to remove through-traffic from towns and villages. Investment policies were clearly influenced by these pressures but considerable credit for the level of Government investment in the road programmes must go to successive Ministers of Transport who, significantly perhaps, were members of the Cabinet.

There were, of course, critics of the motorway programme, some taking the view that whilst it was substantial it was still not enough to meet traffic needs, and others arguing against it on grounds of its being environmentally unacceptable and largely unnecessary if greater use were made of railways.

The programme meant that road engineers, designers and contractors began to gain real experience of motorway construction and there were considerable developments of design skills and construction techniques. The Ministry of

Transport and local authorities had to learn to adapt to the needs of the new situation as planners and managers of large programmes. The evolution of the Road Construction Units was an important step forward in this respect.

The motoring public and road transport operators soon realised that the motorway network was opening up new possibilities for road travel. Journeys could be made more quickly so that productivity on business trips could be increased and leisure travel was changed: for instance it became easy to reach the Lake District from Manchester using the M6. Motorways were, however, not universally liked by drivers, many of whom preferred the all-purpose routes such as the A1, although reasons for this preference were not always clear.

In short, the development of the motorway network in the 1960s was bringing about a major change in transport in the country, the economic and social effects of which were only just beginning to be perceived at the end of the decade.

References

1. MINISTER OF TRANSPORT. *Roads in England and Wales 1959–60.* HMSO, London, 1961.
2. MINISTER OF TRANSPORT. *Roads in England and Wales 1969–70.* HMSO, London, 1970.
3. MINISTRY OF TRANSPORT. *Roads for the future: a new inter-urban plan.* HMSO, London, 1969.
4. MINISTRY OF TRANSPORT. *Roads for the future: the new inter-urban plan for England.* HMSO, London, 1970.
5. SELECT COMMITTEE OF THE HOUSE OF COMMONS. *Sixth report session 1968–69. Motorways and trunk roads.* HMSO, London, 1969.
6. ECONOMIC DEVELOPMENT COMMITTEE FOR CIVIL ENGINEERING. *Efficiency in road construction.* HMSO, London, 1966, 1967.
7. BRITISH ROAD FEDERATION. *Symposium on road administration and finance.* British Road Federation, London, 1966.
8. MINISTER OF TRANSPORT. *Transport policy.* HMSO, London, 1966.
9. MINISTER OF TRANSPORT. *Roads in England 1966–67.* HMSO, London, 1967.
10. BRIDLE R.J. Computers in highway engineering. *The highway engineer,* 1980, **27**, no. 6.
11. KERENSKY O.A. The consulting engineer's view. Part 2, Supervision. *Proceedings of the conference on motorways in Britain.* Institution of Civil Engineers, London, 1971.
12. MAXWELL B. The Great North Road. *Sunday Times Colour Supplement,* 28 April 1963.
13. LOVELL S.M. Suitability of the existing highway organization to deal with an expanding road programme. *Proceedings of the conference on the highway needs of Great Britain.* Institution of Civil Engineers, London, 1957.
14. COBURN T.M., BEESLEY M.E. and REYNOLDS D.J. *The London–Birmingham motorway: traffic and economics.* DSIR road research technical paper no. 46. HMSO, London, 1960.

15. CHARLESWORTH G. and PAISLEY J.L. The economic assessment of returns from road works. *Proc. Instn Civ. Engrs,* 1959, **14**, 229–254.

16. REYNOLDS D.J. *The assessment of priority for road improvements.* DSIR road research technical paper no. 48. HMSO, London, 1960.

17. MINISTRY OF TRANSPORT, SCOTTISH DEVELOPMENT DEPARTMENT and WELSH OFFICE. *Traffic prediction for rural roads.* HMSO, London, 1968.

18. EXPENDITURE COMMITTEE OF THE HOUSE OF COMMONS. *2nd report 1971–72. Motorways and trunk roads.* HMSO, London, 1971.

19. MINISTRY OF PUBLIC BUILDING AND WORKS. *Report of the Committee on the placing and management of contracts for building and civil engineering work.* HMSO, London, 1964.

20. ECONOMIC DEVELOPMENT COMMITTEE FOR CIVIL ENGINEERING. *Contracting in civil engineering since Banwell.* HMSO, London, 1968.

21. SELECT COMMITTEE OF THE HOUSE OF COMMONS. *Twelfth report. Session 1966–67. Road Research.* HMSO, London, 1967.

22. HENRY J.K.M. Selection of route for the Lancaster–Penrith section of M6 motorway. *Proceedings of the 5th world meeting of the International Road Federation.* IRF, London, 1966.

23. LOVELL S.M. Birth of a motorway. *Surveyor,* 1966, **127**, 22 January, 15–19; 29 January, 20–25.

24. MINISTRY OF TRANSPORT, SCOTTISH DEVELOPMENT DEPARTMENT and WELSH OFFICE. *Specification for road and bridge works.* HMSO, London, 1969.

25. MINISTER OF TRANSPORT. *Report of the Committee on Highway Maintenance.* HMSO, London, 1970.

26. SCOTTISH DEVELOPMENT DEPARTMENT and MINISTRY OF TRANSPORT. *Traffic safety code for road works and emergencies on motorways.* HMSO, London, 1962.

27. GINNS H.N. *English motorways—development and progress.* Final report of the Public Works and Municipal Services Congress and Exhibition Council, London, 1966.

28. ROAD RESEARCH LABORATORY. *Report on the 70 m.p.h. speed limit trial.* Special report no. 6. HMSO, London, 1967.

6

1970–1980: the troubled years

Introduction

The last decade opened with the target of 1,000 miles of motorway in Britain well within sight; in fact this target was achieved in 1972. Plans were being made for further extensions to the main inter-urban network to meet forecast future traffic demands. The Labour Government's proposals in 1970 were referred to in the last chapter and the broad strategy for roads was not seriously changed by the Conservative Government which came to power late in 1970. Their programme included the construction of a further 1,000 miles of inter-urban motorways by the early 1980s as part of a primary network of high-standard trunk routes. Both Governments saw a need for increased expenditure on roads in urban areas and were looking to the Urban Motorways Committee, set up in 1969, to advise on how urban roads could be better related to their surroundings.

The aim of an extra 1,000 miles of motorway by the early 1980s turned out to be ephemeral and by 1980 only about half that mileage had been built. One reason was the effect of the marked increase in the price of oil demanded by the Oil Producing and Exporting Countries (OPEC) starting in 1973, which without doubt has led to serious recession in countries of the Western World. Although Britain has to a considerable extent been cushioned from some effects of the oil crisis by North Sea oil and gas the economy has been in serious decline and successive Governments have been seeking economies, notably by cutting capital expenditure programmes, and, as had occurred in similar circumstances in earlier years, the new roads programme did not escape being cut.

Another factor of considerable importance affecting progress with motorway programmes was the delay resulting from Public Inquiries and the effect this had on the ability of the Ministry of Transport to spend its budget.

The Department of the Environment

The Conservative Government elected in 1970 under the Rt Hon. Edward Heath introduced two important changes affecting the administration of roads.

74

The first was the creation of the Department of the Environment (DoE), which brought together under a Secretary of State the former Ministry of Transport, Minstry of Housing and Local Government and Ministry of Public Building and Works. The second was the reorganisation of local government in 1974, which resulted in responsibility for roads and traffic at local government level being vested in fewer authorities and which also changed the system of grants to local authorities for roads.

Under the Secretary of State for the Environment there were three Ministers, one for Housing and Construction, one for Local Government and Development and one for Transport Industries. The responsibility for the location, design and planning of roads of the former Minister of Transport were initially regarded as being "an integral part of land use planning"[1] and to that extent were placed under the Minister of Local Government and Development. However, in 1972 responsibility for roads was transferred to the Minister for Transport Industries and that Minister's role thus moved nearer to that of the former Minister of Transport. Nevertheless overall responsibility for roads still lay with the Secretary of State for the Environment. This state of affairs persisted until the Rt Hon. James Callaghan became Prime Minister of the Labour Government on the resignation of the Rt Hon. Sir Harold Wilson in 1976: then a Department of Transport was separated from the Department of the Environment although certain common services remained under the Department, in particular research.

From 1965 to 1970 the Road Research Laboratory (RRL) had been part of the Ministry of Transport, carrying out programmes approved by the Minister of Transport. When the DoE was created a Directorate-General of Research was formed bringing together several government research establishments including the RRL. The scope of the RRL was extended to include research on broader aspects of transport, notably transport planning, and in recognition of this, in January 1972 the Laboratory was renamed the Transport and Road Research Laboratory (TRRL). About this time the customer/contractor relationship for government research establishments was formally adopted by the Government. This meant that most of the research programme of the TRRL had to meet specific needs of the policy and executive branches of the DoE. The effect of all these changes meant that a smaller proportion of the total effect of the Laboratory was devoted to "road" problems since greater effort was called for to meet requirements in the broader transport field. To what extent this may have resulted in a lack of sufficient research specifically concerned with motorway planning, design and construction, maintenance and use is difficult to say. There is little doubt that more information on these matters would be of value particularly in regard to assessing the impact of motorways on the economy and social life of the community. The comment, remarked on earlier, by the Select Committee in 1958/59[2] that because of lack of sufficient research in earlier years "Britain's first motorways are in the nature of experimental roads" could well be echoed in 1980:

it is uncertain whether sufficient research had been carried out on the motorways that had been built in the previous 20 years to provide sound guidance on policy for future motorways.

One other result of the creation of the DoE was the bringing together in regional organisations of the day-to-day administration of housing, planning, roads and transportations and of the Regional Economic Planning Councils and Boards. In consequence the old Ministry of Transport Divisional Road Engineers were replaced by Regional Controllers (Roads and Transportation). The organisation of the Road Construction Units remained unchanged at that time.

The oil crisis of 1973

The sharp rise in the price of oil imposed by OPEC in the autumn of 1973 triggered a serious energy crisis in the Western World whose economies, particularly that of the USA, are so heavily dependent on oil as a source of energy. In Britain some two thirds of the total energy requirements are supplied by oil and road transport accounts for about a quarter of the total petroleum consumption.

The Government had to consider both short and longer term measures to meet what were clearly not only immediate difficulties but also difficulties reaching into the future. So far as road traffic was concerned there were pressures on Ministers to introduce rationing as a means of securing savings in consumption, but these were resisted and instead a speed limit of 50 mile/h was introduced, initially for a period of 6 months, on all roads which did not have a lower limit in force and there was an increase in the price of motor fuel.

The effect of the crisis on the total distance run by traffic on roads (vehicle-kilometrage) was to reverse the growth on rural roads (excluding motorways) and vehicle-kilometrage on those roads did not reach the 1973 levels again until 1976 (Fig. 6.1). On motorways the rapid growth prior to 1973 slowed down in 1974 but the level of vehicle-kilometrage was still higher than in 1973. After that the rapid growth continued. However, there was a drop in the mean flow on motorways between 1973 and 1974 because the length of motorway increased more in percentage terms than did the vehicle-kilometrage.

There is evidence to show that when allowance is made for inflation, households spent less of their income on buying new motor vehicles in 1975/76 after the oil crisis than before it, but spent about the same proportion of their income on maintaining and running motor vehicles.[3]

The effect of the 50 mile/h speed limit was studied by the TRRL on the M3 and M4.[4] Speeds were at their lowest in December 1973, the mean speed of cars being 15 mile/h below the "normal" speed of 70 mile/h on those motorways. Speeds then started to rise and by September 1974 were back to the normal level. The 50 mile/h limit had been discontinued after 6 months and had reverted to 70 mile/h on motorways in April 1974.

During the 6 month period of the 50 mile/h speed limit there was a reduction in accidents of 40% in daylight and 28% in darkness over and above that likely to be explained by trends with time and seasonal variations and also with reductions in traffic. There were indications that by the end of the experimental period the accident rate in daylight was returning towards expectation. In darkness the reduction persisted through May.

The rise in oil prices affected not only people using the roads but also the contractors who were engaged on contracts let at the time of the price rise. In May 1974 the Government announced *ex gratia* payments to reimburse contractors for costs arising from these unforeseeable price rises on trunk road contracts. Also in 1974 variation of price of contracts using the Baxter formulae came into operation on jobs over 1 year duration.

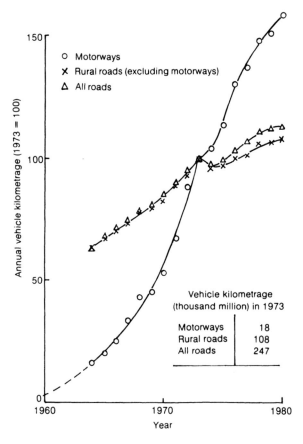

Fig. 6.1 Motorway traffic on roads in Britain (source of data: Transport Statistics Great Britain, HMSO)

Environmental issues

The inter-urban trunk road programme for England in 1971 had six main aims[1]

(1) to achieve environmental improvements by diverting long-distance traffic and particularly heavy goods vehicles from a large number of towns and villages so as to relieve them of noise, dirt and danger

(2) to complete by the early 1980s a comprehensive network of strategic trunk routes to promote economic growth

(3) to link the more remote and less prosperous regions with this new national network

(4) to ensure that every major city and town with a population of more than 250,000 would be directly connected to the strategic network and that towns with a population of more than 80,000 would be within 10 miles of it

(5) to design the network to serve all major ports and airports

(6) to relieve as many historic towns as possible of through trunk road traffic.

Environmental objectives were thus explicitly included in the roads programme and the creation of the Department of the Environment meant that issues relating to the environment could receive proper attention when decisions were being made about schemes in the programme. The need to minimise the damage which some roads could cause to the environment was recognised, as was also the possibility that major road schemes could enhance the environment as well as provide economic benefit. The importance of careful design in relation to the environment can perhaps be seen on the M6 in the Lune Gorge on the M40 where it cuts through the Chilterns and on the M62 over the Pennines with its associated Scammonden Dam.

Environmental issues which were increasingly to the fore in inter-urban road schemes were much more prominent when it came to motorways in urban areas, as will be seen in chapter 9.

In 1972, and arising out of recommendations of the Urban Motorways Committee, the Government published a White Paper, *Development and compensation—putting people first*, setting out its intentions concerning terms of compensation for those people affected by new public works. This was followed by the Land Compensation Act 1973 which among other things permitted highway authorities to fit roads into their surroundings and to mitigate adverse environmental effects. More land could be purchased, extra landscaping and planting carried out and noise barriers or insulation installed to reduce the impact of new roads. The Noise Insulation Regulations 1973 made under the Act enabled dwellings and other buildings used for residential purposes to be provided with insulation against traffic or road construction noise.

Research was initiated into noise produced by traffic under various conditions and into maximum acceptable noise levels. Largely as a result of this work the Noise Insulation Regulations 1975 were made, which require the Department of

Transport to provide double glazing or equivalent compensation for properties which in certain circumstances become subject to noise levels greater than a specified amount (68 dB(A)L_{10}).

Experiments were also made into ways of reducing noise and one of the first of these was with lengths of noise barrier and sound insulation in buildings near the M6 motorway at Perry Barr, Birmingham.

Noise is one of the more readily evaluated environmental factors but several others have been identified as of importance. In 1976 the Department of Transport received a report[5] from a working party under J. Jefferson which had been set up "to draft guidance to Road Construction Units on the location of major inter-urban road schemes with regard to noise and other environmental issues". The report identified area of land taken, noise, vibration, air pollution, visual effects, severence and accidents as environmental factors to be taken into account and recommended that a standard format should be introduced for their presentation. The Department accepted the recommendations.

Public participation

Concern over environmental effects arising from the growth of motor traffic and from the construction of new roads, particularly motorways, to cater for that traffic was augmented in the early 1970s by concern for the availability of resources for road traffic in the future and by a growing awareness of the importance of involving the public in decisions about new roads. The work of Forrester[6] and Meadows[7] in the USA had focused attention on the rate at which non-renewable resources were being consumed and the importance of oil in this connection was brought home in a dramatic way when OPEC raised its prices in 1973. Questions were being asked about the need to build motorways for traffic which might not exist "if the oil ran out".

A step towards providing more information for the public concerned about new road schemes was afforded in the Highways Act of 1971. This empowered the Secretary of State to provide additional publicity about such schemes including: individual notification of occupiers living within 100 yards of the new road; the provision of a statement fully describing the proposal and the reasons for it; and the provision of leaflets describing the statutory procedures, the rights of objectors and the entitlement to compensation. In addition special exhibitions and public meetings could be held where models and large-scale plans could be seen and officials questioned about the proposals.[8]

Many County Surveyors had been urging on the Ministry for several years before 1970 the value, and indeed necessity, of early information to the general public to overcome accusations levelled at the Ministry of secrecy and of minds made up in advance come what may.

In 1973 the Secretary of State issued a consultation paper inviting comments on a proposal that the public should be invited to comment on practical road alternatives before a decision was taken as to which routes would be developed further. The proposal was welcomed and in July 1973 the Secretary of State announced that the procedure would be adopted as a regular stage in trunk road planning. The procedure, which is still used, required the setting out of the main features of alternatives in a consultation document which is circulated to interested local authorities and organisations and the seeking of comments from individual members of the public. A public exhibition is mounted and at least 6 weeks allowed for comments. According to T.P. (later Sir Trevor) Hughes[9] when he was Deputy Secretary Roads and Local Transport at the Department of Transport, there are mixed views as to whether the procedure introduces unnecessary delays or whether it goes far enough in involving the public. He considered that the aim must be on the one hand to involve the public in a way that helps decision-making but is not too complex or costly, and on the other hand to speed up internal administrative processes without reducing the quality of consideration given to all relevant factors.

Public Inquiries

The Public Inquiry provides the statutory base for objections to be made to road schemes and the procedures to be followed in the case of motorway schemes have been referred to earlier. In 1973 the Department of the Environment issued a booklet[10] to help anyone concerned with taking part or being represented at a Public Inquiry concerned with a road proposal which was before the Secretary of State for his decision. A detailed description of the various legal processes involved in new roadworks has been given by H. Woodhouse.[11]

During the 1970s the Public Inquiry procedure into motorway proposals in particular began to be challenged. Public anxiety began to be felt about the scope and conduct of inquiries and people wanted to be sure that there was a genuine need for a new road, that the new route had been thoroughly investigated and that there would be a fair and impartial hearing by the Inspector.

The Government considered that local inquiries about particular schemes could not sensibly be about national policies. To advise on such policies, the Secretary of State for Transport set up an Advisory Committee on Trunk Road Assessment[12] in 1976 under the chairmanship of Sir George Leitch with terms of reference

"(a) to comment on, and recommend any changes in, the Department's method of appraising trunk road schemes and their application, taking account both of economic and environmental factors and of the extent to which these methods give a satisfactory basis for comparison with investment in alternative methods of transport; and

"(b) to review the Department's method of traffic forecasting, its application of the forecasts and to comment on the sensitivity of the forecasts to possible policy changes."

The Committee's report was published in 1978 and its work has been continued by a Standing Advisory Committee on Trunk Road Assessment (SACTRA).

In 1976 the Council on Tribunals joined with the Department of the Environment in carrying out a review of highway inquiry procedures; when the Department of Transport was formed later in 1976 it also took part. Whilst this review was under way the Lord Chancellor, after consultation with the Council on Tribunals, laid rules of procedure at highway inquiries before Parliament and these came into operation in June 1976. The review[13] was completed and presented to Parliament in 1978 and set out the actions which the Government would be taking. This was a Labour Government but the Conservative Government in 1980 also endorsed the recommendations of the review.

Following upon the recommendations of the Leitch Committee and those of the review, there is now a closer and more open examination of road proposals at inquiries. Government's policy for national road planning and their assumptions are explained, as are the techniques of appraising road schemes. The reasons for putting forward particular schemes are considered in depth and the Department's approach is to provide all the necessary factual material on which a scheme depends. In some cases, pre-Inquiry procedural meetings are held by the Inspector to clarify the scope of questions on policy and need.

The final decision on the Department of Transport's road schemes in England is taken jointly by the Secretaries of State for Transport and the Environment (the Secretaries of State for Wales and for Scotland make the decisions on their own schemes). Because of criticism that they had been responsible for appointing their own Inspectors, who could therefore be biased in their favour, it was decided in 1978 as a result of the review that in future all Inspectors would be appointed on the nomination of the Lord Chancellor. This seems to have been well received.

Disturbances at Inquiries

A problem that arose at a number of Inquiries during the 1970s was the disruptive tactics used by certain objectors. One objector who appeared on several occasions was John Tyme, at one time a lecturer at Sheffield Polytechnic, who has described the part he played on those occasions in a book *Motorways versus democracy*[14]. He states as his belief that the motorway trunk road programme "poses a consummate evil" by helping to create a "profligate and wasteful society". He considers that Public Inquiries into motorway proposals deny essential information to people affected, that motorway proposals are entirely without Parliamentary approval and that the Department of Transport is in the hands of a road lobby. In seeking to make his views known at Inquiries he became convinced that "in the face of the (corrupt) alliance between the road lobby and the highway mandarins in Marsham Street, civil disobedience was ... the only means of showing the extent and depth of popular feeling and opposition to the endless proliferation of motorways ... ."

John Tyme's views are clearly controversial and in order that they might be debated with professional engineers the North Western Transport Engineering Group of the Insitution of Civil Engineers arranged two meetings in the winter of 1979/80, at one of which he gave his views on major highway planning and construction of the future; at the other a response to those views was made by A.E. Naylor, the County Engineer of Greater Manchester Council. Tyme explained why he believed that motorways are disastrous in themselves and why he thought that the "auto way of life" was leading to a world-wide calamity. Naylor pointed out the popularity of motor transport among the general public and the freedom of travel that it brought to millions of people. For these reasons he disagreed profoundly with Tyme's view that roads made democracy impossible.

Inquiries and the law

An important legal issue arose out of the Inquiry held in 1973/74 into schemes for the M42 in Bromsgrove and the M40 in Warwickshire. The Inspector refused to allow objectors to cross-examine DoE witnesses about their traffic forecasts. After the Inquiry, but before the Inspector had reported in favour of the schemes, the DoE revised its standards for the design flows of motorways. The objectors sought to reopen the Inquiry so as to challenge the traffic flow figures and took the matter to the Court of Appeal. Lord Denning said that there had been a loss of public confidence in Inquiries in road schemes which had led to protests and, deplorable as some of those protests had been, he thought it essential for the Court of Appeal to do its utmost to see that Inquiries were conducted fairly. After considering this particular case, judgment by the Court of Appeal was reached in favour of the objectors, on the grounds of a failure of natural justice in disallowing cross-examination at the Inquiry and in not reopening the Inquiry on limited grounds; in consequence the schemes were quashed. In 1980 the DoE took the matter to the House of Lords who allowed the appeal by the Department against the decision of the Court of Appeal[15]. It was considered that the decision to construct a national network was an administrative one and Government policy: and it was not open to question at local inquiries concerning a particular section of motorway. Methods used by the Government Department concerned to forecast future traffic needs was also an element in determining Government policy. A local inquiry was not a court of law and an Inspector, although he must be fair, had a discretion to refuse cross-examination by objectors seeking to challenge the validity of the forecast method.

Time taken for preliminary stages

One effect of the changes made in the inquiry process has been the longer time taken to complete Public Inquiries. In 1977 it was reported[16] that whereas the time between first including a motorway scheme in the "preparation pool" and starting construction was some 5 to 7 years in the 1960s, by 1977 it was between

10 and 12. The steps involved in preparation of a major road scheme before work starts have been identified by Shaun Leslie[17] as follows.

Preparation steps which may have to be undertaken for any major trunk road scheme
Up to 30 separate steps may now have to be undertaken before a major trunk road scheme can be started, although some of these steps may be taken together.

(1)	Feasibility study to establish need—not necessary in all cases	1–3 years
(2)	If (1) establishes the need or there is no feasibility study, work starts on broad outlines of scheme	
(3)	Inclusion of scheme in preparation pool which is not a commitment to build	1–2 years
(4)	Work by Road Construction Unit, agent authority and/or consulting engineers on identification of routes, traffic surveys, etc.	
(5)	Public consultation on possible corridors	1 year
(6)	Announcement of preferred corridor	
(7)	Detailed working up of the scheme including economic assessment	1 year
(8)	Submission of alternative routes to Landscape Committee	
(9)	Public consultation on possible routes	1–2 years
(10)	Announcement of preferred route	
(11)	Detailed work on design etc. including economic assessment	1–3 years
(12)	Inclusion of scheme in firm programme but without firm commitment to build	
(13)	Publication of draft line orders	
(14)	If Public Inquiry is necessary because objections cannot be resolved, pre-Inquiry meeting	up to 1 year
(15)	Public Inquiry	
(16)	Submission of Inspector's report to Minister	1½–2 years
(17)	Minister's decision and publishing of order	
(18)	Confirmation of order	6 weeks
(19)	Publication of side road and compulsory purchase orders	up to 1½ years
(20)	If Public Inquiry is necessary because objections cannot be resolved, pre-Inquiry meeting	6 months–1 year
(21)	Public Inquiry	
(22)	Submission of Inspector's report to Minister	
(23)	Minister's decision and publishing of order	

(24) Confirmation of order   6 weeks
(25) Economic review of scheme   ⎫
(26) Preliminary inquiries re tenders   ⎪
(27) Tenders invited   ⎬ up to 1 year
(28) Economic review of scheme   ⎪
(29) Contract let   ⎭
(30) Work starts   6 weeks

Criticism of the present road-planning procedures has been voiced by consulting engineer R.L. Wilson[18] who has advocated new procedures which he claims would cut at least 5 years from the preconstruction period. His proposed procedures are

—public consultation prior to start of study
—preliminary surveys and feasibility study report on issues, need and options
—publication of feasibility study report and 1:2,500 drawings, with limits of deviation on land take
—written observations from public
—inquiry into feasibility study under investigating Inspector
—investigating Inspector reports to Minister and makes recommendations
—Minister decides route to be constructed, giving reasons if Inspector's recommendations not accepted
—detailed surveys and design of selected route leading to land-acquisition plans
—Land Tribunal/Commission negotiates between Department of Transport and landowner for final land take and value.

Finance for trunk roads

From information published in annual reports and White Papers it is not possible to identify the amounts spent on motorways. Figures are given for trunk roads as a whole and although a large proportion of the total trunk road expenditure has been on motorways there has also been a substantial programme of improvements to all-purpose trunk roads.

The expenditure on trunk roads, including motorways, as a proportion of the total public expenditure on roads and inland surface transport, declined during the decade from a little over a quarter to rather less than one fifth. As the total expenditure on transport declined in real terms also, there was thus an even greater fall in the amount spent on trunk roads than the difference in these proportions suggests.

In Table 6.1 are set out the figures published in 1980 by the Government[19] for expenditure on trunk roads in Britain from 1974 to 1980 with forecast figures for 1980/81. Figures for 1971/72 and 1973/74 have been derived from the Government White Paper in 1977[16] after adjustment for changes in the Retail Price Index.

Some of the changes in expenditure on roads reflect changes in successive Governments' views on transport priorities, e.g. greater support for public transport at the expense of road construction and a belief that, although road traffic is likely to continue to increase despite increased costs of motoring and questions over fuel supplies, there is a decreasing need for an inter-urban road programme on the scale of that during the 1960s and early 1970s. Expenditure on road construction appears also to have fallen short of budgeted expenditure. A major influence on the budget for roads must have been the various economic crises during the decade. Leslie[17] has observed that, of ten public spending cuts in the 1970s, since 1973 road expenditure was unique as featuring in every one as follows.

(1) May 1973   Road expenditure cut by £20 million in 1973/74 and £100 million in 1974/75.

(2) December 1973   Road expenditure plans for 1975/76 and 1976/77 cut by £320 million (Public Expenditure White Paper Cmnd 5519).

(3) December 1973   Road expenditure cut by £16 million in 1973/74 and about £150 million in 1974/75.

(4) January 1975   Road expenditure in the period 1975/76 to 1977/78 cut by about £500 million (Public Expenditure White Paper Cmnd 5879).

(5) April 1975   Road expenditure in 1976/77 cut by £62 million.

(6) February 1976   Road expenditure plans cut by £450 million, mostly in 1977/78 and 1978/79 (Public Expenditure White Paper Cmnd 6393).

(7) July 1976   Road expenditure in 1977/78 cut by £87 million.

(8) December 1976   Road expenditure cut by £75 million in 1977/78 and £50 million in 1978/79.

Table 6.1. *Expenditure on trunk roads in Britain: £ million at 1979 prices*

Expenditure	1971/ 72	1973/ 74	1974/ 75	1975/ 76	1976/ 77	1977/ 78	1978/ 79	1979/ 80	1980/ 81
New construction and improvement	690 (485)*	705 (495)*	620	640	547	398	392	404	418
Maintenance	93 (65)*	142 (100)*	86	101	106	101	115	116	112
Total	783	847	707	741	654	498	507	519	530

* Values quoted in reference 16 at 1976 prices.

(9) June 1977   White Paper on Transport Policy announced cuts of
                     £60 million per annum in road construction and £20
                     million per annum in road maintenance for the years at
                     the "end of the decade".
(10) June 1979   Trunk road expenditure cut by £10 million in 1979/80,
                     with further unspecified cuts in local road spending aris-
                     ing from lower cash limits on the rate support grant.

In addition there was a moratorium on the letting of contracts for new local road
schemes from August 1976 to June 1977 and for trunk road schemes from
December 1976 to June 1977 in England. Leslie suggests that roads are
vulnerable to variations in budget policy for various reasons.

—Road spending can be changed merely by stopping new contracts, as happened
  with the 6 month moratorium on letting trunk road contracts at the time of the
  IMF cuts in December 1976.
—The road sector is diffuse with no easily identifiable victim and hence no direct
  political backlash.
—There appears to be no direct employment effect.
—Objectors to a road scheme are usually more vocal than those in favour and
  would be appeased by cancellation of the scheme.

Expenditure on motorways and trunk roads is forecast by the Government to
remain at about the 1979/80 level at constant prices until 1983/84 in Britain as a
whole. It is reckoned by the Government that this will permit the completion of
some 500 miles of motorway and trunk road in England and some 200 miles in
Scotland in the years up to 1984.

Road Construction Units

In July 1978, the Department of Transport issued a discussion paper on the
future organisation for road construction. It was pointed out in the paper that the
trunk road programme would decline in the future and that the opportunity
would arise for an increase in resources for local road building. It was necessary to
review the organisational arrangements for designing and building roads in the
future so as to ensure the most effective use of departmental and local authority
resources of skilled manpower. It was desirable that there should be the maximum
flexibility in deployment of engineering effort between trunk and local schemes.
It was for consideration whether a reversion to an agency basis for schemes in
hand in Road Construction Unit (RCU) Sub-Units and planned to start in the early
1980s would be the best way forward.

This paper was followed by another from the Department in November 1978
concerning staff to handle the tasks currently undertaken by RCU Headquarters
Units. It was concluded that the successful completion of the trunk road pro-

gramme would require, at least until the late 1980s, a substantial number of staff to work under the direction of the Secretary of State; the paper discussed several options for dealing with local authority staff seconded to RCU Headquarters Units. It was noted that the RCU Headquarters Units could possibly be absorbed into a broader regional organisation in the Department. Discussions on these documents took place with local authority associations and unions.

In August 1979 a further study was initiated by the Department of Transport in consultation with Sir Derek Rayner "to examine the work of the Road Construction Units (RCUs)" and a report of the study was published in 1980[20]. The study was carried out by a Principal in the Department of Transport and included interviews with RCUs, with various branches of the Departments of Transport and the Environment, with local authority associations, staff associations, a few other organisations and one individual consulting engineer.

On 6 March 1980, the Minister of Transport announced the publication of the report of the study in the House of Commons. After commenting that the main issue in the report was the future of the Sub-Units he said, in regard to his policy on this, "I am proposing the planned phasing-out of the Sub-Units. I intend in particular to make increased use of consultants who have a large part to play; and also of agency arrangements where the case made for them by the county councils concerned clearly makes good sense".

Discussions on the implementation of this policy followed and provoked strong reaction by local authority engineers in the RCUs, particularly against the takeover of work by consultants. This arose because a few years earlier an agreement had been reached with the previous administration that when the time came for winding up the RCUs as their work load decreased, there would be a progressively increasing role of County Councils as agents for such work as remained. The new Government's policy was, however, to transfer more work to the private sector; and it may be remarked that in the past 20 to 25% of work on major trunk road schemes and motorways had been designed and work supervised by consultants.

To help with the transfer of staff from the RCUs with the minimum disturbance to the road programme the Department of Transport set up a clearing house comprising advisers from unions, local authority associations and the Association of Consulting Engineers under the Chairmanship of Maurice Milne, CB, a former Deputy Director General of Highways in the Department. The clearing house was to be given the responsibility of recommending which consultants from a short list chosen by the Department were likely to offer the best terms and conditions for the staff joining them for any group of schemes being carried out by a particular Sub-Unit. The Department paid regard to the extent of overseas work being carried out or sought by consultants.

Over 100 consulting firms expressed interest in sharing the £2,300 million programme of work then in hand involving some 1,600 engineers and other staff in the 6 RCUs and 16 Sub-Units. By October 1980 a final decision had been taken by Ministers on the work to be retained by counties. The Department put forward a short list of consultants and meetings were held in December 1980 and January 1981 to explain the programme of work to each group of consultants. After this representatives of the clearing house met the staff to set out their proposed method of working and by Easter 1981 the first recommendations were made for firms to be appointed. The Secretary of State then took his decision on the appointments and in so doing gave considerable weight to staff preferences in the selection of a consultant.

The conditions of transfer of staff provided for their being given the statutory redundancy payments by the county authorities with certain other payments being made by the Department of Transport. Consultants were required to pay salaries not less than those obtaining at transfer with other terms as appropriate to their own conditions of employment.

By the time the clearing house ceased operating at the end of October 1981 some 900 staff had been transferred or were to be transferred by the end of the year. Almost all the staff who had been engaged in the Sub-Units had either been transferred to consultants, reabsorbed by the counties for work on schemes retained by them or had taken early retirement. The successful consultants and the Sub-Unit work taken over by them are shown in Table 6.2.

Some engineering matters

Leaving aside the serious problems arising from increased costs and cuts in programmes arising from the oil price rise and other inflationary factors, probably

Table 6.2. Consultants taking over work of Sub-Units

Successful consultant	Sub-Unit package
G. Maunsell	Essex and East Bedfordshire
Brian Colquhoun	Hertfordshire and West Bedfordshire
Sir William Halcrow	Buckinghamshire
Bullen	Durham
Mott Hay and Anderson	Hampshire
Babtie Shaw and Morton	Airedale and Settle ⎫
Pell Frischmann	Kirkhamgate–Dishforth ⎬ West Yorkshire
John Burrows	Lincoln relief road ⎭
Babtie Shaw and Morton	Lancashire
Mander Raikes and Marshall	Devon and Somerset
W.S. Atkins	Surrey
Scott Wilson Kirkpatrick	Derbyshire
Mott Hay and Anderson	Kent
Ove Arup	Warwickshire (main package)
C.H. Dobbie	Warwickshire (small package)
Ward Ashcroft and Parkman	Cheshire
Sir Owen Williams	Staffordshire

the most important issues of an engineering kind affecting motorways during the decade were: the design of steel box-girder bridges; revision of design flow standards; and motorway maintenance.

A number of steel bridges on motorways had been designed on box-girder principles but following the collapse during erection of two large bridges designed on these principles, one in Melbourne over the Yarra River and the other the Cleddau Bridge at Milford Haven in Wales, the Secretary of State for the Environment in association with the Secretaries of State for Scotland and Wales in December 1970 appointed a technical committee to look into the basis of design and method of construction of such bridges. The committee which was under the chairmanship of Dr (now Sir Alec) Merrison found that there was no reason to doubt the soundness of the design provided it conformed to stricter rules which they recommended. The Department of the Environment made these rules available to all engineers engaged in the design of this type of bridge.

In the light of these findings the Department put in hand an assessment of the designs of individual bridges of this kind already built and in use and, pending the outcome of this, placed restrictions on the amount of traffic using those bridges. Where it proved necessary, bridges were strengthened to meet the new requirements. Work proceeded quickly and by 1972 over two thirds of bridges on which restrictions were placed had been investigated, strengthened where necessary and traffic restrictions had been lifted.

In June 1974 the Minister of Transport announced new design standards for roads[21]. It had been observed that the volumes of traffic carried by a number of motorways was well in excess of the then current design flows and that those volumes appeared to be carried in reasonable safety. It was, therefore, argued that standard design flows should be revised upwards. As an example[22] the design capacity for a dual three-lane rural motorway had been 55,000 passenger car units per day or approximately 37,000 vehicles per day. In the new standard a peak-hour flow of 4,800 vehicles per hour in one direction and a total design flow of up to 85,000 vehicles per day, depending on peaking characteristics, were prescribed. The passenger car unit was abandoned as being unnecessarily complicated and a correction applied to the vehicles per day figure depending on the level of heavy vehicles.

The new design flows meant that economies could be obtained. With the new standards, for example, a dual two-lane instead of a dual three-lane motorway might now be deemed adequate in a particular case to carry forecast flows in the design year. A note of caution should be sounded, however. The preliminary stages in the planning of a motorway scheme take 10–12 years before construction can start and the design year to which design flows apply is 15 years after the motorway is open to traffic. Planning is thus starting some 30 years ahead of the time when traffic is expected to reach the design capacity. Fine tuning of forecasting procedures and capacity standards should therefore be viewed with caution and a considerable degree of scepticism.

Caution is also engendered by experience with standards for motorways to date. Initially, in the interests of keeping first costs down, the strengths provided were soon proved to be inadequate and necessitated repairs not only expensive in themselves but also in the delays caused to motorway traffic. The first "hard" shoulders were inadequate in width and strength and they, too, had to be redesigned and new specifications drawn up. With the extensive amount of maintenance and reconstruction taking place, the current standard hard shoulder, which has the same strength as the carriageway, is providing a needed extra lane for traffic in some places when lane closures occur. It is questionable whether this had been envisaged when the revised high standard was drawn up. Some early dual two-lane motorways soon proved inadequate for the traffic they had to carry and early widening was necessary (e.g. the Slough and Maidenhead by-passes; and Preston and Lancaster by-passes which had been built with extra-wide central reservations to allow for future widening). Perhaps the lesson is that economic assessments in these matters need to be tempered by engineering judgment and caution in view of the many uncertainties that exist.

Motorway maintenance, which had been growing in amount through the 1970s, is anticipated to require increasing attention in the 1980s. This is stated in the Government's White Paper on roads in 1980[23] which envisages that striking a balance between building new roads and properly maintaining the existing network will be a continuing feature of the 1980s. Stating that motorways are designed to last about 20 years before needing renewal, the White Paper goes on to say that the road construction programme during the 1960s will, therefore, have to be matched during the 1980s by higher maintenance expenditure.

Once again uncertainties and underprovision have crept in. The White Paper comments that motorways have attracted a far greater proportion of total traffic, particularly the largest heavy goods vehicles, than was forecast in the 1960s when many of the motorways were designed and built. Motorways now carry some 22% of heavy goods mileage and 35% of the heaviest vehicles. As it is the heavy vehicles which cause damage to the road structure this means that road lives will be shorter than anticipated. There is pressure to increase the size and loading of goods vehicles within the EEC. Already through the 1970s the weights of heavy goods vehicles have been increasing: these are matters of concern in relation to the strengths and design lives to be built not only into new motorways but also into the reconstruction of old motorways which are wearing out.

Finally, although not solely concerned with motorways, reference should be made to the work on a Regional Highway Traffic Model (RHTM) which was carried out during the latter half of the 1970s by the Department of Transport. The aims of the project, which cost several million pounds, were "To derive, on a consistent national basis, forecasts of traffic flow on individual links of existing and projected regional road networks for use in the appraisal, design and management of major inter-urban highways. The model is to be capable of providing data for further refinement for more detailed studies of particular schemes and is to be compatible with the National Traffic Model"[24]. (The National Traffic Model was concerned with long distance mixed-mode traffic.) Further reference to RHTM is made in chapter 10.

Into the 1980s

As mentioned earlier, the Government's plans in 1980 looked ahead 4 years, during which some 500 miles of trunk road would be built in Britain. It was not clear how many of these would be motorways.

From the White Paper *Policy for roads: England, 1980*[23] it appears that in February 1980 in England between 60 and 70 miles of motorway were under construction and expected to be completed within 2 years. Schemes in preparation to be included in the main programmes from 1980 to 1983 amounted to 165 miles, with a further 70 miles included for 1984 onwards. Dates when these schemes would be completed were not given. In commenting that dates which had been put on the schemes under construction were meant to be realistic, the White Paper went on to say "We see no point in putting definite dates on construction of schemes from 1984 onwards because uncertainties make any attempt to do so misleading."

Early in the 1960s a clear target of motorway construction was set "1,000 miles by the early 1970s" and this was achieved. In 1970 the Government announced a new target of a further 1,000 miles by the early 1980s, but this was abandoned in later years for reasons which have been discussed. The earlier concept of a motorway network as part of a stategic inter-urban network does not figure so explicitly in plans for the 1980s and a more piecemeal approach seems to be in prospect, with no clear commitment to a motorway programme of the previous kind. There can be no doubt that this approach has been largely the result of the economic recession which has been taking place. In such conditions it is especially important that sound investment criteria are applied to programmes. Individual road projects have been subject to this kind of appraisal for many years and Gwilliam and Wilson[25] have concluded that the British motorway programme has produced "enormous direct benefits to road users". It may reasonably be asked whether the current programme for the 1980s is adequate to meet economically justifiable requirements, whether a policy of improving all-purpose trunk roads rather than building more motorways has been evaluated and, if so, with what results and whether some change in the way road programmes are planned is called for.

The arguments for a Roads Board separate from Government have been rehearsed at intervals ever since the early years of the century. It is extremely unlikely that any Government would agree to surrender its authority over raising and spending of revenue from road users, but there might be a case for setting up a Road, or possibly Transport, Planning Board with responsibility for carrying out

91

studies of the strategic requirements for transport and with putting forward proposals to meet those requirements.

The 1980s, as distinct from the 1960s, started with a substantial number of engineers experienced in motorway design and construction, and with a road construction industry possessing the experience and capacity to undertake motorway projects. With the programmes envisaged for the 1980s at present those resources are unlikely to be used to the full in Britain on new construction and are more likely to be needed to undertake the extensive reconstruction and maintenance of existing motorways.

It seems highly likely that motorways will develop even more as freight-ways in the future and it will be important to monitor developments in this direction as they affect standards of motorway construction and layout.

Energy conservation, particularly in regard to oil supplies, can be expected to lead to changes in vehicle design and use. Motorway traffic could well tend to be polarised between still larger goods vehicles and smaller private cars on the grounds of economy of operation and such a change could have implications for safety on motorways.

Environmentalists can be expected to continue to be vigilant over motorway and indeed other road schemes. The public consultation and inquiry procedures which have been evolved appear to be more acceptable to objectors but they can take a considerable amount of time to complete. It remains to be seen whether the best balance is being achieved by these procedures between the interests of objectors to and promoters of motorway schemes.

References

1. DEPARTMENT OF THE ENVIRONMENT. *Roads in England 1971.* HMSO, London, 1972.
2. SELECT COMMITTEE ON ESTIMATES. *First report session 1958–59. Trunk Roads.* HMSO, London, 1969.
3. CHARLESWORTH G. A note on motoring expenditure shortly before and after the oil crisis of 1973/74. *Traffic engineering and control,* 1978, **19**, No. 10.
4. TRANSPORT AND ROAD RESEARCH LABORATORY. *Transport and road research 1975.* HMSO, London, 1976.
5. DEPARTMENT OF TRANSPORT. *Route location with regard to environmental issues.* Department of Transport, London, 1977.
6. FORRESTER J.W. *World dynamics.* Wright-Allen Press, Cambridge, Mass., 1971.
7. MEADOWS D. *et al. The limits to growth.* A report for the Club of Rome's project on the predicament of mankind. Universe Books, New York, 1972.
8. DEPARTMENT OF THE ENVIRONMENT. *Roads in England 1971–72.* HMSO, London, 1972.
9. HUGHES T.P. Roads policy at national, regional and local levels and the role of motorways. *Proceedings of the conference on 20 years of British motorways.* Institution of Civil Engineers, London, 1980.

10. DEPARTMENT OF THE ENVIRONMENT. *Public Inquiries into road proposals.* HMSO, London, 1973.
11. WOODHOUSE H. The legal framework covering new roadworks. *The highway engineer,* 1977, **24**, No. 11.
12. DEPARTMENT OF TRANSPORT. *Report of the Advisory Committee on Trunk Road Assessment.* HMSO, London, 1978.
13. DEPARTMENT OF TRANSPORT and DEPARTMENT OF THE ENVIRONMENT. *Report on the review of highway inquiry procedures.* HMSO, London, 1978.
14. TYME J. *Motorways versus democracy.* Macmillan, London, 1978.
15. THE TIMES. Motorways: limited scope of local inquiries. Law Report. *The Times,* 11 February 1980.
16. DEPARTMENT OF TRANSPORT, SCOTTISH DEVELOPMENT DEPARTMENT and WELSH OFFICE. *Transport policy.* HMSO, London, 1977.
17. LESLIE S. *Budgeting for roads; the need for reform.* British Road Federation, London, 1979.
18. WILSON R.L. Roads. *New Civil Engineer,* 18 January 1979.
19. CHANCELLOR OF THE EXCHEQUER. *The Government's expenditure plans 1980–81 to 1983–84.* HMSO, London, 1980.
20. DEPARTMENT OF TRANSPORT. *Report of the study of Road Construction Units in consultation with Sir Derek Rayner for the Minister of Transport.* Department of Transport, London, 1980.
21. DEPARTMENT OF THE ENVIRONMENT. *Design flows for motorways and all-purpose roads.* Technical memorandum H6/74. Department of the Environment, London, 1974.
22. WILLIAMS H. *et al.* Standards, specifications and design. *Proceedings of the conference on 20 years of British motorways.* Institution of Civil Engineers, London, 1980.
23. DEPARTMENT OF TRANSPORT. *Policy for roads: England, 1980.* HMSO, London, 1980.
24. DEPARTMENT OF THE ENVIRONMENT. *Regional highway traffic model project report,* Vol. 1. Directorate General Highways, Department of the Environment, London, 1976.
25. GWILLIAM K.M. and WILSON R.L. Social and economic effects of motorways. *Proceedings of the conference on 20 years of British motorways.* Institution of Civil Engineers, London, 1980.

7

Trunk road motorways in England

Introduction

In 1981 there were 1,447 miles of trunk road motorways in use in England located as shown in Fig. 7.1. The distribution of the mileage between the various motorways is shown in Table 7.1. The rate of growth of the motorways is indicated in Table 7.2 which shows the extra mileage coming into use at 5 year intervals since 1960. Almost half the total in use in 1980 had been built by 1970 and the peak period of building was in the 5 years between 1970 and 1975.

The five longest motorways in England are the M1, M4 (the M4 extends into Wales by a further 80 miles), M5, M6 and M62. These are all continuous lengths of motorway whereas the 77 miles of the A1(M) are not.

Out of the total mileage of 1429 in 1980, some 83% was dual three-lane and the remainder dual two-lane, apart from some 3 miles of dual four-lane carriageway on the M5 between junctions 29 and 30. Flexible construction was the most commonly adopted form and only about 15% of the mileage of carriageway had a concrete surface.

The Department of Transport carry out traffic censuses at selected points on the motorway network and in 1979[1] the highest 24 hour traffic flows recorded at those points were at the London end of the M4 and the traffic loading in relation to carrying capacity was high on the dual two-lane elevated section near Chiswick. Other high flows occurred on the M1 between junctions 9 and 10, on the M6 between junctions 11 and 12 and on the M62 between junctions 10 and 11. The lowest traffic volumes were recorded on the M45 and on the M50. The highest volumes of heavy goods traffic occurred on the M1, the M6 and the M62.

By 1980 traffic volumes on some motorways, particularly near the major conurbations, were reaching or even exceeding the flow levels recommended for design purposes by the Department of Transport,[2] and as a result serious congestion was occurring at these places in peak hours. Furthermore not only was design capacity being reached but the design life of many of the road pavements was being attained earlier than had been anticipated. The life of a road pavement depends on the wheel loads and frequency of application of those loads. The damaging effect

Table 7.1. Trunk road motorways in use in England 1981 (total 1447 miles)

Motorway	Length: miles	Motorway	Length: miles	Motorway	Length: miles
M1	194	M27	27	M63	11
M2	25	M40	31	M66	6
M3	41	M42	8	M67	3
M4	121	M45	6	M69	16
M5	168	M50	21	M180	27
M6	234	M53	12	M181	2
M10	2	M54	5	M271	2
M11	53	M55	12	M606	2
M18	30	M56	37	M621	4
M20	40	M57	10	A1(M)	77
M23	18	M58	11	A3(M)	5
M25	39	M61	22	A41(M)	2
M26	8	M62	108	A627(M)	4

increases in proportion to the number of applications of wheel load, but in proportion to approximately the fourth power of those loads. Consequently private cars and similar vehicles are of little relevance to design; it is the wheel (or axle) load, in particular of the heavy lorries, and number of repetitions of those loads which matter. When the earlier motorways were being designed the forecasts of the loading of heavy vehicles expected on them were underestimated so that repairs become necessary earlier than predicted. This was particularly the case on the M1 and M6 but also applied to some other sections of motorway.

In their *Policy for roads: England 1980*[3] the Department of Transport commented on this and stated that "Motorway maintenance will require increasing attention" and went on to say that the growth in the road construction programme in the 1960s would have to be matched during the 1980s by higher maintenance expenditure because the earlier roads were reaching the end of their designed life, after which renewal became necessary. The motorway maintenance programme for 1980/81 put forward for schemes exceeding £500,000 included substantial lengths of the M1, M4, M5 and M6. This programme was a follow-on to earlier programmes on these and other motorways.

Table 7.2. Mileage of motorway in use in England, 1960/80

	1960	1965	1970	1975	1980
Additional mileage in previous 5 years	121	251	300	500	257
Total in use: miles	121	372	672	1172	1429

Scale of miles
0 10 20 30

96

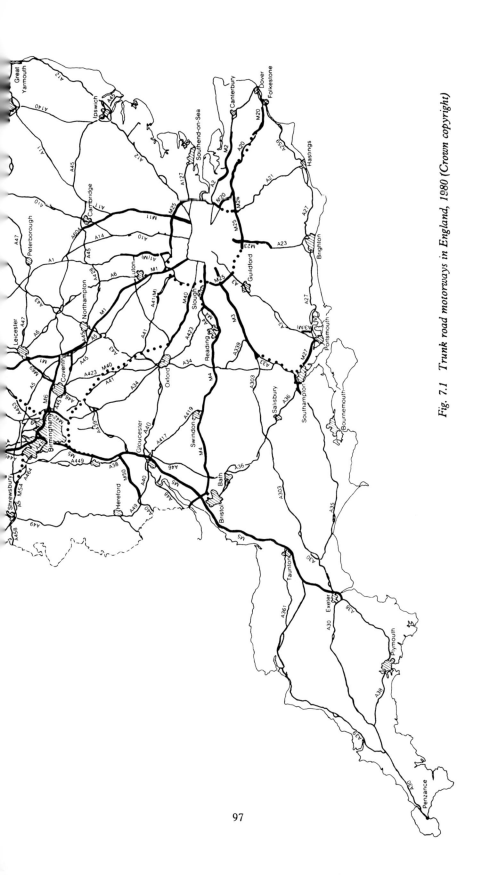

Fig. 7.1 Trunk road motorways in England, 1980 (Crown copyright)

97

Motorway contracts

In Table 7.3 are summarised some brief details of the trunk road motorways contracts in England. Most of this information has been extracted from records kindly made available by the Department of Transport. Where possible, missing data in those records have been filled in from various other sources such as press releases and consultants' brochures.

The roads were all built for the Ministry (now the Department) of Transport as highway authority. In some cases the Minister appointed County Councils to act as his agents for the location, design and supervision of construction of motorways, in others consultants were employed. With the formation of the Road Construction Units and county Sub-Units, while the value of work with consultants continued at much the same level, the Sub-Units handled a higher proportion of the expanding programme. The column headed "Engineer" lists the agent primarily concerned.

The column headed "Contractor" gives the main firm involved. Quite often advance contracts were let, for example, for preliminary earthworks and bridge works, but these are for the most part excluded as there is some uncertainty about providing complete information on these. Contracts usually started a month or two after the date the contracts were let and commonly took 2 to 3 years to complete; the average length of contracts was about 6 miles.

The cost data are mostly for the tender price at the time contracts were let but in a few cases other data, e.g. estimates of cost in *Policy for roads: England, 1980,* have been used. The tender price covers only the main contract; the final cost of construction would be higher when all other items were included.

An indication of changes in total cost of motorway construction with time can be gained from Table 7.4 (p. 124). These lengths are small samples in relation to the total mileage of motorways which has been built and the results need to be treated with caution. It does seem that, within the margins of error in the samples, construction costs in the late 1970s were, in real terms, not dissimilar from those in the early 1960s. The low cost of sample 1 was no doubt in part due to the lower standard of design adopted for that early motorway.

Selected motorways

The location, design and construction of the motorway system has thrown up a wide variety of problems and issues. As an illustration of the nature of some of these matters a brief description follows of features of the five longest motorways, the M1, M4, M5, M6 and M62.

M1, London–Yorkshire motorway

The M1 runs from the North Circular Road A406 at Staples Corner in London to the Leeds city boundary and its construction can be considered in four main stages: from the North Circular Road to Berrygrove; from Berrygrove to Crick;

from Crick to Aston; and from Aston to Leeds. Some information about these stages of construction is given in Table 7.3. Nine service areas have also been built namely, from the north, Woólley Edge, Woodall, Trowell, Leicester Forest, Watford Gap, Rothersthorpe, Newport Pagnell, Toddington and Scratchwood.

The first stage to be built was that between Berrygrove and Crick and details of the design and construction were given in papers to the Institution of Civil Engineers in 1960[4]. According to J.F.A. Baker, then Chief Engineer at the Ministry of Transport, the London–Birmingham motorway was given priority because of the "immediate and very substantial relief which it could give to . . . the two heavily overloaded trunk roads A5 and A6". He went on to say that the 74 miles of the London–Birmingham motorway to Crick constituted the "first full-scale motorway to be constructed" in the UK and was in fact the southern part of the London–Yorkshire motorway, the M1.

The southern section from Berrygrove where the M1 joins the A41 to Beechtrees was built with a dual two-lane carriageway and by 1980 congestion at peak times on this section was severe. At Beechtrees the M1 joins the M10, also a dual two-lane carriageway, which runs for a short distance southeast to join the A5 at Park Street. These lengths of M1 and M10 constitute the St Albans by-pass and were designed for the Ministry of Transport by the Hertfordshire County Council (County Surveyor, C.H. ffolliott). The carriageways were of 11 in thick reinforced concrete on a sub-base normally 7 in thick and were the first motorways to be built with concrete surfaces. Because of heavy rain during construction problems arose with a hoggin sub-base where it was used by construction traffic soon after laying.

North of Beechtrees to Pepperstock, the motorway was also designed for the Ministry by Hertfordshire County Council and was also of concrete construction, but the carriageway was dual three-lane as is the rest of the motorway.

From Pepperstock north to Crick, design was carried out by consulting engineers Sir Owen Williams and Partners[5]. These consultants had been commissioned in 1951 by the Ministry of Transport to carry out studies of a route for the London to Yorkshire motorway between St Albans and Doncaster, and in 1955 they were appointed to prepare a scheme for the length from Pepperstock to Crick with a short spur, the M45 connecting the M1 to the Dunchurch by-pass. The scheme was published in September 1955 and confirmed in 1956. Originally it was planned to provide dual two-lane carriageways but this was changed before the scheme was published to dual three-lane. This increased the overall cost by 20% and the land used by 10%, but was estimated to add at least 50% extra traffic capacity to the road.

The Ministry asked if construction could be completed in 19 months, i.e. in two summers instead of the three originally considered, and tenders were sought with these alternative periods of completion on a fixed price basis. The 55 mile length of route was divided into four sections for which tenders were sought and

text continues on page 124

Table 7.3. Trunk road and motorway contracts in England

Motorway	Motorway section (interchange no.)	Length: miles	Engineer	Main Contractor	Contract let	Open	Standard: D2=dual 2 lane D3=dual 3 lane (F=Flexible; C=Concrete)		Cost: £ million (tender price)
M1	Leeds (44)–Stourton (43)	0.5	Leeds CC	Tarmac	Early 1971	Dec. 1972	D3	F	0.5
	Stourton–East Ardsley (41)	5	Yorks. WRCC	A. Monk	Mar. 1965	Oct. 1967	D3	F	5.4
	East Ardsley–Tinsley (34)	23	Yorks. WRCC	Sir Alfred McAlpine/ Leonard Fairclough consortium	Jan. 1965	Oct. 1968 Aug. 1967– Oct 1968	D3	F	3.9
	–Wakefield	4							
	–Darton	7		Costain	July 1966	Oct. 1968			7.3
	–Tankersley	7		Dowsett	July 1966	Oct. 1968			6.7
	–Blackburn	3		A. Monk	Apr. 1966	June 1968			3.6
	–Meadowhall	2		Holland Hannan with Cubitts	Apr. 1966	June 1968			2.5
	Tinsley viaduct strengthening works		Freeman Fox	Cleveland Cleveland	Feb. 1965 Mar. 1977	June 1968			4.2 3.5
	Tinsley–Aston (31)	6	Yorks. WRCC	Dowsett	June 1965	Oct. 1967	D3	F	6.0
	Thurcroft–Barlborough (30)	8	Sir Owen Williams	Tarmac	Oct. 1965	Nov. 1967	D3	F	4.7
	Barlborough–Pinxton (28)	13	Sir Owen Williams	John Laing	July 1965	Nov. 1967	D3	F	12.6
	Pinxton–Nuthall (26)	10	Sir Owen Williams	G. Wimpey	Dec. 1964	May 1967	D3	F	5.5
	Nuthall–Sandiacre (25)	6	Sir Owen Williams	R.M. Douglas	Aug. 1964	Nov. 1966	D3	F	4.6
	Sandiacre–Kegworth (24) Trent structures	6	Sir Owen Williams	G. Wimpey Brims	Apr. 1964	May 1966	D3	F	3.1 1.0

100

Kegworth–Markfield (22)	11	Sir Owen Williams	Sir Robert McAlpine	July 1963	Nov. 1965	D3	F	6.5
Markfield–Crick (18)	26	Sir Owen Williams			Nov. 1965	D3	F	16.3
–Kirby Muxloe	5		A. Monk	Dec. 1962				3.3
–Whetstone	6		R.M. Douglas	Oct. 1962				4.3
–Crick	15		G. Wimpey	Aug. 1962				8.7
Crick–Pepperstock (10)	50	Sir Owen Williams	John Laing	Mar. 1958	Nov. 1959	D3	F	20.2 (final cost)
Pepperstock–Beechtrees (7)	12	Herts. CC	Tarmac	Mar. 1958	Nov. 1959	D3	C	4.5
Beechtrees–Berrygrove (5)	5	Herts. CC	Cubitts and Fitzpatrick with Shand	Mar. 1958	Nov. 1959	D2	C	1.3
Berrygrove–Brockley (4)	4	Herts. CC	Fitzpatrick	Apr. 1964	Nov. 1966	D3	C	3.8
Brockley–Page Street (2) railway bridges	4	W.S. Atkins	Holland Hannan with Cubitts	Oct. 1963	May 1967	D3	C	11
Brockley Hill interchange main and ancillary works			Cementation	Apr. 1964				
			Marples Ridgway	June 1964				
Page Street–North Circular Road A406 at Staples Corner (1)	3	W.S. Atkins			N'bound May 1975 S'bound Jan. 1977	D3	C	
Five-ways interchange main works			Cementation	June 1968	July 1970		C	1.6
			Costain	May 1972	July 1977	D3	C	4.3
Staples Corner interchange	1		Taylor Woodrow	Oct. 1972	Aug. 1976	D3/D2	F	5.0

continued overleaf

Table 7.3 (Cont.)

	Motorway section (interchange no.)	Length: miles	Engineer	Main Contractor	Contract let	Open	Standard: D2=dual 2 lane D3=dual 3 lane (F=Flexible; C=Concrete)	Cost: £ million (tender price)
M2	Medway Bridge		Freeman Fox with Robert F. Earley	Christiani Nielson with S.L. Kier	Mar. 1961	Sept. 1963		2.3
	Three Crutches (1)–Medway Bridge	2		Christiani Nielson and S.L. Kier with Sydney Green	Sept. 1963		D2 F	1.0
	Medway Bridge–Stockbury (5)	11	Freeman Fox with Robert F. Earley	G. Wimpey			D2 F	6.0
	Stockbury (5)–Faversham (7)	12	Freeman Fox with Robert F. Earley	John Laing			D2 C	4.7
M3	Sunbury (1)–Lightwater (3) Thames Bridge	13	SERCU (Surrey SU)	A.E. Farr Sir W. Arrol	Jan. 1971 Nov. 1968	July 1974 Mar. 1971	D3 F	12.7 0.5
	Lightwater–Hawley (4)	4	Posford Pavry with SERCU (Surrey SU)	A.E. Farr	Oct. 1968	June 1971	D3 F	5.6
	Hawley–Basingstoke (6)	18	SERCU (Hants SU)	W. and C. French	Dec. 1968	June 1971	D3 F	9.2
	Winchfield railway bridge Basingstoke–Popham (8)	6	Hants CC	Mears A. Monk	Oct. 1968 Dec. 1968	Oct. 1970 June 1971	D3 F	0.8 6.3
M4	Chiswick flyover (1)	0.5	Sir Alexander Gibb	Marples Ridgway		Sept. 1959	D2 F	
	Chiswick elevated section	1	Sir Alexander Gibb	Kier with Christiani Nielson	June 1962	Mar. 1965	D2 F	5.0

continued overleaf]

Section	No.	Engineer	Contractor			Code		Mileage
Boston Manor–airport spur (4)	7	Sir Alexander Gibb	Costain with Higgs and Hill	Nov. 1962	Mar. 1965	D3	C	6.4
Airport spur–Langley (5)	4	Sir Alexander Gibb	Holland Hannan and Cubitts with Sydney Green	Mar. 1963	Mar. 1965	D3	C	3.3
Slough by-pass (5)–(7) widening	6	Bucks. CC ERCU (Bucks. SU)	Higgs Hill and Costain Amey Asphalt	Apr. 1961 Oct. 1969	Mar. 1963 Oct. 1971	D2 D3	F F	4.1 2.2 (incl. widening Maidenhead by-pass)
Maidenhead by-pass (7)–(9) New Thames Bridge widening	4	Berks. CC ERCU (Bucks. SU)	John Laing and Horseley with Thomas Piggott Amey Asphalt	Apr. 1959 Oct. 1969	May 1961 Sept. 1971	D2 D3	F F	2.8 (as above)
Holyport (9)–Winnersh (10) Reading-Wokingham link interchange A329 (M)	7	Sir Alexander Gibb	Costain W. and C. French	Dec. 1969 Sept. 1971	Dec. 1971 Feb. 1973	D3 D2	F C	4.5 1.8
Winnersh–Theale (12)	11	Sir Alexander Gibb	Costain	Jan. 1970	Dec. 1971	D3	F	10.8
Theale–Wickham (14)	20	Sir Alexander Gibb	Sir Lindsay Parkinson	Dec. 1969	Dec. 1971	D3	F	9.2
Wickham–Liddington (15)	12	Sir Alexander Gibb	A. Monk	Nov. 1969	Dec. 1971	D3	F	7.2
Liddington–Wootton Bassett (16)	7	Sir Alexander Gibb	W. and C. French	May 1969	Nov. 1971	D3	F	6.5
Wootton Bassett–Tormarton (18)	23	Sir Alexander Gibb	Sir Alfred McAlpine	June 1969	Nov. 1971 (part in June 1971)	E3	F	8.9
Tormarton–Almondsbury (20) Tormarton–Hambrook Hambrook–Almondsbury	11		Sir Alfred McAlpine with Leonard Fairclough	Apr. 1965 June 1964	Nov. 1966	D3 D3	F F	5.3 2.1

Table 7.3 (Cont.)

Motorway	Motorway section (interchange no.)	Length: miles	Engineer	Main Contractor	Contract let	Open	Standard: D2=dual 2 lane D3=dual 3 lane (F=Flexible; C=Concrete)	Cost: £ million (tender price)
M4 (contd)	Severn Bridge, Wye Bridge and approaches (20)–(22)	8	Mott Hay and Anderson		Mar. 1961	Sept. 1966	D3 F	
	Severn Bridge substructure			Associated Bridge Builders	May 1962			6.1
	Severn Bridge superstructure and Aust viaduct			John Howard	May 1963			2.0
	Wye Bridge and viaduct		Freeman Fox	Cleveland	May 1963			1.9
	Eastern approach road			Costain	July 1963			2.4
	Western approach road			Martin Cowley with Fitzpatrick	Mar. 1964			1.7
					Nov. 1965			0.8
M5	M6–West Bromwich (1)	5	Sir Owen Williams	W. and C. French	June 1967	May 1970	D3 F	5.8
	West Bromwich–Oldbury (2)	2	Sir Owen Williams	Sir Lindsay Parkinson	Dec. 1967	May 1970	D3 F	6.8
	Oldbury–Quinton (3)	4	Sir Owen Williams	Christiani/Shand consortium	May 1967	May 1970	D3 F	5.9
	Quinton–Lydiate Ash (4) widening	6	Worcester CC MRCU	Tarmac A. Monk	Aug. 1963 Oct. 1978	Nov. 1965 Apr. 1980	D3 F D3 F	4.3 3.7

104

Section		Engineer	Contractor					
Lydiate Ash–Strensham widening	26	Worcester CC MRCU	A. Monk / R.M. Douglas / Amey Roadstone	May 1960 / Jan. 1979 / Aug. 1979	July 1962	D2 / D3 / D3	F / F / F	9.0 / 1.7 / 5.0
Strensham–Bredon Bridge	1	Freeman Fox with Robert F. Earley	Christiani/Shand consortium	July 1967	June 1970	D3	F	1.6
Bredon Bridge–Tredington	5	Freeman Fox with Robert F. Earley	Costain	July 1968	June 1970	D3	F	3.4
Tredington–Brookthorpe (12)	12	Freeman Fox with Robert F. Earley	Cementation with Leonard Fairclough	Apr. 1969	Apr. 1971	D3	F	10.0
Brookthorpe–Eastington (13)	6	Freeman Fox with Robert F. Earley	Costain with Sydney Green	May 1969	Apr. 1971	D3	F	5.5
Eastington–Michael Wood	8	Freeman Fox with Robert F. Earley	G. Wimpey with J.L. Kier					
Michael Wood–Almondsbury (15)	8	Freeman Fox with Robert F. Earley	G. Wimpey with J.L. Kier	Oct. 1969	Dec. 1971	D3	F	11.4
Almondsbury interchange		Freeman Fox with Robert F. Earley	Costain	Mar. 1964	Aug. 1966	D3	F	1.9
Filton by-pass (16)–(17) widening	2	Gloucester CC	Gloucester CC / Costain		May 1963 / July 1969	D2 / D3	F / F	
Cribbs Causeway (17)–Avonmouth (18)	4	Freeman Fox with Robert F. Earley	A.E. Farr	Feb. 1967	Aug. 1969	D3	F	3.7
Avonmouth Bridge (18)–(19)	1	Freeman Fox with Robert F. Earley	Fairfield Mabey	July 1969	May 1974	D3	F	4.2
Easton (Gordano)–Clapton Wick (20)	5	Freeman Fox with Robert F. Earley	Cementation	Jan. 1970	Jan. 1973	D3	F	5.7

continued overleaf

Table 7.3 (Cont.)

Motorway	Motorway section (interchange no.)	Length: miles	Engineer	Main Contractor	Contract let	Open	Standard: D2=dual 2 lane D3=dual 3 lane (F=Flexible; C=Concrete)		Cost: £ million (tender price)
M5 (contd)	Clapton Wick–St George's (21)	9	SWRCU Freeman Fox with Robert F. Earley	John Laing	Oct. 1969	Jan. 1973	D3	F	10.7
	St George's–Erithmead (22)	9	SWRCU Freeman Fox with Robert F. Earley	A.E. Farr with Bovis	Nov. 1969	Jan. 1973	D3	F	8.0
	Edithmead–Dunball (23)	5	SWRCU (Somerset SU)	W. and C. French	Feb. 1971	Aug. 1973	D3	F	7.5
	Dunball–Huntworth (24)	5	SWRCU (Somerset SU)	Cementation	May 1971	Dec. 1973	D3	F	5.3
	Huntworth–Blackbrook (25)	6	SWRCU (Somerset SU)	A. Monk	Apr. 1973	Nov. 1975	D3	F	5.7
	Blackbrook–Chelston (26)	7	SWRCU (Somerset SU)	Cementation with R. McGregor	Jan. 1972	Apr. 1974	D3	C	5.0
	Chelston–Willand (28)	11	SWRCU (Somerset SU)	Tarmac	Oct. 1974	Oct. 1976	D3	C	12.5
	Killerton	10	SWRCU with Freeman Fox	Bovis	Apr. 1973	Oct. 1975	D3	F	4.8
	Poltimore Bowles–Sandygate (30)	4	SWRCU with Freeman Fox	Bovis	Apr. 1973	Oct. 1975	D3	F	4.9

106

Sandygate–Pearces Hill (31)	4	SWRCU with Freeman Fox	Cementation	May 1974	May 1977	D3	F	12.9
Carlisle by-pass (44)–(42)	7	Cumberland CC	Tarmac	Nov. 1968	Dec. 1970	D3	F	7.0
Carlisle (42)–Penrith (41)	13	Cumberland CC	Dowsett	Feb. 1969	July 1971	D3	F	6.9
Penrith by-pass	7	Cumberland CC	Sir Alfred McAlpine with Leonard Fairclough	Sept. 1966	Nov. 1968	D3	F	7.7
Hackthorpe–Thrimby	3	Scott Wilson Kirkpatrick	Tarmac	Dec. 1967	Sept. 1969	D3	F	1.4
Thrimby–Tebay (38)	9	Scott Wilson Kirkpatrick	Christiani/Shand consortium	Aug. 1968	Oct. 1970	D3	F	7.9
Tebay–Killington (37)	9	Scott Wilson Kirkpatrick	John Laing	Oct. 1967	Oct. 1970	D3	F	11.7
Killington–Farleton (36)	8	Scott Wilson Kirkpatrick	W. and C. French	Aug. 1968	Oct. 1970	D3	F	5.4
Farleton–Carnforth (35)	8	Scott Wilson Kirkpatrick	W. and C. French	June 1968	Oct. 1970	D3	F	4.9
Lancaster by-pass (35)–(33) widening	11	Lancs. CC	Sir Lindsay Parkinson A. Monk	July 1957 Mar. 1966	Apr. 1960 Jan. 1967	D2 D3	F F	3.2 0.8
Lancaster (33)–M55 (32)	14	Lancs. CC	Sir Alfred McAlpine/ Leonard Fairclough consortium	Aug. 1962	Jan. 1965	D3	C	9.5
Preston by-pass (32)–(29) Samlesbury Bridge High Walton Bridge widening	8	Lancs. CC	Tarmac Cleveland Dorman Long G. Wimpey	June 1956 July 1965	Dec. 1958 Mar. 1966	D2 D3	F F	2.4 0.3 0.2 0.5

continued overleaf

Table 7.3 (Cont.)

Motorway	Motorway section (interchange no.)	Length: miles	Engineer	Main Contractor	Contract let	Open	Standard: D2=dual 2 lane D3=dual 3 lane (F=Flexible; C=Concrete)		Cost: £ million (tender price)
M6 (contd)	Preston (29)–Thelwall (21)	26	Lancs. CC	Sir Alfred McAlpine/ Leonard Fairclough consortium	Feb. 1961	July 1963	D3	F	15.3
	Gathurst viaduct	0.1		A. Monk	Sept. 1959	July 1963	D3	F	0.8
	Winwick link road	1		Cubar	Aug. 1962	July 1963	D2	F	0.4
	Thelwall Bridge	1	Lancs. CC	Leonard Fairclough	Sept. 1959	July 1963	D3	F	5.0
	Thelwall Bridge–Holmes Chapel (18) bridges	16	Cheshire CC Scott Wilson Kirkpatrick	Tarmac	May 1961	Nov. 1963	D3	F	8.6
	Holmes Chapel–Bartholmey (16)	10	Scott Wilson Kirkpatrick	Sir Lindsay Parkinson	June 1961	Nov. 1963	D3	F	5.8
	Bartholmey–Hanchurch (15)	10	Staffordshire CC	John Laing	Sept. 1960	Nov. 1963	D3	F	5.0
	Hanchurch–Stafford by-pass (14)	11	Staffordshire CC	John Laing	Sept. 1960	Dec. 1962	D3	F	5.0
	Stafford by-pass (14)–(13) Creswell viaduct	6	Staffordshire CC	John Laing J.L. Kier	June 1960	Aug. 1962	D3	F	5.0
	Dunston (13)–Shareshill (11)	8	Sir Owen Williams	John Laing	Dec. 1963	Mar. 1966	D3	C	5.6

	Shareshill–Darlaston (10)	5	Sir Owen Williams	Sir Alfred McAlpine/Leonard Fairclough consortium	Sept. 1964	Sept. 1966	D3	F	4.9
	Darlaston–Bescot (9)	2	Sir Owen Williams	Taylor Woodrow	Feb. 1967	Apr. 1970	D3	F	9.4
	Bescot–Rayhall triangle (8)	3	Sir Owen Williams	R.M. Douglas	May 1968	May 1972	D3	F	3.0
	Rayhall–Great Barr (7)	1	Sir Owen Williams	R.M. Douglas			D3	F	
	Great Barr (7)–Castle Bromwich (5)	8	Sir Owen Williams						
	Perry Barr			R.M. Douglas	Jan. 1969	Nov. 1971			5.2
	Gravelly Hill (6)			A. Monk	Aug. 1968	Apr. 1972			8.2
	Bromford			Marples Ridgway	Jan. 1969	Nov. 1971			10.2
	Bromford–Maxstoke	5	Sir Owen Williams	Sir Alfred McAlpine	Apr. 1969	Feb. 1971	D3	F	3.6
	Maxstoke–Ansty (2)	12	Sir Owen Williams	G. Wimpey/Kier consortium	Feb. 1969	June 1971	D3	F	9.7
	Ansty–M1 at Catthorpe	12	Sir Owen Williams	John Laing	Sept. 1968	Oct. 1971	D3	F	8.6
M10	M1 link	2	Herts. CC	Tarmac	Mar. 1958	Nov. 1969	D2	C	incl. in M1
M11	Redbridge (3)–Loughton (6)	6	ERCU with W.S. Atkins	W. and C. French	Sept. 1973	Apr. 1977	D3/D2	F	11.8
	Loughton–S. Harlow (7)	8	ERCU with W.S. Atkins	Dowsett	Oct. 1974	Apr. 1977	D3	C	8.8
	S. Harlow–A120 (8)	10	ERCU with W.S. Atkins	Fitzpatrick	Oct. 1972	June 1975	D3	C	7.1
	A120–Quendon (9)	7	ERCU with W.S. Atkins	Sir Alfred McAlpine (Northern)	May 1977	Nov. 1979	D2	C	7.9

continued overleaf

Table 7.3 (Cont.)

Motorway	Motorway section (interchange no.)	Length: miles	Engineer	Main Contractor	Contract let (P = programme)	Open	Standard: D2 = dual 2 lane D3 = dual 3 lane (F = Flexible; C = Concrete)		Cost: £ million (tender price) (E = estimated)
M11 (contd)	Quendon–Stump Cross (10)	8	ERCU with W.S. Atkins	Tarmac	May 1977	Nov. 1979	D2	C	9.8
	Cambridge Western bypass (10)–(14)	8 / 6	ERCU (Beds. SU)	Bovis / Amey Roadstone	Jan. 1977 / July 1977	Feb. 1980 / Feb. 1980	D2 / D2	F / F	8.5 / 7.4
M18	Thurcroft (1)–Wadworth (2)	10	Sir Owen Williams	W. and C. French	Jan. 1966	Nov. 1967	D3	F	5.1
	Wadworth viaduct Wadworth (2)–Armthorpe (4)	8	NERCU (W. Yorks. SU)	Dowsett	Oct. 1976 / Dec. 1976	Dec. 1978 / Dec. 1978	D2 / D2	F / F	2.4 / 9.5
	Armthorpe–Hatfield (5)	4	NERCU (W. Yorks. SU)	A. Monk	Oct. 1975	Aug. 1977	D2	F	4.7
	Hatfield–Thorne (6)	3	NERCU (W. Yorks. SU)	Sir Alfred McAlpine	Aug. 1970	June 1972	D3	F	4.8
	Thorne–East Cowick (7)	5	NERCU (W. Yorks. SU)	W. and C. French	Apr. 1973	Sept. 1975	D3	F	2.6
M20	Swanley–West Kingsdown	6	SERCU (Kent SU)	Sir Alfred McAlpine (Northern)	Mar. 1975	May 1977	D3	F	9.1
	West Kingsdown–Wrotham	5	SERCU (Kent SU)	Dowsett	July 1976	Feb. 1980	D3	C	10.3
	Ditton by-pass	7	SERCU (Kent SU)	Costain	Dec. 1969	Dec. 1971	D3	C	4.5

	Section	No.	Consultant	Contractor					
	Maidstone by-pass west (4)–(6)	4	Kent CC with Scott Wilson Kirkpatrick	Sir Robert McAlpine	Mar. 1959	Dec. 1960	D2	F	2.3
	Maidstone by-pass east (6)–(7)	3	Kent CC with Scott Wilson Kirkpatrick	Costain	Apr. 1958	Sept. 1961	D2	F	
	Maidstone–Ashford (9)	14		Scheme temporarily suspended					
	Ashford–Sellindge	8	Colquhoun with Williams	Dowsett	Sept. 1978	Dec. 1981	D3	C	14.9
	Sellindge–Folkstone (12)	7	SERCU (Kent SU)	Tarmac	Sept. 1978	Oct. 1981	D2/D3	C	13.8
M23	Hooley (7)–Merstham (8)	2	R. Travers Morgan	W. and C. French	Jan. 1972	Dec. 1974	D3	F	2.6
	Bletchingley (8)–Pease Pottage (11)	15	R. Travers Morgan	W. and C. French	Feb. 1972	Nov. 1975	D3	F	11.9
M25	Gatwick link	1	SERCU (Surrey SU)	W. and C. French	Apr. 1974	Nov. 1975	D2	F	1.6
	Dartford (1)–Swanley (3)	5	SERCU (Kent SU)	John Laing	May 1974	Apr. 1977	D3	C	5.5
	Swanley–Dunton Green	7	SERCU (Kent SU)		P 1982/83		D3		24.3 (E)
	Dunton Green–Sundridge Rd	2	SERCU (Kent SU)	Cementation	Sept. 1977	July 1980	D3	F	7.2 (E)
	Sundridge Rd–Westerham	4	SERCU (Kent SU)	Gleeson	Dec. 1976	Nov. 1979	D3	C	6.2
	Westerham–Godstone (6)	5	SERCU (Surrey SU)	Bovis	July 1976	Nov. 1979	D3	F	8.4
	Godstone–Reigate (8)	6	SERCU (Surrey SU)	W. and C. French	Jan. 1972	Feb. 1976	D3	F	10.4
	Reigate–Leatherhead Leatherhead interchange	5	SERCU with W.S. Atkins		P 1982/83 P 1982/83		D3		10.0 (E) 15.7 (E)

continued overleaf

111

Table 7.3 (Cont.)

Motorway	Motorway section (interchange no.)	Length: miles	Engineer	Main Contractor	Contract let (P = programme)	Open	Standard: D2 = dual 2 lane D3 = dual 3 lane (F = Flexible; C = Concrete)	Cost: £ million (tender price) (E = estimated)
M25 (contd)	Leatherhead–Wisley advance bridges	4	SERCU with W.S. Atkins	Leonard Fairclough	July 1981		D3	1.2
	Wisley interchange advance construction				P 1982/83			11.0 (E)
	New Haw viaduct		SERCU (Surrey SU) Gifford	A. Monk Balfour Beatty	Feb. 1980 June 1979			1.6 3.7
	Wisley–Chertsey (11)	6	SERCU with W.S. Atkins	Balfour Beatty	July 1981		D3 C	20.7
	advance bridges		SERCU (Surrey SU)	Leonard Fairclough	Nov. 1978	Sept. 1980		1.2
	Chertsey–Thorpe (12) Chertsey link	2	SERCU (Surrey SU)	Bovis	July 1978 Apr. 1976	Oct. 1980 Dec. 1977	D3 F	7.6 2.2
	Thorpe–Egham (13)	2	SERCU (Surrey SU)	Bovis/Fairclough consortium	July 1974	Dec. 1976	D3 F	9.9
	Egham–Yeoveney (14)	1	SERCU (Surrey SU)	Bovis	Jan. 1979	Oct. 1981	D3 F	6.4
	Yeoveney–airport spur	2	SERCU with W.S. Atkins	Balfour Beatty	Sept. 1980		D4 F	14.8
	Runnymede Bridge	0.2	Ove Arup	Leonard Fairclough	June 1977	July 1980	D4 F	1.8
	Airport spur–M4 (15)	2	SERCU with W.S. Atkins		P 1982/83		D4	32.0 (E)

	Section		Consultant	Contractor					
	M4–Denham (17)	5	ERCU with Halcrow		P 1982/83		D3		23.5 (E)
	Denham–Maple Cross (18)	6	ERCU with Halcrow		P 1982/83		D3		28.5 (E)
	Maple Cross–Hunton Bridge (21)	6	ERCU with Halcrow	Costain	Aug. 1973	Feb. 1976	D3	C	5.8
	Micklefield Green–A405 (22)	6	ERCU with Halcrow		P 1982/83		D3		33.6 (E)
	A405–A1 (23)	7	ERCU with Halcrow		P 1982/83		D3		27.0 (E)
	A1–A111 (24)	3	ERCU with Halcrow	Balfour Beatty	Apr. 1973	Sept. 1975	D3	C	4.9
	A111–A10 (25)	5	DTp (GLRT)	Sir Alfred McAlpine	May 1979	1981	D3	C	15.8
	A10–M11 (27)	8	ERCU (Essex SU)						
	Stage 1			Tarmac	July 1980		D3	F	28.6
	Stage 2			Tarmac	May 1981		D3	F	13.1
	Stage 3			John Laing	May 1981		D3	F	29.1
	M11–A12 (28)	8	ERCU (Essex SU)						
	Stage 1			Costain	Sept. 1980		D3	F	22.1
	Stage 2			John Laing	Dec. 1980		D3	C	19.9
	A12–A13 (31)	9	ERCU with Mott Hay and Anderson						
	Stage 1			John Laing	Nov. 1978		D3	F	11.0
	Stage 2			John Laing	Aug. 1979		D3	F	7.2
	Stage 3 (Dartford Tunnel)			Costain	Sept. 1980	Dec. 1981	D3	C	31.1
M26	Dunton Green–Wrotham	8	SERCU (Kent SU)	Cementation	Sept. 1977	Sept. 1980	D2	F	14.2
M27	Cadnam (1)–Ower (2)	3	SERCU (Hants SU)	John Laing	July 1973	Aug. 1975	D3	F	3.0
	Ower–Chilworth (4)	10	SERCU (Hants SU)	Sir Alfred McAlpine	Jan. 1973	Dec. 1975	D3	C	8.3

continued overleaf

113

Table 7.3 (Cont.)

Motorway	Motorway section (interchange no.)	Length: miles	Engineer	Main Contractor	Contract let (IP=in preparation)	Open	Standard: D2=dual 2 lane D3=dual 3 lane (F=Flexible; C=Concrete)	Cost: £ million (tender price) (E=estimated)
M27 (contd)	Chilworth–Stoneham		SERCU with Mott Hay and Anderson	Cementation	Oct. 1981		D3 F	12.5
	Stoneham advanced bridges		SERCU with Mott Hay and Anderson	A. Monk	Apr. 1981			1.2
	Stoneham–Hedge End	7			1981/82			22.0 (E)
	Hedge End–Windhover (9)	2	SERCU (Hants SU)	Amey Roadstone	Apr. 1976	Feb. 1978	D3 F	3.7
	Windhover–Funtley (10)	3	SERCU (Hants SU)	John Laing	May 1972	Mar. 1976	D3 C	6.6
	Funtley–Portbridge (12)	9	SERCU (Hants SU)	Marples Ridgway with Amey Roadstone John Laing	Feb. 1973	Mar. 1976	D3 F	9.5
	advance earthworks				Jan. 1971		D3	3.2
M40	Knaves Beech interchange	1	ERCU (Bucks. SU)	Sydney Green	Jan. 1971	May 1972	D2 F	0.3
	Gerrards Cross by-pass (1)–(2)	7	ERCU (Bucks. SU)	Amey Asphalt/Leonard Fairclough consortium	July 1971	Aug. 1973	D3 C	5.4
	Beaconsfield by-pass (2)–(3)	1	ERCU (Bucks. SU)	Amey Asphalt/Leonard Fairclough consortium	Feb. 1969	Mar. 1971	D3 F	2.0
	High Wycombe by-pass Loudwater–Handycross (4)	5	Bucks. CC	G. Wimpey	Apr. 1966	Mar. 1969	D3 F	3.4
	Loudwater viaduct			Reed and Mallik	Jan. 1967	Mar. 1969	D3 F	1.7

Section	No.	Engineer	Contractor			Type	Class	Length
Handycross–Stokenchurch (5)	7	Bucks. CC	S. Green/Holland Hannan and Cubitts/Kier consortium	June 1964	June 1967	D2	F	4.7
Stokenchurch–Lewknor (6)	2	ERCU (Oxford SU)	Gleeson	Feb. 1972	Mar. 1974	D2	C	5.6
Lewknor–Waterstock (7)	7	ERCU (Oxford SU)	Gleeson			D3	C	
Waterstock–Birmingham	60	MRCU		IP 1984 onwards		D3, D2		140.0 (E)
M42								
Polesworth section	7			IP 1982/83		D2		16.6 (E)
Kingsbury section	6			IP 1982/83		D2		14.8 (E)
Water Orton section	5			IP 1982/83		D3		22.9 (E)
Coleshill (4)–Monkspath (1) Solihull section	10	MRCU	R.M. Douglas	Apr. 1974	Nov. 1976	D3	F	16.6
Umberslade section	6			IP 1982/83		D3		16.5 (E)
Alvechurch section	5			IP 1982/83		D3		13.1 (E)
Catshill section	5			IP 1982/83		D3		9.4 (E)
M45 M1 (17)–Dunchurch (1)	6	Sir Owen Williams	John Laing	1958	Nov. 1969	D2	F	
M50 Ross spur motorway	21	Worcestershire CC Gloucestershire CC Herefordshire CC Sir Alexander Gibb Scott Wilson Kirkpatrick W.S. Atkins	A.E. Farr R.M. Douglas Tarmac		Nov. 1960 (junction 1 to M5 in July 1962)	D2	F	6.0

continued overleaf

Table 7.3 (Cont.)

Motorway	Motorway section (interchange no.)	Length: miles	Engineer	Main Contractor	Contract let	Open	Standard: D2 = dual 2 lane D3 = dual 3 lane (F = Flexible; C = Concrete)		Cost: £ million (tender price)
M53	Mersey Tunnel–Bidstone Moss		Mott Hay and Anderson	Sir Alfred McAlpine/ Leonard Fairclough consortium	Oct. 1968				5.3
	Bidstone Moss–Hooton	11	G. Maunsell	Sir Alfred McAlpine/ Leonard Fairclough consortium	July 1969	Feb. 1972	D3	F	11.6
M54	Wellington by-pass (5)–(7)	5	MRCU	Gleeson	Dec. 1972	Dec. 1975	D3	C	6.4
	Shifnal section	5	Sir Owen Williams	A. Monk			D2		11.8
	Donington section	4	Sir Owen Williams	R.M. Douglas			D2		8.1
	Codsall section	5	Sir Owen Williams	Sir Alfred McAlpine			D2		13.1
	Featherstone section	4	Sir Owen Williams	Tarmac			D2		13.3
M55	Preston Northern by-pass Peel–Lancaster Canal Lancaster Canal–Broughton	12	NWRCU (Lancs. SU)	Sir Alfred McAlpine/ Leonard Fairclough consortium	Apr. 1973	July 1975	D3	F	13.6
M56	Powey Lane–Stoak	2	NWRCU (Cheshire SU)	Sir Alfred McAlpine (Northern)	Sept. 1978	Mar. 1981	D2	C	4.3

						D3/D2	F	
Stoak interchange	1	NWRCU (Cheshire SU)	Percy Bilton	Mar. 1978	Mar. 1981			4.8
Stoak–Hapsford (14)	3	NWRCU (Cheshire SU)	Sir Alfred McAlpine (Northern)	Mar. 1978	Mar. 1981	D3	F	5.4
Hapsford–Preston Brook (11)	8	NWRCU (Cheshire SU)	Christiani/Shand consortium	Mar. 1968	Sept. 1971	D3	F	12.5
Weaver viaduct		Husband	Christiani Nielson with Lehane Mackenzie and Shand	Apr. 1968	Sept. 1971	D3	F	3.1
Preston Brook–Lymm (9)	6	NWRCU (Cheshire SU)	Marples Ridgway	Sept. 1972	July 1975	D3	F	6.3
Lymm–Bowden (8)	5	NWRCU (Cheshire SU)	Robert McGregor	Sept. 1972	Dec. 1974	D3	F	4.6
Bowden–Wythenshaw (4)	6	NWRCU (Cheshire SU)	Holland Hannan with Cubitts	July 1969	Jan. 1972	D3	F	6.7
Sharston by-pass	4	Howard Humphreys						
west	1		Peter Lind	Jan. 1973	May 1975	D2	F	1.2
east	3		Sir Alfred McAlpine with Leonard Fairclough	Dec. 1971	Mar. 1974	D3	F	5.0
M57								
A59–A580	4	Lancs. CC	Reed and Mallik	1970	1972			3.8
A580–A57	4	Lancs. CC	Sir Alfred McAlpine/ Leonard Fairclough consortium	1972	1974			6.9
A57–A5080	2	Lancs. CC	Sir Alfred McAlpine/ Leonard Fairclough consortium	1973	1976			

continued overleaf

117

Table 7.3 (Cont.)

Motorway	Motorway section (interchange no.)	Length: miles	Engineer	Main Contractor	Contract let	Open	Standard: D2=dual 2 lane D3=dual 3 lane (F=Flexible; C=Concrete)		Cost: £ million (tender price)
M58	Aintree–Melling	4	NWRCU (Lancs. SU)	Sir Alfred McAlpine/ Leonard Fairclough consortium	Apr. 1978	Sept. 1980	D2	F	12.1
	Bickerstaff section	4	NWRCU (Lancs. SU)		Apr. 1978	June 1980	D3	F	9.7
	Skelmersdale–M6 widening	3	Lancs. CC NWRCU (Lancs. SU)	Dowset Percy Bilton	Jan. 1976	1970 Sept. 1977	D3	F	2.1 2.3
M61	Preston M6–Chorley (8)	5	NWRCU (Lancs. SU)	Sir Alfred McAlpine with Leonard Fairclough	Dec. 1967	Nov. 1969	D3	F	6.8
	Chorley–Horwich (6)	8	NWRCU (Lancs. SU)	Sir Alfred McAlpine with Leonard Fairclough	May 1968	Nov. 1969	D3	F	3.6
	Horwich–A580 (1)	9	NWRCU (Lancs. SU)	Sir Alfred McAlpine with Leonard Fairclough Costain	Jan. 1969	Dec. 1970	D3	F	12.4
	Worsley Braided interchange (1) (advance contract)				Jan. 1968	Feb. 1969			0.6
M62	Queens Drive (4)–Tarbock (6)	4	NWRCU (Lancs. SU)	Sir Alfred McAlpine/ Leonard Fairclough consortium	Oct. 1973	Nov. 1976	D3	F	11.7

Tarbock–Risley (10)	13	NWRCU (Lancs. SU)	Sir Alfred McAlpine/ Leonard Fairclough consortium	Sept. 1971	Dec. 1973	D3	F	15.9
Risley–Worsley M63 (12)	7	NWRCU (Lancs. SU)	Sir Alfred McAlpine/ Leonard Fairclough consortium	Apr. 1972	Aug. 1974	D3	F	6.6
advance contracts			Sir Alfred McAlpine with Norwest					
Eccles interchange		NWRCU (Lancs. SU)	Leonard Fairclough	Dec. 1969	Nov. 1971	D3	F	3.5
Eccles–Worsley (13) (originally M63)	1	Lancs. CC	Gee, Walker and Slater	Apr. 1957	Oct. 1960	D2	F	
Worsley Court House–A580	1	Lancs. CC	Reed and Mallik	Oct. 1968	Oct. 1970	D3	F	2.2
Worsley–Whitefield (17)	5	NWRCU (Lancs. SU)	A. Monk	May 1968	Sept. 1970	D3	F	5.1
advance bridgeworks			Costain	Aug. 1966	Aug. 1968			3.0
advance roadworks		Lancs. CC	Robert McGregor	Mar. 1966	Nov. 1967			0.9
Whitefield–Moss Moor (22)	13	NWRCU (Lancs. SU)	Sir Lindsay Parkinson	Nov. 1968	May 1971	D3	F	12.4
Rakewood Bridge			Reed and Mallik	June 1966	Jan. 1969			1.3
Besses o'th' Barn Bridge		British Rail	Leonard Fairclough					0.8
advance bridgeworks		Lancs. CC	Costain					1.6
Milnrow–Rakewood		Lancs. CC	Sir Alfred McAlpine/ Leonard Fairclough consortium	Mar. 1967	Dec. 1968	D3	F	2.4
Moss Moor–Outlane (24)	8	Yorkshire WRCC with Rolfe, Kennard and Lapworth	Sir Alfred McAlpine	Sept. 1966	Dec. 1970	D3	F	10.5
Moss Moor–Pole Moor including Scammonden Dam						D3	F	

continued overleaf

119

Table 7.3 (Cont.)

Motorway	Motorway section (interchange no.)	Length: miles	Engineer	Main Contractor	Contract let (IP = in preparation)	Open	Standard: D2=dual 2 lane D3=dual 3 lane (F=Flexible; C=Concrete)		Cost: £ million (tender price) (E=estimated)
M62 (contd)	Outlane Moor–Outlane		NERCU (W. Yorks. SU)	W. and C. French	Apr. 1969	Dec. 1970	D3	F	1.4
	Outlane–Hartshead (25)	7	NERCU (W. Yorks. SU)	W. and C. French	May 1970	Dec. 1972–May 1973	D3	F	10.1
	Hartshead–Gildersome (27)	7	NERCU (W. Yorks. SU)	Dowsett	May 1970	Dec. 1972–May 1973	D3	F	7.6
	Gildersome–Lofthouse (29)	6	NERCU (W. Yorks. SU)	Dowsett	June 1968	Dec. 1970	D3	F	5.9
	Lofthouse–Ferrybridge (33)	12	NERCU (W. Yorks. SU)	Dowsett	Feb. 1968	Aug. 1974	D3	F	11.2
	Ferrybridge–Pollington	9	NERCU (W. Yorks. SU)	Sir Alfred McAlpine	Sept. 1972	Aug. 1974–Oct. 1974	D3	F	5.7
	Pollington–Rawcliffe (35)	4	NERCU (W. Yorks. SU)	W. and C. French	Apr. 1973	Sept. 1975	D3	F	5.8
	Rawcliffe–Balkholme west roads east roads Ouse Bridge	7	NERCU with Scott Wilson Kirkpatrick	Sir Alfred McAlpine Clugston Redpath Dorman Long/ Costain consortium	Apr. 1973 Apr. 1973 Dec. 1972	Mar. 1976 May 1976	D3	F	3.1 2.7 6.7

	Balkholme–Caves (38)	6		NERCU (Durham SU)	Sir Alfred McAlpine (Northern)	Apr. 1974	Jan. 1976	D3	C	6.1
M63	Stretford (1)–Eccles (7)	5		Lancs. CC	Gee Walker and Slater, and A.E. Farr with G. Dew		Sept. 1960	D2	F	5.3
	Sale–Northenden (7)–(11)	4		NWRCU (Cheshire SU)	Sir Alfred McAlpine with Leonard Fairclough	Feb. 1972	Sept. 1974	D3	F	9.1
	Stockport east–west by-pass stage 2 / stages 4 and 5	2.6	0.6 / 2	L.G. Mouchel	Balfour Beatty / John Laing	June 1979 / Feb. 1980	(1982) / (1982)	D3/2 / D3/2	F / C	6.1 / 10.7
M65	Whitebirk–Hyndburn	3		Babtie Shaw and Morton		IP 1982		D3	F	25 (E)
	Hyndburn–Burnley	8		Lancs. CC	Cementation / Sir Alfred McAlpine with Leonard Fairclough	June 1981 / Aug. 1981		D3 / D3/2	F / F	17.4 / 21.4
M66	Bury eastern by-pass north / south	9	6 / 3	NWRCU (Lancs. SU)	Sir Alfred McAlpine with Leonard Fairclough / Sir Lindsay Parkinson	Aug. 1975 / Jan. 1973	May 1978 / May 1975	D2 / D3	F / F	15.0 / 4.5
	Middleton–Denton	11		L.G. Mouchel		IP 1984 onwards		D3/D2		61.0 (E)
	Denton–Portwood	5		Ward Ashcroft and Parkman		IP 1982/83		D3/D2		38.2 (E)
M67	Hyde by-pass	3		Sir William Halcrow	Leonard Fairclough	May 1975	Mar.1978	D3	F	11.5
	Denton relief road (stage 1)	1		Sir William Halcrow	Sir Alfred McAlpine (Northern)	July 1978	Sept. 1981	D3	F	10.1

continued overleaf

121

Table 7.3 (Cont.)

Motorway	Motorway section (interchange no.)	Length: miles	Engineer	Main Contractor	Contract let	Open	Standard: D2 = dual 2 lane D3 = dual 3 lane (F = Flexible; C = Concrete)		Cost: £ million (tender price)
M69	Coventry section	8	MRCU	Dowsett	Apr. 1975	July 1977	D3	F	12.5
	Leicester section	8	MRCU	Sir Alfred McAlpine (Southern)	Dec. 1974	Nov. 1976	D3	C	9.8
M180	Thorne–Sandtoft (2)	5	NERCU (W. Yorks. SU)	A. Monk	Apr. 1976	Oct. 1978	D3	F	4.8
	Sandtoft–Trent	5	NERCU (W. Yorks. SU)	Sir Alfred McAlpine (Northern)	Oct. 1976	Oct. 1978– July 1979	D3	C	6.8
	Trent Bridge	0.2	NERCU (W. Yorks. SU)	Cementation	Dec. 1976	July 1979	D3	F	3.3
	Trent–Scunthorpe (3) and M181 link	4	NERCU (W. Yorks. SU)	A.F. Budge	June 1976	Dec. 1978– July 1979	D3/D2	F	4.4
	Scunthorpe southern by-pass (3)–(4)	8	NERCU with Scott Wilson Kirkpatrick	Balfour Beatty with Clugston	Oct. 1976	Nov. 1978	D2/D3	F	10.6
	Brigg by-pass (4)–(5)	5	NERCU with Scott Wilson Kirkpatrick	Sir Alfred McAlpine (Northern)	Apr. 1975	Sept. 1977	D3	F	6.8
M271	Nursling link	2	SERCU (Hants. SU)	Sir Alfred McAlpine (Southern)	Jan. 1973	Dec. 1975	D2/D3	C	incl. in M27 Ower– Chilworth

122

Road	Location	No.	Authority	Contractor	Start	Open	Class		Length
M602	Eccles by-pass	3	Lancs. CC	Leonard Fairclough	Dec. 1969	Nov. 197?	D2	F	8.0
M621	Gildersome–Leeds	4	NERCU (W. Yorks SU)	W. and C. French	Sept. 1971	Nov. 197?	D2/D3	F	2.9
A1(M)	White Mare Pool–Blackfell (originally A194(M))	4		Brims	Oct. 1967	Mar. 1970	D2	F	1.6
	Birtley by-pass	2	NERCU	Robert McGregor	June 1968	Mar. 1970	D2	F	2.3
	Chester-le-Street–Carrville	6	Durham CC	A.M. Carmichael	Oct. 1967	Sept. 1969	D2	F	2.9
	Carrville–Bowburn	5				July 1969	D2	F	
	Bowburn–Bradbury	7	Durham CC	Cementation	Oct. 1966	Jan. 1969	D2	F	3.8
	Bradbury–Aycliff	5	Durham CC	A.M. Carmichael	Aug. 1965	Sept. 1967	D2	F	3.4
	Darlington by-pass + A66(M)	13	Durham CC	Dowsett	Mar. 1963	May 1965	D2	F	5.2
	Doncaster by-pass	15 13	WRCC WRCC with	Cubitts/Fitzpatrick/ Shand	May 1959	July 1961	D2	F	5.0
		2	Notts. CC	Sir Robert McAlpine	May 1959	July 1961	D2	F	1.5
	Baldock by-pass	7	Herts. CC	A. Monk	May 1965	July 1967	D2	F	3.5
	Stevenage by-pass	7	Herts. CC	Martin Cowley		May 1962	D2	F	1.8
	Welwyn–Lemsford	3	ERCU (Herts. SU)	A.F. Budge	Apr. 1972	May 1973	D3	F	2.2
	Roestock–South Mimms	3	ERCU (Herts. SU)	Higgs and Hill	Sept. 1976	May 1979	D2	F	3.6
A3(M)	Horndean–Bedhampton	5	SERCU (Hants SU)	Gleeson	Dec. 1976	Nov. 1979	D2/D3	F	11.0
A41(M)	Tring by-pass	2	ERCU (Herts. SU)	Mears	July 1973	July 1975	D2	F	1.8

123

in the event John Laing and Son Ltd were successful tenderers for each of the four sections.

As with the St Albans by-pass, the wet summer of 1958 gave rise to construction problems. There was considerable difficulty with earthworks because of the wet and one of the suggestions by the contractors after the work was completed was that where a high rate of progress was called for, provision should be made in the Bill of Quantities for the cost of importing free-draining sub-base material for use when unfavourable weather conditions demanded it.

This section of motorway was constructed with a dry lean concrete base 14 in thick along the whole length over a 6 in thick sub-base. Hot rolled asphalt was used for both base course (2½ in) and wearing course (1½ in). Shoulders were 8 ft wide and of grass initially, but these were clearly inadequate both in width and strength and one half were changed to be of a stone-based surface treated type. Later the Ministry standard was changed to require construction to be the same as for the main carriageways and for the width to be increased to 10 ft.

Bridges over the motorway were to a standard design and although they provoked some criticism of their appearance, perhaps because of the relatively "heavy" design from using reinforced concrete, this died down with time. Standardisation was important in enabling the contract to be completed within the tight time limits set.

An account of the maintenance problems which arose early in the life of this first stage of the M1 was given by the County Surveyors of Hertfordshire and Northamptonshire in 1966[6]. About a year after opening of the motorway, crazing

Table 7.4. *Changes in total construction costs per mile for dual three-lane carriageways**

Motorway†	Length: miles	Construction period	Cost/mile: £ million at 1979 prices
(1) M1, M45 Luton–Crick	54	1958/59	1.96
(2) M1 Crick–Stanton	44	1962/66	2.61
(3) M1, M18 Stanton–Wadworth	43	1964/68	2.79
(4) Sections of M25, M67, M180	35	Completed 1978/80	2.5

* Approximate adjustment to costs made using Retail Price Index.

† (1)–(3) Sir Owen Williams and Partners. *London–Yorkshire motorway.*[5]

(4) Department of Transport. *Policy for roads: England, 1980.*[3]

of the asphalt surfacing of the slow lane in Northamptonshire became noticeable and was found to be caused by stripping of binder from the base course asphalt because of the presence of water. Local repairs were carried out but by the summer of 1963 it was evident that a major programme of strengthening and resurfacing over the next 3 or 4 years was necessary. A standard method of repair was adopted which included: excavation and removal of all defective material; provision of extra drainage by inserting a 4 in diameter porous concrete drain below formation level adjacent to the nearside concrete haunch with outlets across the hard shoulder; replacement of defective lean concrete base by a bitumen bound base; replacing defective concrete in the haunch by base course asphalt; and laying a 1½ in wearing course of hot rolled asphalt across the full width of the carriageway and marginal strips.

On the concrete sections in Hertfordshire, there was some spalling and cracking of the carriageway but the general condition of the concrete had remained good. Small areas of spalling were repaired using a epoxy resin sand mortar. Larger areas were replaced with a concrete containing small aggregate for a depth about ¾ in and with cement mortar for ½ in to ¾ in depth. Longitudinal cracking occurred where a wooden fillet placed at the base of the slab to induce cracking along a sawn joint had been displaced, probably during placing and compacting of the concrete. Repairs involved breaking out the concrete, inserting a jointing material and resealing.

Other maintenance problems mentioned by the Surveyors were: replacement of hard shoulders; settlement of embankments; slips on embankments; drainage of the central reservation; winter maintenance; maintenance of grassed areas; maintenance of traffic signs, road markings, maintenance of skidding resistance of the surface (grooving was being tried on the concrete sections); and experiments with surface dressings, crash barriers and signing of road works during maintenance operations.

As has been described in chapter 4, the Road Research Laboratory in conjunction with the University of Birmingham carried out a study of the traffic and economic aspects of constructing this stage of the M1. The study, which was not connected with the decision by the Ministry of Transport to build the motorway, gave a first indication of the nature of benefits which could be obtained from motorway construction.

In 1960 Sir Owen Williams and Partners were asked by the Ministry to prepare a scheme for extending the M1 northwards from Crick to Yorkshire. This scheme took the M1 to Thurcroft to the east of Sheffield from where another motorway, the M18, continued to the Doncaster by-pass A1(M).

From Crick, the motorway runs alongside the line of the old Rugby to Leicester railway, thus reducing the effects of land severance. Further north the motorway runs through the Charnwood Forest where there was considerable opposition to the intrusion of the motorway, but the alternative of taking the motorway through agricultural land was considered to be even less desirable. The motorway reaches a high point of 730 OD at the Forest.

In Nottinghamshire, Derbyshire and Yorkshire the motorway runs for some 40 miles through coalfields, and engineering problems arose from shallow and open cast mining and the subsidence effect of deep mining. Regrading and landscaping colliery waste tips for the motorway did, however, enable the appearance of the area to be improved.

Flexible construction was adopted throughout on the recommendations in the Road Research Laboratory's Road note 29 issued in 1960[7]. For the northern half of the route in the coalfields (Stanton to Doncaster) flexible designs only were prepared, but for the southern half from Crick to Stanton both flexible and rigid designs were drawn up. The tenders submitted favoured the flexible designs. The total design thickness of these pavements was maintained at 24 in. Hot rolled asphalt was used in the wearing course (1½ in) and base course (2½ in) and coated chippings were rolled into the wearing course. Composite bases 10 in thick and less were used between Crick and Stanton, some incorporating lean concrete, but from Stanton to Doncaster fully bituminous bases only were used because of the need to accommodate possible ground movements caused by mining.

The M1 carries on through Yorkshire as the Aston–Sheffield–Leeds motorway, and the Ministry of Transport appointed the West Riding of Yorkshire County Council (Engineer and Surveyor, S.M. Lovell) to locate the route, to carry out detailed design and to supervise its construction with the exception of a bridge over the River Calder and the Tinsley viaduct.

The line of route put forward was confirmed in 1962 and detailed design followed[8]. Topography and the presence of the Yorkshire coalfield had to be taken into account both in design and during construction. Considerable subsidence occurred over substantial lengths whilst construction was going on; in the Rockley area a drop of 10½ ft was recorded between 1961 when design started and 1968. The severity of subsidence due to mining is further illustrated by a drop in level of some 9 ft which occurred on the M1 near Markham colliery in Derbyshire. 100,000 ft of exploratory boreholes were drilled to find old mine workings, and excavations below formation level of up to 24 ft in depth were carried out to explore shallow mines and bell workings. During construction some 50,000 tons of coal were excavated. As was the case in the Derbyshire–Nottinghamshire area, landscaping included reshaping colliery shale tips visible from the motorway.

The pavements were of flexible construction and consisted for the most part of 8 in tarmacadam base on which was laid 4 in of hot rolled asphalt. Precoated chippings were rolled into the wearing course.

Design of the Calder Bridge was put out to open competition and the joint winning design was submitted by A.A.W. Butler and M.V. Woolley in association with E.W.H. Gifford. Subsequently consultants E.W.H. Gifford and Partners were appointed to supervise construction of the bridge[9]. This is of in situ reinforced concrete divided longitudinally into two bridges. The main span over the river is 240 ft. There was a major collapse óf the bridge during construction caused by the falsework.

The Tinsley viaduct is a two-level structure. It was built by Cleveland Bridge and Engineering Co., on a steel structure designed by Freeman Fox and Partners. It was preferred by the Ministry of Transport on cost grounds to a reinforced concrete structure proposed by the West Riding County Council (WRCC). The decision provoked a serious row between the Ministry and the County Council. The viaduct is some ¾ mile long and has a 20 span upper deck carrying the dual three-lane M1 and an 18 span lower deck carrying the dual two-lane A631 with a central service road. Steel box piers support the main cross boxes between the longitudinal girders on which the reinforced concrete in situ decks sit. As a result of the Merrison enquiry into the design of steel box girder bridges, restrictions were placed on traffic using the viaduct until any necessary strengthening following the "Merrison rules" was carried out. Work started on the strengthening programme in 1973 and took 6 years to complete; it is said to have cost twice the original cost of the WRCC design.

The Aston—Leeds section ended at Stourton and was opened to traffic along its whole length in 1968 (parts were opened in 1967). The route was carried on into the urban motorway system within Leeds city by the Leeds City Council in 1972.

In 1964, a few years after the opening of the Berrygrove—Crick stage of the M1, contracts were let for the extension southwards of the motorway from Berrygrove. The section from Berrygrove to Brockley was designed for the Ministry by Hertfordshire County Council (County Surveyor, J.V. Leigh) and consisted of two 36 ft wide reinforced concrete carriageways on a lean concrete base. The paving train used laid carriageways to the full 36 ft width in a single pass. Included in the contract was the dualling of a 1 mile section of the Watford by-pass. This section was opened to traffic on 28 October 1966. From Brockley south the motorway is known as the Hendon urban motorway. Contracts for the section from Brockley to the Five-ways junction at Page Street were let in 1964 and consultants appointed to design and supervise the works were W.S. Atkins and Partners[10]. Advance bridge works were carried out by Holland, Hannan and Cubitts, the Brockley Hill interchange was built by Cementation Co. Ltd, and the main and ancillary works were undertaken by Marples Ridgway Ltd. The first 1½ miles south from Brockley Hill were built to rural motorway standards and the motorway runs largely in cutting at depths of up to 40 ft with the aim of preserving the aesthetics of the area. South of Scratchwood, the motorway crosses the Deansbrook on a 177 ft long viaduct and from about this point southwards urban motorway standards were adopted for design. Between Deansbrook and Mill Hill there is a retaining wall some 1½ miles long and of up to 40 ft in height. This form of construction was adopted so as to avoid the demolition of two streets of houses and shops. At Mill Hill the motorway is carried on a 476 ft long viaduct. The Hendon urban motorway was opened by the Rt Hon. Barbara Castle on 24 May, 1967.

The final section from Page Street to the North Circular Road at Staples Corner was also planned, designed and construction supervised by consultants W.S. Atkins and Partners. This firm had submitted a report to the Ministry of Transport recommending the southern extension of the motorway to the North Circular Road at Staples Corner in 1962. After it was agreed to go ahead with the extension, the first step was to design and construct the Five-ways interchange with the A1 and A41 at Page Street. This interchange was constructed in stages and a prefabricated solution was adopted because of the large amounts of traffic in the area affected by the construction. Tenders for prestressed concrete and steel/concrete composite were invited and the prestressed solution offered by Cementation Construction Ltd was accepted in 1968.

The complex interchange at Page Street involved nearly ½ mile of elevated structures with two-lane carriageways. All the elevated works are of precast concrete and a subway and footbridge are incorporated to allow safe pedestrian access to Hendon aerodrome.

A Public Inquiry was held into the proposals for Staples Corner in 1970 and work started there in 1971. Contracts for the rest of the motorway were let in 1972. The final section of the motorway was opened in two stages: northbound carriageways in 1975 and southbound in 1977.

By 1971 anxiety was being expressed about traffic conditions on the dual two-lane section of the motorway between Beechtrees and Berrygrove and it is interesting to trace the events leading to work starting on the widening of this short length of road. In answer to a Parliamentary Question in the House of Lords in March that year it was stated that the Minister was "actively considering the problems arising from using this 6 miles of dual two-lane carriageway of the M1".

In March 1972 the Minister announced that the M1 between Berrygrove and Breakspears was to be widened to give four lanes in each direction by building a new four-lane southbound carriageway and using the existing carriageways to provide four lanes northbound. Draft proposals were published in May 1973 for improvements between Beechtrees and Berrygrove and Public Inquiries were held that year. In December 1974 the Parliamentary Under-Secretary to the Ministry of Transport said that statutory processes were being delayed "by the current review of the standard to which the motorway is to be constructed". A year later revised draft proposals were put forward in which it was stated that following the introduction of revised standards of design flows for motorways, four lanes were not fully justified until the M25 London orbital road was completed. Three lanes were therefore proposed but with bridges of sufficient width to take four lanes. Another Public Inquiry followed in July 1976 and in November 1978 the Secretaries of State for Transport and for the Environment announced new proposals which omitted new interchanges at Beechtrees, Breakspear and Waterdale. The Inspector at the Public Inquiry in 1976 had concluded that the Orders should not go ahead but the Secretaries of State had decided otherwise. As a result the existing M1 would become the northbound carriageway and a new three-lane southbound carriageway would be built. A scheme was being prepared by the Hertfordshire Sub-Unit for the Eastern Road Construction Unit.

The decision by the Secretaries of State was queried in an adjournment debate in the House of Commons on 23 January 1979 because of the rejection of the Inspector's findings. Objectors at the Inquiry had preferred an "on-line" widening to a new route as giving fewer environmental problems. In October 1979 objectors appealed to the High Court against compulsory purchase orders issued by the Minister, but this appeal was later withdrawn and in an oral answer in Parliament in February 1980 the Minister said that the way was clear for work to proceed. A contract for £27 million was awarded to John Laing and Co. Ltd, and work started in October 1980. It was expected to take 3 years to complete.

M4, London–South Wales motorway

The M4 constitutes the east–west link in the south in the motorway network in England. Starting from Chiswick in the west of London the motorway passes through the outer suburbs of the capital; near West Drayton there is a short motorway link southwards to London Heathrow Airport. There then follow by-passes to Slough and Maidenhead with a link, the A423(M) near Holyport, to the A4 trunk road between Maidenhead and Reading. This link was part of the Maidenhead by-pass before the M4 was extended westwards from Holyport. A little farther west there is a connection to the A329(M) which runs between Reading and the A329 near Wokingham. From then on the motorway passes near Newbury and Swindon to the Bristol area, where there is another motorway link, the M32, into Bristol. Shortly after is the Almondsbury interchange and connection to the M5, followed within another few miles by the Severn Bridge, the Wye Bridge and Chepstow. The continuation westwards into Wales is described in chapter 8.

As can be seen from the brief details in Table 7.3, sections in the east and the Severn Bridge in the west were some of the earlier works undertaken in the Ministry of Transport's first motorway programme. For most of its length in England the motorway was designed and construction supervised by consulting engineers Sir Alexander Gibb and Partners for the Ministry of Transport and the South Eastern Road Construction Unit[11,12].

Service areas are provided along the route at Heston, Membury, Leigh Delamere and Aust and there are toll booths at the eastern end of the Severn Bridge.

The M4 joins the London road system via the A4 at Chiswick and improvements to the A4 in the area were carried out in the late 1950s; the Cromwell Road extension was opened in 1958 and the Hammersmith flyover in 1961. The Chiswick flyover which marks the start of the motorway was opened in 1959. Three years later contracts were let for construction of the next section of the motorway running west, but before this, in 1961, work had to be carried out on the Great West Road to provide space for the construction of that section.

For some 1½ miles from the Chiswick flyover the motorway is on viaduct and was built in this way so as to avoid a considerable amount of destruction of houses and factories. For over a mile the viaduct is built of reinforced concrete surfaced with rolled asphalt. The deck is a 5 in thick reinforced concrete slab laid over precast prestressed concrete beams which sit on cross head beams at the top of concrete columns founded on 4 ft diameter bored piles extending downwards for some 50 ft into the London clay. Because of restrictions on the site and to minimise obstruction to traffic during construction a special gantry was designed to lift beams into place on the cross heads.

The remainder of the viaduct is of steel, and this form of construction was used in part to avoid excessive dust which might have arisen whilst building was in progress and which could have had serious consequences for the Beecham Group premises nearby where medical materials were being made under sterile conditions. The main span of this part of the viaduct is of welded lattice truss construction using high yield stress steel and is built on a curve. The whole of the steel section has a reinforced concrete slab deck 7½ in thick.

The carriageways on the viaduct are dual two-lane with a 4 ft central reservation and 4 ft wide verges; road heating is provided along the length of the viaduct and on slip roads to minimise the risk of ice formation and skidding. Traffic on the viaduct is monitored by loop detectors in the carriageway and by television surveillance by remote control from Hounslow police station. These precautions were taken because it was recognised that, if an accident occurred, the absence of hard shoulders could lead to traffic hold-ups. In the event experience has shown that the lack of traffic capacity on the viaduct does lead to serious congestion when breakdowns and accidents occur. A report by the Road Research Laboratory issued in 1969[13] showed that in 1965/67 the accident rate on the elevated section was 4 times as high as on the main part of the motorway westwards to Maidenhead and the accident rate on the eastbound carriageway on the elevated section was over twice that on the westbound carriageway. The accident situation was much the same 10 years later and traffic congestion was a regular occurrence in the morning peak on the approach to the two-lane elevated section[14].

From the viaduct to Langley at the eastern end of the Slough by-pass, the motorway was built with dual three-lane carriageways and 10 ft wide hard shoulders. Up to and including the airport spur the carriageways were constructed of reinforced concrete on a granular sub-base. Each carriageway was laid in two passes 26 ft and 12 ft wide by trains of self-propelled units; texture was given to the surface by transverse brushing with a wire broom. This section of the motorway was provided with street lighting along its length and was the first substantial length of motorway to be lit in this way.

From the airport spur to Langley, and indeed for the rest of its length, the motorway is of flexible construction. The section to Langley was built with 1½ in wearing course and 2½ in base course of hot rolled asphalt with precoated chippings rolled into the surface. Various bases were laid on a gravel sub-base in a full-scale trial carried out by the Ministry of Transport in conjunction with the Road Research Laboratory.

The Slough by-pass and the Maidenhead by-pass were built originally with dual two-lane carriageways. The Buckinghamshire County Council (County Surveyor, E.N. Frankland) were agents of the Ministry of Transport for the Slough by-pass and for 2 miles of the Maidenhead by-pass. Berkshire County Council (County Surveyor, K.P. Brow) were agents for the remainder of that by-pass but with consulting engineers Freeman Fox and Partners and Scott Wilson Kirkpatrick and Partners responsible for some of the bridges. On both by-passes the surfacing had a 1½ in wearing course of rock asphalt with precoated chippings on a 2½ in gravel asphalt base course. The bridge over the Thames near Bray (consultants Freeman Fox and Partners) has a main span of 270 ft with a superstructure consisting of high tensile steel girders with mild steel cross frames and all-welded joints.

Studies carried out by the Road Research Laboratory in 1965[15] (LN/927/NCD) showed that traffic on the by-passes had increased after opening at a rate of 20% a year compared with a growth rate of 8% a year on all-purpose roads in the south-east of England. Traffic on the parallel trunk road A4 had been reduced by 45%. It was estimated that in economic terms the by-passes were yielding an annual return on capital of some 20%.

The Maidenhead by-pass ended in the west at a roundabout junction with the A4, but when the M4 came to be extended to Wales a new connection was made near Holyport and the western end of the Maidenhead by-pass: from that interchange to the A4 is now the A423(M). A new link was made from the interchange to the A308 to replace an earlier connection from the M4 at Bray. In 1961 the Ministry of Transport appointed consultants Sir Alexander Gibb and Partners to investigate possible routes between the Maidenhead by-pass and the A46 at Tormarton, from where the motorway was already planned to continue to the Severn Bridge.

In 1938 the County Councils of Berkshire and Wiltshire had identified a possible line of a route between Holyport and Tormarton to relieve traffic on the A4, and in the 1950s the Ministry of Transport began looking afresh at a possible route for a motorway. Berkshire County Council in 1960 proposed to the Ministry that the County should be appointed to act as their agents for a route in Berkshire but, as indicated above, the Ministry decided to use consultants.

The consultants were asked to seek a more direct route than that which the Counties had had in mind and over 1,000 miles of possible lines were examined before the 80 miles of route finally built were decided upon. Initially the Ministry appears to have favoured a route north of Reading and leading across the Ridgeway to the north of Swindon. The consultants, however, narrowed the choice down to two broad alternatives: one, the so-called "modified direct" route passed south of Maidenhead Thicket and Wargrave, north of Reading, south of Hampstead Norris and Lambourn, across the Wanborough Plain and then south of Stanton St Quentin and Acton Turville to Tormarton. The other line was the "modified southern" route which went from Holyport south of Reading, through the Enborne Valley, north of Kintbury, through Hungerford and Aldbourne to the Wanborough Plain and thence as with the direct route to Tormarton.

There were difficulties with both these proposals, particularly with the direct route north of Reading where traffic problems would be created in Reading and over its two bridges across the Thames. Reading County Borough Council favoured a route to the south of the city, and eventually a compromise route was chosen which followed the southern route to the A33 to the south of Reading and then passed to the north of Theale and Hermitage to follow the spine of the Downs south of the Lambourn Valley (there had been objections to the direct route interfering with racehorse training near Lambourn) to join up with the direct route above the Wanborough Plain. Various sections of this route were published by the Minister between 1966 and 1968 and, after Public Inquiries in 1969, work started on the controversial sections in 1969/70. The sections farther west had begun earlier as there were fewer problems with the line of route.

In selecting the route, the consultants attempted "to avoid doing violence to the existing scene". Straights were avoided and the only embankment higher than 30 ft is that of 40 ft at Hooker's Gate where the motorway crosses the railway; the deepest cut, which is near Yattendon, is only 36 ft. Particular care was taken over locating the route over the Berkshire Downs and through the amenity area of Coate Water near Swindon.

The whole of this length of the motorway is rural in character and is built over a variety of soils including London clay, chalk, Kimmeridge clay, Oxford clay and oolitic limestone. Several materials were used to construct the upper 6 in of sub-base, e.g. crushed limestone in the section between Tormarton and Wootton Bassett, and cement bound granular, crushed limestone and soil cement in the stretch from Liddington to Wickham. The remainder of the sub-base was mostly natural gravel from local sources.

For the most part the base used was 7 in lean concrete and 3 in of tarmacadam road base. The base course was laid with 2½ in of either dense bitumen macadam, dense tarmacadam or rolled asphalt. The wearing course was everywhere 1½ in rolled asphalt with precoated chippings rolled in.

Bridges are of reinforced concrete and of steel. At Welford the motorway crosses the River Lambourn and the B4000 on a viaduct of five spans of 80 ft at a height of 40 ft over the flood plain. The viaduct consists of welded steel plate girders with a reinforced concrete deck acting compositely.

From Tormarton to Almondsbury the motorway passes to the north of Bristol with a connection into the city via the M32. The interchange with the M5 at Almondsbury is briefly described later when discussing the M5. From that interchange the M4 runs on and across the Severn Bridge and then the Wye Bridge into Wales.

The River Severn had long posed a major obstacle to a direct route between London and South Wales and several schemes were put forward for bridging the river in the 100 years or so up to the outbreak of World War II[16]. In 1943 the County Surveyor of Gloucestershire, E.C. Boyce, advocated a high level bridge 6,000 ft in length between Aust and Beachley, the site eventually chosen for the present bridge. In May 1945 the Ministry of Transport assumed responsibility for a bridge as a trunk road and consultants Mott Hay and Anderson in association with Freeman Fox and Partners were appointed to design a scheme.

The Severn estuary has a tidal range between 45 and 50 ft at its maximum, with swift tidal currents. To allow shipping to continue to use the estuary, the navigational authorities required any bridge to have a clear span of 3,000 ft with a headroom above high water level of 120 ft: this called for a long span suspension bridge[17]. The narrowest relevant stretch of the river is between Aust on the east side and the Beachley peninsular between the Severn and River Wye, and this was the site recommended for the crossing. An Order fixing the line of the bridge was confirmed by the Minister of Transport in July 1947 and covered a scheme for 8 miles of new trunk road between the A38 near Almondsbury to the A48 near Haysgate in Monmouthshire. The Severn was to be crossed by a suspension bridge with a main span 3,300 ft long, 120 ft above high water and there was to be a bridge over the Wye. The scheme as eventually built to carry the M4 consists on the eastern approach of the three-span Aust viaduct from a cutting in the cliffs to the main bridge abutment. There is then a 1,000 ft side span, a 3,240 ft main span and another 1,000 ft side span to the Beachley peninsular where the motorway continues on viaduct to the River Wye, which it crosses on a cabled stayed bridge which has a 770 ft long main span with two 285 ft side spans. After that the motorway is carried on viaduct to the Newhouse interchange with the A466.

Although there seemed early prospect after the war of a bridge being started, economic circumstances intervened and, when there was an up-turn in the economy, the Government switched priorities in favour of the bridge over the Forth in Scotland. The design of that bridge was based very largely on work done originally on the design of a bridge across the Severn which followed American practice for suspension bridges and incorporated a bridge deck using open lattice trusses. By the time the Severn Bridge came to the fore again the designer, Sir Gilbert Roberts, had developed revolutionary new ideas for suspension bridges and these were accepted for the new bridge.

Essentially, Roberts's idea was to combine various elements in the lattice truss and independent deck panels into an integral box unit the top of which formed the road deck. These units were then designed to have a shape which was aerodynamically stable, tests being carried out at the National Physical Laboratory wind tunnel to determine what that shape should be. The box girder finally adopted was 10 ft deep at the centre, 75 ft wide with sloping sides and with cantilever decks on either side for cycle track and footway. Mild steel was used throughout except for the top deck for which high tensile steel was used. Transverse diaphragms and longitudinal stiffeners were provided and all joints were welded. Box units were assembled and welded up in 70 ft long sections nearby in the River Wye at a former ship-yard. The units were made watertight, launched into the river and towed to the bridge site where they were lifted into position and hung from the main suspension cables. An inclined system of hangers was adopted to damp out unwanted oscillations which model tests showed could occur at low windspeeds. The new design provided a saving of some 20% in steel compared with the original design.

The suspension cables are 20 in in diameter containing over 8,300 parallel galvanised steel wires; the towers carrying these cables are hollow rectangular steel boxes standing 400 ft high above solid concrete piers. Bolting flanges were provided inside the towers in the light of experience with the Forth Bridge, where problems had arisen with bolts on the outside. The Aust pier is founded on a limestone outcrop and work on it was intertidal for more than half of the time; no cofferdam was needed. The Beachley pier rests on two 60 ft diameter cylinders and cofferdams were needed during construction. Anchorages for the cables are of the gravity type and consist of massive blocks of concrete of sufficient weight to resist the pull of the cables. The steel deck plate was coated with sprayed zinc as a protection against corrosion before the surfacing of 1½ in hand-laid mastic asphalt was applied. Since the bridge was opened problems with the deck structure have necessitated a substantial repair and maintenance programme.

The Wye bridge and viaduct uses a similar form of streamlined box section deck construction and is continuous over its supports with a single break for expansion near the centre. On the viaduct sections the deck is carried on splayed steel hinged trestles but the bridge itself is of the stayed girder type using a cable system on the longitudinal centre line. At each end of the main span is a 96 ft high hollow rectangular section steel tower pivoted at its base carrying the cable which consists of 20 galvanised wire spiral strands 2½ in in diameter. The cable over each tower passes into the deck of the centre and side spans at a distance of 255 ft from the tower and is anchored within a system of diaphragms.

By 1978, twelve years after the bridges were opened to traffic, an average of 33,000 vehicles per day were crossing over them[18].

M5, Birmingham–Exeter motorway

In the north the M5 starts at the Ray Hall triangular junction with the M6 to the north-west of Birmingham, passes through West Bromwich and Warley and forms in effect a western by-pass to the Birmingham area. To the south-west of Birmingham, Department of Transport plans in 1980 included a junction with the projected extension of the M42 running south of Birmingham. Farther south, at Twyning, the M5 and M50 join, so providing one connection between the Midlands and South Wales. Farther south still, the M5 and M4 join at Almondsbury providing another connection to South Wales and also a connection to London. The motorway then carries on south to the west of Bristol, through Somerset to Devon, and ends to the south of Exeter where there are connections into Devon and Cornwall via the A38 and A30. The motorway thus forms a significant part of the national motorway network, important both to industrial traffic and to holiday traffic to the West Country.

The motorway was planned and designed for the Ministry of Transport and South Western Road Construction Unit in part by County Councils and in part by consulting engineers. Some details about the motorway are given in Table 7.3.

Starting in the north, there are service areas at Frankley, Strensham, Michael Wood, Gordano, Taunton Deane and Exeter. At Gordano there is a picnic area as well as services and there is a rest area at Brent Knoll, a little to the north of junction 22.

The 11 miles or so of the M5 south from the junction with the M6 at the Ray Hall triangle to Quinton were planned, designed and construction supervised by consultants Sir Owen Williams and Partners as part of the Midland Links project[19]. The route threads its way through industrial and residential areas and includes substantial lengths on viaduct and also appreciable lengths in retained cutting. The viaducts, as on the rest of the Midland Links road, are of a standardised composite design. The deck consists of in situ reinforced concrete slab acting compositely with steel beams supported on reinforced concrete cross beams and circular concrete columns. Where possible, longitudinal spans of 50 ft have been used with a maximum permitted span of 150 ft. Each cross beam is supported on four columns at 28 ft centres transversely. Depending on the longitudinal span, the steel beams were either I-section girders of high yield steel or welded mild steel or were welded steel box girders.

Where there are retained cuttings and retained embankments, the retaining walls are of mass concrete faced with precast facing blocks which also served as shuttering. At Blackheath, Warley the motorway passes along 1,400 ft of retained cutting with a maximum height of 35 ft.

Canals have figured prominently in the location of this section of the motorway. At the northern end near Ray Hall triangle an aqueduct was built to carry the Tame Valley Canal over the motorway and in Oldbury, where the motorway runs on viaduct for some 2 miles, the Birmingham Canal was reconstructed and diverted to run longitudinally underneath for part of this length.

From Quinton to Twining, the Worcestershire County Council (County Surveyor, W.R. Thomson) acted as agents for the Ministry of Transport for the design and supervision of construction of the motorway. The County began work on design of the Quinton to Lydiate Ash section in August 1961 and included with design of the motorway were the Quinton link and Halesowen by-pass extension, two class I roads connecting with the motorway at the Quinton interchange. The motorway was built with dual two-lane carriageways within an effective total width of 105 ft. In the light of earlier experience the drainage system was made more positive by shedding rain-water to gulleys at the back of the 10 ft wide paved hard shoulders. The road pavement was also constructed without the use of preformed haunches which had led to the penetration of rain-water on earlier projects. Substantial earthworks were involved during construction and some 3,000,000 cubic yards of earth had to be moved, some of it from areas of boulder clay which included large pockets of waterlogged silt. The cutting at Chapman's Hill has a vertical depth of 80 ft and the embankment at Lyeclose a height of 60 ft.

Within a few years of opening, traffic on this section was giving rise to congestion and in March 1975 the Minister of Transport announced proposals for widening the road to dual three-lane carriageways within the existing motorway boundaries. The widening was completed 5 years later.

The 26 mile section from Lydiate Ash to Twining was the first part of the M5 to be built. Designed and supervised during construction by Worcestershire County Council it also was built with dual two-lane carriageways and 9 ft wide hard shoulders. The sub-base was formed from nearly 500,000 cubic yards of granular material across the full formation width and the pavement consisted of an 8 in cement-bound granular base with a hot rolled asphalt base course of 2½ in and wearing course of 1½ in laid on top. The hard shoulders were constructed to the same specification as the carriageways except that the wearing course was 1½ in of dense tarmacadam surface dressed.

Lack of traffic capacity became apparent on this dual two-lane section and to some extent this was eased by the provision of crawler lanes. Widening and reconstruction of the stretch between Warndon (junction 6) and Lydiate Ash (junction 4) was included in the Department of Transport *Policy for roads: England, 1980*[3] as an item in the main programme for 1982 and 1983.

In 1959 consultants Freeman Fox and Partners[20] were appointed by the Minister of Transport to report on the line of route from Twyning south through Gloucestershire to Edithmead in Somerset, and in 1964 they were appointed to design and supervise its construction which they carried out in association with Robert F. Earley. This was apart from the 2 mile long section of motorway built to replace the prewar Filton by-pass by Gloucestershire County Council (County Surveyor, R.A. Downs) as agents for the Minister of Transport and opened in

1963. This originally had dual two-lane carriageways but these were widened to three-lane carriageways in 1969; extra width had been provided initially in the central reservation to allow for this.

Statutory procedures to establish the route took place between 1964 and 1969 and only two short lengths had to go to Public Inquiry. Ten compulsory purchase orders were required and Public Inquiries were held into six of these. The draft proposals were confirmed in all cases with minor adjustments.

Since 13 miles of the route pass over highly compressible alluvial soils and peat, and to help with design, trial embankments were built from which data on consolidation were obtained. As a result of the trials, with which the Road Research Laboratory was associated, a specified surcharge and its period of application were derived which guarded against residual settlement of the subsoil. Pile-loading trials were also made in connection with the design and construction of piled foundations for bridges.

South from Twining the motorway crosses an alluvial flood plain north of the River Avon at Bredon on an embankment which was surcharged for 21 months before the construction of drainage and paving. The motorway crosses the River Avon on a 567 ft long five-span steel bridge and crosses an overflow channel on a three-span bridge. Near Tewkesbury the route crosses areas liable to flooding from streams near the River Severn.

Continuing south the motorway passes between Gloucester and Cheltenham below a three-level interchange. Because many diversions of services were necessary a large culvert for those services was constructed at Piffs Elm in advance of the main works. Near junction 12 the old Stroudwater Canal was filled in on each side of the motorway and the route runs along the main runway of the disused Moreton Valence airfield. A considerable amount of excavation and fill was required from then on to the Almondsbury interchange, including a 30 ft deep sandstone cutting near Tytherington.

The sections of the route between Twining and Almondsbury were opened between 1970 and 1971. Delays in starting work were raised in an adjournment debate in the House of Commons in March 1967. The Joint Parliamentary Secretary explained that delays had been incurred partly because soil surveys had indicated that soil conditions were worse than anticipated, partly because of difficulties in locating junctions and partly on account of statutory processes.

The Almondsbury interchange between the M5 and M4 was opened by HM the Queen in September 1966. It is a four-level structure occupying some 80 acres of land and includes some 7 miles of road. The three bridges of which it is comprised pass over each other at various angles but with a common vertical axis; it is 65 ft from the lowest to the highest road level. The bridge carrying the M5 is 130 ft long and that carrying the M4 300 ft long and the main beams of these bridges are welded steel-plate girders encased in concrete[21]. A little to the south of this interchange is a subsidiary one providing a junction to the A38 and the start of the

Filton by-pass.

From the western end of the Filton by-pass to the Avonmouth interchange, where there is a link to the Portway A4, there is a mile-long cutting of about 60 ft maximum depth at Hallen. Additional width was provided in the cutting to permit the construction of a crawler lane on the northbound carriageway; the gradient of the motorway is 3.7% in the cutting.

A trial embankment was constructed at the Avonmouth interchange in 1965 and records were made of settlement and porewater pressures. The information obtained was used on the design of the motorway and side embankments. Temporary surcharging of the embankments on the weak alluvial plain was carried out for 11 months.

After the interchange the motorway crosses the River Avon on the 4,550 ft long Avonmouth bridge with a 100 ft clearance over high water. The bridge has a 570 ft long main river span with two side spans of 370 ft each and 17 approach spans with lengths ranging between 100 ft and 240 ft. The superstructure of the three main spans consists of twin welded steel box girders which were fabricated in 60 ft sections at Chepstow, carried by pontoon to the site and lifted into place. In addition to dual three-lane carriageways and hard shoulders the bridge has a cycle track and footway within an overall width of 132 ft 6 in.

Delays occurred during construction of the bridge, which was started in 1969. In reply to a Parliamentary Question on 22 June 1972 the Minister said delays had occurred because of the need to check the box girder structure against the Merrison rules "and other difficulties". The latter presumably referred to labour troubles because in answer to a further Parliamentary Question in February 1973 in the House of Lords it was stated that "negotiations are proceeding between the contractor and the unions representing the men". Another Parliamentary Question about the bridge was asked in the House of Commons on 25 March 1973 and in reply it was said that steel work was approaching completion. In May 1974 the bridge was opened to allow a single lane in each direction but it was some 6 months later before it was fully open to traffic.

South of the bridge the motorway passes into the area of the Clevedon Hills. On sidelong ground in the hills the motorway is mainly in rock cutting and there are split-level carriageways with up to 30 ft difference in level. In adjacent valleys at Wynhol there are two parallel viaducts about 1,600 ft long and 100 ft high[22]. In the hills some 2,000,000 cubic yards of rock were excavated with a maximum depth of cutting of 100 ft. A substantial amount of fill was imported, including a large amount of pulverized fuel ash brought in by rail from South Wales. At the Clevedon interchange, piles coated with a bitumen slip layer were used for the first time in England[23].

After crossing the Mendip Hills the route crosses the Somerset Levels. The embankments on the weak soils were surcharged for 12 months and lightweight fill was used on the high embankments.

From Edithmead to the Devon county boundary, the Somerset County Sub-Unit (County Surveyors, A.S. Turner and F.D.J. Johnson) of the South Western Road Construction Unit were responsible for design and supervision of contract work and the Devon County Sub-Unit (County Surveyor, M.J. Hawkins) and Freeman Fox and Partners were responsible for sections in Devon.

Public Inquiries were held in 1970 into the proposals for the route south from Edithmead in Somerset. Objections were raised on grounds of interference with agriculture and commercial enterprises, of close proximity to residential areas and of aggravation of flooding in the area. Schemes were approved by the Minister and work started on the sections between Edithmead and Huntworth in 1971. As with the section to the north of Edithmead, problems were encountered with the compressible alluvium deposits in the area and accounts of some of the investigations carried out into the embankments built on the soft ground were given at a symposium of the British Geotechnical Society in 1973[24]. At Huntworth the motorway runs along a 17 span viaduct over the River Parrett, the Bristol–Exeter railway line and the Bridgewater and Taunton Canal. It is a steel box girder structure some 4000 ft long and was the first such structure to be built from the start according to the Merrison rules.

The line of route from Huntworth to Willand was fixed by the Minister in May 1971 and work on the section from Huntworth to Blackbrook started in 1973. Work on the next section, the Taunton by-pass between Blackbrook and Chelston, had started earlier in 1972. This section and the length from Chelston to Willand are constructed of concrete. The Taunton by-pass was opened in 1974 and it was not long before complaints began to arise from drivers about the condition of the southbound carriageway. Four years after opening, the concrete slabs of the carriageway began to break up and reconstruction became necessary; repairs were completed in July 1980. The cause seems to have been that the sub-base was too thin to allow proper drainage through it. Water seeped in through the joints and at the interface with the black-top hard shoulder and this led to softening of the Keuper Marl sub-grade. The northbound carriageway had been used as a haul road during construction and had therefore been built with a very much thicker sub-base; no comparable problems have occurred on this carriageway. The next section south to Willand was also built with a much thicker sub-base and with a thicker concrete pavement and no similar troubles have been experienced on this length either.

South of Willand a by-pass had been built to Cullompton in 1967/69 by Devon County Council as part of trunk road A38 but with the intention that the by-pass would be incorporated into the M5. This took place in 1975 after suitable improvements had been made to bring the by-pass up to modern motorway standards.

A Public Inquiry was held in April 1971 into the line proposed for the motorway from the Cullompton by-pass to Poltimore and objections were raised to the proposed taking of agricultural land for the motorway on the Killerton Estate of the National Trust. There appeared to be little alternative to this and the Minister confirmed the route in February 1972. Some lengths of the motorway in this area cross flood plains where there are weak alluvial soils. Where embankments were built in these places the top soil was left in position and was covered with a protective layer of crushed rock. For embankments over 10 ft high longitudinal rock-filled stability trenches were provided and, to reduce disturbance of the soil, the roots of trees and hedges were left in the ground after cutting to ground level.

The 3 mile stretch from Poltimore to Sandygate was considered at a Public Inquiry in July 1972 and the Minister decided to keep to the published route in December that year. There are two junctions on this section only 1 mile apart and the junction with the A30 includes a four-span bridge over which the motorway passes.

The route of the final section of the M5 from Sandygate to Pearce's Mill together with link roads to the A30 and A38 was considered at a Public Inquiry in February 1973 and most of the objections at the Inquiry were to the route of the A30 through Ide. The Minister confirmed the route of the M5 in September 1973 and work started in June 1974.

After the Sandygate interchange the motorway crosses under the Exeter–Exmouth railway line and then crosses over the River Exe and the Exeter Canal on the 2,250 ft long concrete Exe viaduct. Each carriageway of the viaduct is on a separate but contiguous 11-span structure and is supported on prestressed concrete box beams. After running for a short distance on embankment the motorway then crosses on the 1,000 ft long five-span Exminster bridge, which is essentially of the same design as the Exe viaduct except that the two structures carrying the carriageways are more widely separated in order to accommodate a wider central reservation[25]. Finally the motorway climbs to a 100 ft deep cutting to Pearces interchange where it joins the A38 trunk road to Plymouth.

M6, Carlisle–Catthorpe motorway

The M6 is one of the motorways most intensively used by heavy industrial traffic in Britain. Together with the southern end of the M1 it provides a direct motorway link between London and the Midlands on the one hand and between the Midlands through Lancashire to Scotland on the other. It is, indeed, the only direct motorway link between the Scottish road system and the English motorway network.

Lancashire County Council through their Surveyor and Bridgemaster, Sir James Drake, were to the forefront in the evolution of the motorway. On 30 April 1948 the *Manchester Guardian* carried a report of a scheme devised by Drake for a motorway between points near Carnforth and Warrington "which has a high Government priority." For most of its length it was to have dual two-lane carriageways 24 ft wide but dual three-lanes were needed in places and these would have 32 ft wide carriageways. Ten years later in 1958 the first section of motorway in Britain, the 8 mile long Preston by-pass on the M6, was opened to traffic.

Some details about the whole motorway are given in Table 7.3. Starting from the junction of the A7 and A74 north of Carlisle the M6 runs south first along the Carlisle by-pass, then along a 13 mile stretch to the Penrith by-pass. In all, these constitute some 27 miles of motorway and were designed and supervised as agents for the Ministry of Transport and the North Western Road Construction Unit by Cumberland County Council (County Surveyor, F.L. Broughton).

For the next 36 miles or so to Carnforth the route passes through mountainous country between the Lake District and the Pennines and the location and design of the motorway through this area was a matter of some complexity. The Minister of Transport appointed consultants Scott Wilson Kirkpatrick and Partners to select a route and to design and supervise the construction of the motorway between Penrith and Carnforth. The consultants were required to investigate a range of alternative routes taking into account economic and social factors.

Alternative routes for the motorway fell into "direct" routes over the mountains, or longer but lower level routes through the Lune Gorge to the south of Tebay.[26,27] An important factor in considering alternatives was the effect of weather, particularly the incidence of fog on the higher ground. To help in this evaluation a meteorological survey was carried out of visibility, temperature and snowfall. Of possible routes over the mountains the one selected as the best was only 1½ miles longer than the most direct line. It entailed tunnelling for 1⅓ miles and climbed to a maximum altitude of 1160 ft. The best route through the Lune Gorge, the Killington route, was some 2½ miles longer than the best route over the mountain but its maximum altitude was 1040 ft. The final choice lay between these two routes.

The Killington route was judged to offer a small advantage in service to the local community and in land use and the incidence of snow and ice was much the same on both routes. The product of hours of reduced visibility and mileage was also much the same, but the incidence of bad visibility on the Killington route was estimated to be only two thirds of that on the other route. The meteorological survey showed that under the prevailing weather conditions the incidence of poor visibility at a given altitude south of the mountains corresponded with that at an altitude 500 ft higher to the north. This meant that on the route with a tunnel through the mountains there would be considerable periods when motorists travelling south would enter the tunnel in good visibility but emerge in cloud.

It was estimated that the cost of the direct tunnel route would be some 15% greater than the Killington route but that the reduced operating costs on the direct route would offer a return of 9% on the extra cost involved in building it. On balance overall it was concluded that the Killington route was the one to adopt and this was accepted by the Minister. Interestingly, the Romans and the railway engineers chose routes through the gorge, whereas the A6 takes a more direct route climbing to an altitude of 1400 ft on Shap Fell.

From Hackthorpe to Thrimby the motorway runs through farm and parkland but joins the Penrith by-pass on a 70 ft high embankment. Between Thrimby and Tebay the motorway reaches its highest point in the moors near Shap and on both sides of this high point the carriageways are separated. Land values were low and savings in earthworks were obtained by fitting carriageways to the contours whilst at the same time keeping to reasonably uniform gradients for ascending traffic. Separation also gave opportunities for grazing for easier snow clearing and for better landscaping. North of Shap the carriageways are separated for 2½ miles, the climbing southbound gradient being kept constant; south of Shap the northbound carriageway has a constant climbing gradient and the carriageways are separated for some 4½ miles.

From Tebay to Killington the route passes through the steep-sided Lune Gorge. Through most of the gorge and on the southern approaches to it the carriageways are stepped with a vertical separation of up to 30 ft. This was done to economise on earthworks and was not continued at the northern end where deep rock cuts and heavy bridging made it uneconomic[28]. A substantial amount of rock-cutting (about 1,000,000 cubic yards) was involved in building the road through the gorge and extensive rock-bolting had to be employed to stablise the rock faces on the steep cutting profiles adopted.

The Killington to Farleton section passes through farmsteads and hill pastures. There is a long climb in the northbound direction to the Killington reservoir and there is a 65 ft high embankment near Killington. Farther south towards Farleton there are two lengths of stepped carriageway.

The final section to Carnforth and the Lancaster by-pass runs in part alongside the Lancaster Canal and immediately north of the Carnforth interchange the canal was diverted to pass under the motorway and clear of the interchange.

The line of the motorway between Carnforth and Penrith passes through extensive areas of boulder clay and it was doubted whether this material when excavated in cuttings could be used in embankments because of its high moisture content brought about by the wet climate. Importing fill would have been expensive and so the consultants in collaboration with the Road Research Laboratory carried out experiments with a trial embankment of the wet fill into which drainage layers were incorporated. The trial confirmed that it would be possible to use the boulder clay to form embankments and that the rate of dissipation of porewater pressure could be controlled by the spacing of the drainage layers. It was also found that the total settlement would be small because of the high stone and sand content of the clay[29]. Because of the quality of the materials and the heavy rainfall in the area, a method specification was used for earthworks with vertical face excavation and substantial rock drainage layers.

Some 78 bridges and underpasses were built and extensive use was made of prestressed precast beams.

From Carnforth south through Lancashire the motorway was designed and construction supervised by Lancashire County Council as agents for the Ministry of Transport (County Surveyor and Bridgemaster, Sir James Drake)[30]. This part of the motorway was built in four main sections: in chronological order of com-. pletion, the Preston by-pass, the Lancaster by-pass, the length from Preston to the Cheshire boundary and finally the section joining the Preston and Lancaster by-passes. There were few objections to the motorway in the planning stages and in only three cases were Public Inquiries considered necessary by the Minister of Transport; these were in the southernmost section.

Starting in the north of the county, the Lancaster by-pass runs south from Carnforth for some 11 miles. This by-pass was originally built with dual two-lane carriageways with grassed hard shoulders but the shoulders were paved in 1964 and the carriageways widened to three lanes in 1967, the extra lanes being built on the central reserve which had been made wide enough to allow for this in the original design. A particular feature of the by-pass is the reinforced concrete bridge over the River Lune near Lancaster. This comprises two parallel single span arches 10 ft apart with a clear span over the river of 240 ft; the total length of the bridge is 400 ft.

The section between the Lancaster and Preston by-passes was the last to be opened and was built in reinforced concrete. It is one of only two sections along the whole length of the M6 (the other is in Staffordshire) to have a concrete surface. It was built with dual three-lane carriageways, the 36 ft width of carriageway slab being laid by concreting train in one operation. The 10½ in thick slabs were laid in two layers. The lower 7½ in layer was laid on plastic sheeting placed over the base and reinforcement was laid on top of the 7½ in layer. The top 3 in layer was of air-entrained concrete with ¾ in maximum gauge granite aggregate. Expansion joints were normally spaced 480 ft apart, with contraction joints 40 ft apart.

The Preston by-pass, like the Lancaster by-pass, was built originally with dual two-lane carriageways but with sufficient width in the central reservation to allow widening to three lanes if this should prove necessary, as indeed it did in 1966. Reference was made in chapter 4 to problems which arose after the by-pass was opened. The shoulders were grassed and soon proved unsatisfactory and were replaced by hardened paved shoulders. A temporary surfacing of cold asphalt was laid with a view to a permanent surfacing being laid after settlement had occurred. This surfacing proved unsatisfactory and it was replaced in the summer of 1959 by a permanent surfacing of 4 in two layer hot rolled asphalt; the idea of temporary surfacings was dropped in future work. The road base was 9 in of wet mix but the precipitation was such that the moisture content could not be controlled at the point of compacting; 2% of cement was therefore added to give adequate strength.

Because the by-pass was the first motorway in Britain it generated a lot of public interest and its building was televised by the BBC on 15 August 1957, when it rained all day. It is said that every supplier of materials wanted to get in on the act and a programme which was only on television for 1 hour stopped the job for about 3 days while the record deliveries that had come to site were sorted out.

The southernmost section from the Preston by-pass to Thelwall at the Cheshire boundary is some 26 miles long. The carriageways were constructed with precoated chippings rolled into a 1½ in wearing course of hot rolled asphalt on a 2½ in base course also of hot rolled asphalt. The base was either 10 in of dense bitumen macadam or 3½ in of dense bitumen macadam on 6½ in of cement-bound gravel. The motorway traverses some 10 miles of the Lancashire coalfield and in those areas the 10 in dense bitumen macadam was used.

In the mining area not only had subsidence due to deep mine working to be catered for but also there were many shallow mines and old workings to locate and deal with. Mineworkings down to 15 ft below formation level were excavated and filled and where they were between 15 and 30 ft below they were rafted over, as were old deep mine shafts.

This section of motorway includes two large bridges, the Gathurst viaduct to the west of Wigan and the Thelwall Bridge at the southern end between Lancashire and Cheshire.

The Gathurst viaduct carries the motorway over road, river, canal and railway and is 800 ft long rising to 87 ft above normal level of the River Douglas. There are six spans, four of 150 ft and one at each end of 100 ft. The deck is of reinforced concrete and the bridge rests on 19 in diameter bored cast in situ reinforced concrete piles.

The Thelwall Bridge is over 4,400 ft long and takes the motorway over the Manchester Ship Canal and the River Mersey. It crosses the canal at a height of 93 ft, with a centre span over the canal of 336 ft and one on either side of 180 ft. Including the approaches there are 36 spans in all, ten on the north, twenty on the south and three each over the canal and River Mersey. Some of the piles used are over 150 ft long with a wide diameter. The bridge is 92 ft wide between parapets, allowing dual 36 ft wide carriageways with 1 ft marginal strips on each side, a central reservation of 8 ft and two 4 ft verges.

South from Thelwall to Holmes Chapel, Cheshire County Council (County Surveyor and Bridgemaster, C.G. Day) acted as agents for the Ministry of Transport for the design and supervision of construction of the motorway. In addition on this section, consultants Scott Wilson Kirkpatrick and Partners were appointed to design and supervise bridges. These consultants were also appointed to design and supervise work on the whole of the next section south from Holmes Chapel to the Staffordshire border.

Before work on the north Cheshire section began, a new bridge taking the Chester–Manchester railway line over the motorway was built for British Railways to their design by contractors Dews and Co. of Oldham. As a result of the high water table over most of the area, dewatering by well points was necessary over 2 miles to enable drainage systems to be laid. The longest bridge on the section is that of 270 ft over the River Dane.

The line of the south Cheshire section was selected by the Ministry of Transport in association with the Cheshire County Council. There were no serious problems in locating the route and only two old cottages had to be demolished during construction. The route lies through rolling open country for the most part and the main problems during construction were with earthwork operations in places where the sandy ground was saturated and where there were ponds and boggy areas.

From the Staffordshire–Cheshire boundary to junction 13 at the southern end of the Stafford by-pass the agents appointed to design and supervise works were the Staffordshire County Council (County Surveyor, F. Jepson). The first section south to Hanchurch passes through hilly country and involved extensive earthworks; some 2,750,000 cubic yards of excavation was required. Near Madeley at Walton's Wood a serious slippage occurred over some 400 yards during the construction of an embankment. This was due to slip planes some 38 ft below the original ground surface, which were much lower than the depth normally reached in soil survey borings. Considerable extra excavation and drainage were required to correct the trouble.

Carrying on south of Hanchurch and along the Stafford by-pass to Dunston, one of the most interesting features is the 2/3 mile long Creswell viaduct to the west of Stafford, which crosses the River Sow, the Stafford–Crewe railway and a wide peat bog. The viaduct consists of a series of bridges separated by linking embankments, one bridge having five spans, the second four spans and the third three. The embankments are built on 15 in thick concrete rafts supported on piles and the fill is contained in part within retaining walls under the side slopes.

Parts of this section of road were to attract much higher volumes of heavy traffic earlier than expected and failures began to occur before the design life was reached. In February 1976 in reply to a Parliamentary Question in the House of Commons about repairs to the M6 in Staffordshire the Minister stated that they "had to repair this section of the M6 relatively soon after the last repair because of deformation in the wheel tracks of a certain stretch in 1972 which was causing considerable danger". The main weaknesses appear to have been as-dug gravel in the sub-base and its overlying cement-bound gravel base[31].

The final stretch of the M6 south from the Stafford by-pass at Dunston passes to the West of Cannock to West Bromwich and the triangular links with the M5 at Ray Hall, after which it swings eastwards to the north of Birmingham joining the Aston Expressway, A38(M), at Gravelly Hill. Continuing eastwards the motorway joins the M42 near Coleshill, joins the M69 to the north-east of Coventry and finally ends on the M1 at Catthorpe. Consultants Sir Owen Williams and Partners were appointed first by the Ministry of Transport and then the Midlands

Road Construction Unit to carry out the planning, design and supervision of construction of the whole of this stretch of motorway together with a short length of the M5, the whole being known as the Midland Links motorway.[19]

Almost 70% of the cost of the whole project was incurred in the route through the Birmingham conurbation, a brief description of which is included in chapter 9.

Of the rural sections, a short length south of Dunston was constructed with a reinforced concrete surface, but all other surfaces were of hot rolled asphalt. In the section to the north of Coventry precautions had to be taken in design against mining subsidence.

The interchange with the M1 at Catthorpe allows movement on to the M6 from the London direction of the M1 and from the M6 southwards on to the M1 south towards London. Other movements between the M6 and M1 are not catered for at the interchange.

Brief mention needs to be made of the build-up of traffic in the Midlands area. In 1973[32] it was reported to Staffordshire County Council that traffic flows on the M6 were well above the theoretical capacity and that there had been many "shunt" accidents. It was believed that new links then being completed round Birmingham to the M6 would give completely unacceptable traffic conditions. A few years later congested conditions on the motorway system in the West Midlands had become a regular feature during peak periods, particularly where the A38(M) and M6 slip roads merge and on the M6 between junctions 10 at Bentley and 9 at Bescot. Essentially difficulties were arising where the demand from traffic wishing to enter the motorway was greater than the capacity for entry and where exit capacities were reduced by high circulating flows on interchanges, resulting in traffic queues on exit slip roads reaching back on to the motorway proper. These problems had not been resolved in 1980.

Along the motorway there are 10 service areas, starting in the north at Southwaite, followed by Tebay, Killington, Burton (west), Forton, Charnock Richard, Knutsford, Keele, Hilton Park and Corley.

M62, Lancashire–Yorkshire motorway

The M62 runs from the outskirts of Liverpool in the west, through south Lancashire to Manchester where it serves in part as an outer by-pass on the west and north of the city, then climbs steeply on to the moors between Lancashire and Yorkshire, where it is the highest motorway in Britain, and descends on the east through industrial West Yorkshire near Bradford and Leeds and thence towards Kingston upon Hull on the east, but stopping some 16 miles short of that city near North Cave where it joins the A63 all-purpose trunk road.

The possibility of providing a good road connection between Lancashire and Yorkshire across the Pennines had been discussed in the 1930s, but no real action occurred until the Ministry of Transport invited the County Councils of Lancashire and the West Riding of Yorkshire to investigate and put forward proposals for a motorway between the conurbations of South East Lancashire and West Yorkshire. This meant not only locating a route through heavily built-up areas in both counties but also finding a way across the mountainous terrain in between. First contracts for work were let in 1966 and the first section of the route was open to traffic in 1970.

On the Lancashire side, the Lancashire County Council (County Surveyor and Bridgemaster, Sir James Drake) acted as agents for the Ministry of Transport until 1967 for the planning, design and supervision of construction of the motorway; thereafter the North Eastern Road Construction Unit took overall responsibility with the Lancashire County Council Sub-Unit (successive County Surveyors, J.H. Dean, Sir James Drake, J.R. Ingram and H.L. Yeadon) carrying on the work done by the County Council.

In Yorkshire a similar arrangement occurred with the West Riding County Council (Engineer and Surveyor, S.M. Lovell) carrying out planning, design and supervision of construction until the North Eastern Road Construction Unit was formed when the West Yorkshire Sub-Unit (County Surveyor, J.A. Gaffney) took on the work formerly done by the West Riding County Council.

Besides forming the major motorway link between west and east in the northern counties, the M62 also has connections with the major north–south routes: with the M6 at the Croft interchange, with the M1 at Lofthouse and with the A1 at Ferrybridge. There are also motorway links near Liverpool with the M57; near Manchester with the M63, M602, M61, M66 and A627(M); near Bradford with the M606; near Leeds with the M621; and near Rawcliffe with the M18.

On the Lancashire side two service areas, Burtonwood and Birch, are provided and in Yorkshire there is one at Hartshead.

Some details about the 108 mile long route are given in Table 7.3.

It had been planned at one time that the M62 would start in Liverpool at the proposed inner ring motorway, but after that proposal was dropped the sections of the M62 into the city from Queens Drive were also dropped in 1976 so that the route now starts at Queens Drive at junction 4. The section east from Queens Drive to Tarbock first went to Public Inquiry in September/October 1967 and objections were raised on the grounds of substantial disturbance through property demolition and loss of amenity. The Inspector concluded the Inquiry in favour of the Minister's proposals and in 1970 the Minister fixed the line of route. Further Public Inquiries into side road proposals and compulsory purchase orders took place in January 1972 and a contract for work to start was eventually let in August 1973. This section of route opened in 1976 and joined the Tarbock to Risley section which had been opened in 1973. In this area precautions had to be taken during design against possible subsidence caused by mining operations.

The Tarbock–Risley contract included construction of the Croft interchange where the M62 and M6 join. Because the existing M6 was at a level which was the lowest capable of draining into the local watercourse system, the M62 and connecting links had to be built above that level. The interchange comprises six overbridges and five underbridges and seven of the bridges incorporate prestressed pretensioned concrete box beams.

From Risley to Worsley[33] the route crosses the soft peat mosses of Chat Moss in south Lancashire where railway engineers experienced difficulties in the 19th century. In order to provide a stable foundation for the motorway some 2,000,000 cubic yards of peat had to be excavated, in places up to a depth of 20 ft. Stabilisation of the sides of the motorway was accomplished by the construction of slag buttresses. The Eccles interchange connects the M62 with the M63 and M602 motorways and was built as part of the M602 Eccles by-pass contract. The decks of the bridges at this interchange are steel beams with in situ reinforced concrete slabs and the bridges are built on pile foundations. There were limits on the choice of site for this interchange imposed by proximity to an Eccles Corporation housing site, the Liverpool and Manchester railway and the Worsley Court House interchange.

From Worsley to Whitefield the route passes through a heavily industrialised area and was the first section of the M62 to be opened (apart, that is, from a length of the Stretford–Eccles by-pass now incorporated into the M62 but which was originally part of the M63 and which was opened in 1960). Mine shafts, disused canals and railways, old sewage works and slag heaps had to be dealt with during construction. At Besses o' th' Barn a new railway bridge was built by British Railways to carry the Manchester–Bury line over the M62 and A665 and the motorway crosses the River Irwell on a 200 ft single skew span steel box girder bridge.

Between Whitefield and the county boundary on Moss Moor the motorway rises some 600 ft in five miles and crosses at its higher point at Windy Hill through a 100 ft deep rock cutting, rock from which was used in construction of the Scammonden Dam further to the east. Sections in the higher parts have concrete channels in the verges to trap falls of loose rock and to carry off heavy rain and melted snow. This section of route also includes the Rakewood viaduct which carries the M62 over Longden End Valley to the south of Littleborough. The viaduct has six spans, four of 150 ft and two of 120 ft, and is equipped with an automatic wind gauge connected to the police headquarters.

From the county boundary eastwards across the high moors several possible routes were considered in the planning stage and eventually the choice was narrowed down to two, a "high level" and a "low level" route[27,34]. The high level route reached a maximum height above sea level of 1,350 ft near the county boundary compared with 1,220 ft for the low level route, and the average height of the latter route fell to below 1,000 ft over the next 2 to 3 miles and rose only slightly above that where the two routes joined at Pole Moor some 6 miles away from the county boundary. Climate at these altitudes was an important factor in choice of route and in order to provide meteorological data about the area a network of weather stations was set up in January 1962. From the information gathered at these stations it was concluded that the high level route would have a 30 to 40% greater incidence of fog, a 10% greater incidence of frost and a 20% greater incidence of snow than the low level route. Also high winds were much more frequent at the higher levels. On the basis of these data it was decided to adopt the low level route.

At the eastern end of this route at Dean Head a cutting of up to 180 ft was necessary, and rock excavated there was also used in the construction of the nearby Scammonden Dam which serves as an embankment to carry the motorway and also forms a dam for a reservoir from Dean Head Clough. The dam was built jointly by the Ministry of Transport and the Huddersfield County Borough Council because of its dual purpose. The embankment is some 7,000 ft long, 220 ft high, 129 ft wide at the top and has a maximum width at the base of 1,100 ft.

Snow has always been a major problem on roads across the Pennines and it was decided at the design stage to carry out snow trials in relation to the Scammonden embankment and to the Dean Head cutting. Two sections of full-size motorway embankment were built at Scammonden with varying side slopes and it was found that a side slope of about 1:5 was sufficiently streamlined to minimise deposition of snow on the embankment.

A model of the Dean Head cutting was tested in a wind tunnel at the National Physical Laboratory to assess the effects of snow and it was found that in deep cuttings space was the key factor in minimising deposition of snow on the carriageway. As a consequence designs of the cutting were widened out at formation level and berms introduced all the way up the sides.

Other areas where snow was prevalent were provided with lightweight plastic-covered mesh fences in place of the normal motorway fencing to reduce the effect of drifting[35]. It was also found that the normal type of tensioned beam used on central reserves could cause snow to drift and trials were carried out with tensioned cable barriers as an alternative.[36]

Trials were also carried out to find suitable designs of fencing for use on Scammonden Dam to reduce the effect of wind pressures, particularly on high-sided vehicles. A slatted fence placed on the upstream berm significantly reduced wind effects on vehicles crossing the dam.

Because construction was going to require a considerable amount of rock cutting, a £150,000 rock trial was carried out to determine the optimum method of blasting and of extracting the rock for laying in embankments. The rock trials were carried out as part of the excavation of the Dean Head cutting and the material extracted was used in a trial embankment at Moselden, which was later incorporated into the motorway. As a result of these trials it was possible to specify the most satisfactory size of material and layer thickness for the embankments.[37]

A striking feature over the road through the Dean Head cutting is the Scammonden Bridge. This is a fixed spandrel arch with a span of some 400 ft and carries the A6025 road at a height of about 150 ft above the motorway. The design chosen minimised disturbances in air through the cutting and snow drifting.

To the east of the Dean Head cutting the climbing gradient across Moselden Pastures is limited to a maximum of 3%. The gradient down hill has a maximum of 4% and carriageways were separated to make economies in earthworks.

From the Outlane interchange the motorway runs eastwards along the top of the mountain ridge and then passes to the south of Elland avoiding built-up areas around Ainley Top. On this stretch the road passes alternately from short deep cuts to high embankments. The interchange at Ainley Top is unusual in having two roundabouts on opposite sides of the motorway connected by ¼ mile of dual carriageway; one roundabout collects the motorway and some side-road traffic and the other distributes it to the A629 and A643.

After Ainley Top the motorway continues east across the reinforced concrete arch Whitehaughs Bridge and then within a few miles drops 480 ft to cross the River Calder, the Calder and Hebble Navigation Canal and a railway. The crossing is made by the Kirklees viaduct, which is 870 ft long with six spans of continuous reinforced concrete deck acting compositely with steel box girders supported on reinforced concrete columns.

From Kirklees viaduct to Hartshead the route passes through old sand and gravel workings to the Clifton interchange, and then through the 55 ft deep Clifton cut before reaching Hartshead.

A few miles further on, after passing through the 60 ft Cleckheaton cutting, the M62 connects with the M606 spur to Bradford at Chain Bar and then continues through an area of deep cuttings and high embankments, where there are both shallow and deep mine workings, to the Gildersome interchange. This provides a connection to the M621 spur to Leeds. A few miles further on is the Lofthouse interchange where the M62 connects with the M1 which, in addition to providing a main route to the south, provides another link northwards to Leeds.

In January 1967 the Minister of Transport (the Rt Hon. Barbara Castle) announced in the House of Commons that she had decided to make a scheme for the M62 to join the A1 at Ferrybridge; from there to Humberside traffic would use the trunk road network. In 1970 a Public Inquiry was held into proposals for side roads and compulsory purchase on the Lofthouse–Ferrybridge section and a decision was finally taken on the route in 1971.

The route passes through a mining area and some 750,000 cubic yards of colliery shale from National Coal Board tips were used as fill and tip areas were reshaped. For part of this section alternative tenders were obtained, with contractors being required to give a price based on the one hand on using colliery shale fill and on the other on using fill of their own choice.

The section from Lofthouse to Ferrybridge also includes a 380 ft long steel box

Plate 1   Before construction of the M6 through the Lune Gorge

Plate 2   After construction of the M6 through the Lune Gorge

Plate 3   Split-level carriageways on the M5 in Cleveland

Plate 4   Wind barrier on the M6 at the Scammonden Dam

Plate 5   Severn Bridge on the M4

Plate 6   Friarton Bridge on the M85

Plate 7   Gravelly Hill interchange between the M6, A38(M) and A5127 in Birmingham

Plate 8   Contra-flow working during road maintenance on the M4

girder bridge (built to the new rules post-Merrison) over the River Calder and a 230 ft long bridge over the Aire and Calder Canal.

Although originally it was planned for the M62 to end at Ferrybridge, an extension eastwards to Rawcliffe was announced in April 1971 and a Public Inquiry was held in 1971. In May 1972 the Minister of Transport fixed the line of route which made some modification to the original proposals to meet objections at the Inquiry. Further extension of the route to Balkholme and North Caves followed and the route now ends at this point where it joins the A63 road to Hull.

At the Whitley interchange, where the motorway links to the A19, a reinforced earth wall was constructed using lightweight hexagonal glass fibre reinforced cement panels as permanent shuttering. The reinforcing consists of horizontal strips of galvanized steel and glass fibre tied to the front face.

At Rawcliffe the M62 joins the M18, which runs south to the M1 and which also has connections with the M180 running east to South Humberside and with the A1(M) Doncaster by-pass.

To the north of Goole the motorway crosses the River Ouse. The bridge was designed and built by Redpath Dorman Long–Constain consortium under the supervision of consulting engineers Scott Wilson Kirkpatrick and Partners. It is a plate girder bridge ¾ mile long with 29 spans and the central span has 75 ft headroom over the navigable waters. It has dual three-lane carriageways with a central reservation and hard shoulders. Work, which started in 1973, was delayed by the three-day working week, but even so the bridge was opened to traffic on 24 May 1976.

The Balkholme–Caves section has two lengths of continuously reinforced concrete pavement which were the first to be laid on a motorway in Britain. This form of construction was used at the eastern end where the motorway was built over a disused railway embankment comprising a variable depth of compressible material.[38] The remainder of the carriageways were built of unreinforced concrete using a slipform paving train.

There is no direct motorway connection to the new Humber Bridge but the A63 links the northern approach to the bridge at Hessle to the M62 at North Cave.

Studies were initiated at the University of Leeds by the Department of Transport into certain economic and other effects of the M62[39]. One conclusion reached in the studies was that "there are undoubted substantial benefits to the initial traffic and some substantial environmental benefits to residents on the initial road network." Other results of these studies are considered further in chapter 12. As regards environment effects it is of interest to record a comment in the *Goole Times* of 3 October 1975 to the effect that "peace came to Cowick and Snaith" with the opening of the M62 (Pollington to Rawcliffe).

References

1. DEPARTMENT OF TRANSPORT, WELSH OFFICE and SCOTTISH

DEVELOPMENT DEPARTMENT. *Transport statistics 1969–1979.* HMSO, London, 1980.

2. DEPARTMENT OF TRANSPORT. *Design flows for motorways and all-purpose roads.* Directorate General of Highways technical memorandum H6/74. Department of Transport, London, 1974.

3. DEPARTMENT OF TRANSPORT. *Policy for roads: England, 1980.* HMSO, London, 1980.

4. INSTITUTION OF CIVIL ENGINEERS The London–Birmingham Motorway. *Proc. Instn Civ. Engrs,* 1960, **15**, 317–410.

5. SIR OWEN WILLIAMS AND PARTNERS. *London–Yorkshire motorway.* Sir Owen Williams and Partners, London, 1973.

6. LEIGH J.V. and SANDERS R.N. The motorway—some years later. *J. Instn Mun. Engrs,* 1966, **93**, 358–363.

7. ROAD RESEARCH LABORATORY. *A guide to the structural design of flexible and rigid pavements for new roads.* Road note 29. HMSO, London, 1960.

8. WEST RIDING COUNTY COUNCIL. *The completion of the M1.* West Riding County Council, Wakefield, 1968.

9. E.W.H. GIFFORD AND PARTNERS. *Calder Bridge 1968.* E.W.H. Gifford and Partners, Southampton, 1968.

10. W.S. ATKINS AND PARTNERS. *Hendon urban motorway, southern extension of the M1.* W.S. Atkins and Partners, Epsom, 1965.

11. SIR ALEXANDER GIBB AND PARTNERS. *M4, London–South Wales, Chiswick–Langley Special Road.* Ministry of Transport, London, 1965.

12. SIR ALEXANDER GIBB AND PARTNERS. *London–South Wales motorway, M4, Holyport–Tomarton.* SERCU, London, 1974.

13. SABEY B.E. *Accidents on motorway, M4, Chiswick to Maidenhead: March 1965–December 1967.* Report LR 245. Road Research Laboratories, Crowthorne, 1969.

14. WOOTTON JEFFREYS AND PARTNERS. *M4 (Heston): system enhancements.* Wootton Jeffreys and Partners, Brookwood, 1980.

15. DUNCAN N.C.D. *Traffic studies on the Slough and Maidenhead by-passes.* Road Research Laboratory, Harmondsworth, 1965, LN/927/NCD.

16. ROLT L.T.C. *The Severn Bridge.* Gloucestershire CC, Gloucester, 1966.

17. ROBERTS SIR GILBERT. Design and construction of the Severn Bridge. *Proceedings of the 5th world meeting of the International Road Federation.* International Road Federation, London, 1966.

18. DEPARTMENT OF TRANSPORT. *Transport statistics 1968–1978.* HMSO, London, 1979.

19. SIR OWEN WILLIAMS AND PARTNERS. *Midland Links motorways.* Sir Owen Williams and Partners, London, 1972.

20. FREEMAN FOX AND PARTNERS. *M5 Motorway in Gloucestershire and Somerset.* Freeman Fox and Partners, London, 1971.

21. KERENSKY O.A. and DALLARD N.J. Four-level interchange at Almondsbury. *Proc. Instn Civ. Engrs,* 1968, **40**, 295–320.

22. SURRIDGE K.J. and BURGESS P.J.O. The construction of the M5 Wynhol

viaduct. *Proceedings of the Concrete Society 4th annual convention.* Concrete Society, London, 1971.

23. CONTRACT JOURNAL. Bitumen coated piles make UK debut on M5. *Contract J.,* 1972, **5**, No. 247.
24. McKENNA J.M. *et al.* Field instrumentation in geotechnical engineering. *Proceedings of symposium of the British Geotechnical Society.* Butterworths, London, 1974.
25. ATKINSON I. M5 crosses the Exe. *Contract J.,* 1976, **3**, No. 270.
26. HENRY J.K.M. Selection of route for the Lancaster–Penrith section of the M6 motorway. *Proceedings of the 5th world meeting of the International Road Federation.* International Road Federation, London, 1966.
27. GAFFNEY J.A. and HENRY J.K.M. Special problems encountered in the design and construction of the M62 in the West Riding and the M6 in Westmorland. *Proceedings of the conference on motorways in Britain.* Institution of Civil Engineers, London, 1971.
28. HALLS P.N. *et al.* Design of Lancaster–Penrith section of M6 motorway. *Proceedings of the 5th world meeting of the International Road Federation.* International Road Federation, London, 1966.
29. GRACE H. and GREEN P.A. The use of wet fill for the construction of embankments for motorways. *Clay fills.* Institution of Civil Engineers, London, 1978.
30. DRAKE J. *M6 in Lancashire.* Lancashire CC, Preston, 1965.
31. RIDGWAY G. Battered M6 rebuilt after only 15 years. *New Civil Engineer,* 21 July 1977, No. 252.
32. SHELBOURN J.L. *Traffic conditions on M6 motorway.* Staffordshire CC, 1973.
33. NORTH WESTERN ROAD CONSTRUCTION UNIT. *Lancashire–Yorkshire motorway M62, Croft–Worsley section.* NWRCU, 1974.
34. LOVELL S.M. England's mountain motorway. *Proceedings of the 5th world meeting of the International Road Federation.* International Road Federation, London, 1966.
35. INSTITUTION OF HIGHWAY ENGINEERS. Welded wire mesh fencing. *J.Instn Highway Engrs,* 1973, **20**, No. 2.
36. OLIVER F.R. Tensioned cable safety barrier M62. *Highway Road Construction,* 1974, **42**, No. 1769.
37. FORRESTER G.R. and HUNTER G.S.R. Rockfill. *J.Instn Highway Engrs,* 1971, **18**, No. 12.
38. CONTRACT JOURNAL Cracking down on bad soil conditions. *Contract J.,* 1975, **266**, No. 5007.
39. GWILLIAM K.M. and JUDGE M.J. The M62 and trans-Pennine movement 1970–77. Implications for regional and transport planning. *Proceedings of the Regional Studies Association conference on transport and the regions.* Regional Studies Association, London, 1978.

8

Trunk road motorways
in Wales and in Scotland

Introduction

In 1980 out of a total of some 1,600 miles of trunk road motorway in use in Britain there were about 128 miles in Scotland and 65 in Wales.

Responsibility for trunk roads in Scotland, previously exercised by the Minister of Transport, was transferred to the Secretary of State for Scotland on 1 April 1956. Similarly responsibility for trunk roads in Wales was transferred to the Secretary of State for Wales on 1 April 1965. The powers of the Secretaries of State and procedures followed are similar to those of the Minister in England but there is a difference in the administrative set-up affecting motorways in particular[1]. In England it was decided to create the Road Construction Unit organisation to carry out the motorway programme. In Scotland and in Wales this was not thought to be necessary and the motorway programmes in those countries have been handled through consultants and agent authorities on "traditional" lines.

In Scotland the Secretary of State's responsibilities are administered through the Scottish Development Department in Edinburgh; the Chief Road Engineer functions within that Department and combines the duties of the former Divisional Road Engineer and those corresponding to Headquarters' engineering staff in England.

In Wales a similar arrangement applies, the engineering aspects of the Welsh trunk road programme being administered by the Director of the Transport and Highways Group in Cardiff.

Wales

Economic considerations

The only motorway in Wales is the M4 which, when complete, will run for 80 miles from the Wye Bridge westwards through industrial South Wales to Pont Abraham on the A48 to the north-west of Swansea near Pontardulais (Fig. 8.1).

A detailed case for improvements on economic grounds of the South Wales road system was put forward by Brunner[2] in 1949. He pointed out that the economy of South Wales had, since the rapid development of mining and industry, especially

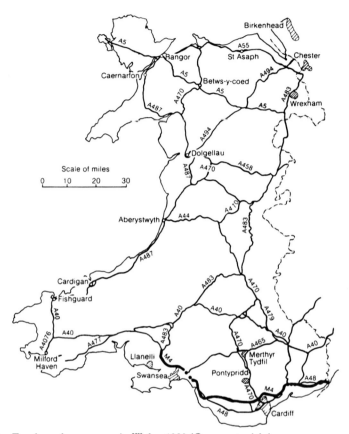

Fig. 8.1 Trunk road motorways in Wales, 1980 (Crown copyright)

in the latter half of the nineteenth century, been essentially an export economy based on transport through the ports to overseas markets or to other parts of Britain. Changes in the economy had taken place between the wars and after World War II, and Brunner argued that industry in South Wales had to look inwards towards Birmingham and that improved communications were required. He considered that "In the case of South Wales road modernisation not only is there an unanswerable economic case based merely on reducing the costs incurred by the present traffic, but, as the prosperity and whole pattern of development not only of South Wales but also of Birmingham ultimately rests on such modernisation there is ... an overwhelming case for giving it top priority in the nation's programme of capital development."

Some 20 years after Brunner's paper, the Welsh Office were saying much the same thing. In a policy statement in 1978[3] it was noted that the economy of Wales had undergone great changes in the post-war years with a substantial decline in the steel and coal industries as well as agriculture; one of the keys to future pros-

159

perity was good communications. Better roads were demonstrably important in attracting new industrial development. "The excellent access provided by the M4 to the Midlands and the South of England was one of the key factors in ensuring that the Ford Engine Plant came to Bridgend rather than elsewhere in Europe". Better roads helped firms already working in Wales and encouraged tourism but the kind of road to be provided in any particular area had to be judged on its merits. Sometimes a length of motorway might be appropriate, but often by-passes and minor improvements would suffice. A "systems" approach to a solution based on a motorway network does not seem to have been considered.

Road planning in South Wales

Dennis Hall has suggested that the history of the M4 probably started in 1823 when the Postmaster General invited Thomas Telford to advise on improvements to the mail coach route between London and Milford Haven. Among Telford's recommendations was a bridge across the Severn at about the site of the present suspension bridge opened in 1966. Telford's proposal was not accepted and it was railway rather than road communications which were to be developed later in the nineteenth century.

Soon after World War I, local authorities revived the idea of constructing a bridge across the Severn estuary to ease traffic congestion in Chepstow and at the A48 bridge across the Wye. In 1935 this idea was taken further by Gloucestershire and Monmouthshire County Councils who promoted a Parliamentary Bill to bridge the estuary. This Bill was rejected by a Parliamentary Select Committee in 1936 in deference to opposition led by the Great Western Railway Company.

Ten years later in 1946 the Government announced its 10 year plan for roads, referred to in chapter 3, which specifically included the Severn Bridge, but it was not until 1961 that construction started and not until 1966 that the bridge was opened to traffic.

There appear to have been considerable arguments about where road improvements should take place in South Wales. A South Wales Regional Survey Committee set up by the Ministry of Health in 1921 recommended improving the road from Cardiff to Bridgend via Llantrisant to take account of changes in the location of population and industry. The line subsequently chosen for the M4 some 50 years later followed this philosophy. The Trunk Road Act of 1936, however, included the A48, not the route through Llantrisant. In 1943 Glamorgan County Council made proposals for a motorway broadly following the line eventually adopted for the M4 but terminating at Margam. The Ministry of Transport plans in 1946 envisaged the M4 ending on the A48 at Tredegar Park to the west of Newport with the route continuing westward on an improved but all-purpose A48. The Glamorgan County Council continued to press for a motorway along the line of their earlier proposal and this was included in their Development Plan. There seems to be little doubt that their action safeguarded the line of the route and was of great help with planning procedures when the M4 came in due course to be built, and credit for this must to in large measure to E.J. Powell and D. Farrar, successive County Surveyors of Glamorgan at the time.

Meanwhile, in 1946, the Ministry of Transport appointed consultants to draw up plans for by-passes to Newport, Port Talbort and Neath under trunk road legislation; it was not until 1949 that the Special Roads Act became law and that Act included an Order covering the Port Talbot by-pass.

These road proposals had been concerned with the mouths of the Valleys, but there was local pressure for improvement to the route along the heads of the Valleys and for a link from that route to the Midlands. These pressures appear to have been reinforced by the Lloyd Committee set up by the Government in 1953 to advise on ways of encouraging industrial development in South Wales. That Committee saw a need for a better road system and, no doubt as a result of its recommendations, priority was given to construction of the M50 Ross motorway in the motorway proposals put forward by the Government in 1955. Construction of the M50 started in 1958 and the road was opened to traffic in November 1960. The Heads of the Valleys road, though not a motorway, was competed in 1966. In subsequent years improvements were made to existing trunk roads, e.g. the A449 though not a motorway is constructed almost to motorway standards and provides a high capacity link between the M4 and the M50.

M50, the Ross motorway[4]

The Ross motorway is not in Wales but as it formed an essential part of the strategy evolved for road communications between Wales and the Midlands and north of England a brief description of the road seems appropriate here.

The motorway runs from the Ross by-pass in Herefordshire in the west to the M5 near Strensham in Worcestershire in the east. It is some 21 miles long with dual two-lane carriageways and at the time of completion in 1960 cost some £6 million. There are two major bridges along its length, one over the River Severn at Queenhill and the other over the River Wye at Bridstow.

The motorway has been regarded as one of the most scenically attractive in Britain, passing as it does through picturesque countryside affording fine views of the Malvern Hills and the mountains of Wales and colourful in the spring from wild daffodils. Landscape treatment of the motorway was based on recommendations of the Advisory Committee on the Landscape Treatment of Trunk Roads.

It was forecast in 1960 that traffic on the motorway in 1961 would average 10,800 passenger car units (pcu) a 16 hour day; in 1978 traffic on the Worcestershire section was recorded[5] as 9,370 vehicles in 24 hours which, on the basis of the composition of the traffic and the pcu values used in 1960, amounted to some 16,400 pcu. After making a small allowance for the probable difference in traffic in a 16 hour and 24 hour day, the growth rate over 17 years is on average only about 2% compound per year.

Table 8.1. *The M4 motorway in South Wales*

Section	Length: miles	Engineer	Contractor	Contract let	Opened	Standard	Cost: £million at Nov. 1980 prices
Newhouse–Coldra	11.9	Mott Hay and Anderson G. Maunsell and Partners	Fitzpatrick and Son (Contractors)	1963	Mar. 1967		27.0
Newport by-pass	6.7	Sir Owen Williams and Partners	Sir Robert McAlpine and Sons (South Wales) Sir Lindsay Parkinson and Co.	Aug. 1962 Apr. 1963	May 1967	D2	67.50
Newport by-pass widening		Sir Owen Williams and Partners	*Tredegar Park–Malpas:* Reed and Mallik *Caerleon–Coldra:* Brunswick	May 1978 Apr. 1980	Apr. 1980 Autumn 1981	D2 to D3	9.97
Tredegar Park– St Mellons	5.0	Sir Owen Williams and Partners	Gleeson Civil Engineering	Nov. 1975	Oct. 1977	D3 to Castleton D2 from Castleton	29.10
Castleton–Coryton	7.5	Howard Humphries and Partners	Wimpey–Fairclough consortium	Oct. 1977	July 1980	D2	28.53
Coryton–Miskin	5.2	Mid-Glamorgan CC	Wimpey–Fairclough consortium	Sept. 1975	Dec. 1977	D3	51.99
Miskin–Pencoed	7.0	Mid-Glamorgan CC	Cementation/Costain joint venture	Sept. 1975	Dec. 1977	D3	58.46

Bridgend northern by-pass	8.3	Freeman Fox and Partners	Advance works: Bovis Civil Engineering Ogmore viaduct: Balfour Beatty E. and W. road works: Cementation/Costain joint venture	Oct. 1977 June 1978 Nov. 1978	Sept. 1981	D3	35.25
Pyle by-pass I	4.7	West Glamorgan CC	Bovis Construction	Apr. 1975	Nov. 1977	D2 Groes to Margam D3 Margam to Pyle	55.71
Pyle by-pass II	0.6	Mid-Glamorgan CC	R.M. Douglas Construction	June 1976	Nov. 1977	D3	
Port Talbot by-pass	4.4	Sir Owen Williams and Partners	A.E. Farr	Feb. 1963	July 1966	D2	30.58
Baglan–Lon Las	5.9	Sir Owen Williams and Partners		After 1984		D2	51.75
Morriston by-pass	4.0	Swansea County BC	Advance works: R.M. Douglas John Laing Construction Co.	Aug. 1969	1972	D2	27.44
Pontardulais by-pass	8.4	W.S. Atkins and Partners	Sir Alfred McAlpine (Northern) Ltd	July 1974	Apr. 1977	D2	64.60
Total	79.6						537.88

Evolution of the M4

The development of a modern road link from the Severn Bridge across Monmouth and Glamorgan to the Swansea area appears to have been approached by the Ministry of Transport in the 1950s and early 1960s in a somewhat piecemeal fashion with bits of motorway, some by-passes and some up-grading of existing roads. When responsibility for trunk roads and motorways was transferred to the Secretary of State for Wales, a more positive attitude to modernisation of the road link, following the earlier proposals of the Glamorgan County Council, seems to have emerged. Thus in a Welsh Day debate on 30 November 1967 the Secretary of State announced that the Government was taking over the "mid-Glamorgan" road as a new road extending the M4 to Bridgend and, as Table 8.1 shows, the M4 really evolved during the 1970s and was a priority project so far as the Welsh Office was concerned.

Table 8.1 gives information about the engineers and contractors responsible for various sections of the motorway together with a note on the standard widths and costs of construction at November 1980 prices. This information is amplified a little in the following paragraphs.

Newhouse–Coldra. This section constituted the approach to the crossing of the estuary from the Newport by-pass. Some problems were encountered on the 9 mile stretch between Crick and Coldra when cracks appeared in concrete beams on the Coldra viaduct and in an overbridge near Caerwent, but these were apparently repaired without undue difficulty[6].

Newport by-pass[7]. In March 1945 Sir Owen Williams and Partners were invited by the Ministry of Transport to undertake a preliminary study of the possibility of constructing, to motorway standards, a by-pass of the A48 at Newport. A scheme was selected and Orders were laid in 1946 under the Trunk Roads Act and a Public Inquiry was held in 1947; 2 years later the scheme was scheduled under the Special Roads Act of 1949. Although design work proceeded to near tender stage the scheme was deferred in 1952 on economic grounds, and it was not until 1960 that the consulting engineers were again asked to proceed with the scheme but incorporating the most modern motorway standards.

The line adopted passes on the northern side of Newport between Coldra and Tredegar Park and includes a major bridge across the River Usk and twin tunnels at Crindau a little to the west of the Usk Bridge.

The by-pass was one of the first urban motorways in Britain and the Crindau tunnel the first motorway tunnel in Britain.

Traffic growth on the by-pass appears to have exceeded expectations and in April 1978 a contract was let to Reed and Malik under the supervision of consultants Sir Owen Williams and Partners for widening the carriageway from dual two-lane to dual three-lane between Tredegar Park and Malpas. Work on this section was completed in 1980. East of the Malpas interchange capacity restraints are imposed by the Crindau tunnels and Usk Bridge which would be difficult and expensive to widen. But a second widening scheme from the interchange east of the tunnels (Caerleon) to the Coldra interchange began in April 1980. The work was carried out by Brunswick Contractors (Cardiff) Ltd, and supervised by Sir Owen Williams and Partners; it was scheduled for completion in Autumn 1981.

Tredegar Park–St Mellons. This scheme was published on 7 September 1971 and there were only 15 objections to the line selected. The line was fixed on 29 August 1973 without a Public Inquiry.

Castleton–Coryton. As far as statutory procedures were concerned this was the most contentious along the whole length of motorway. The scheme was published in April 1974 and 176 objections were received.

Coryton–Pencoed. In 1968 the Secretary of State for Wales added a new road, the Llantrisant radial running from Gabalfa in Cardiff to Capel Llanilltern to the west where it would join the proposed line of the M4[8]. This proposed new road passing through the outer parts of the built-up area of Cardiff ran into serious opposition and the strategy was abandoned in 1971 and the Secretary of State moved directly to the route to the north which was largely clear of the built-up area.

The proposed line of the M4 between Capel Llanilltern and Pencoed was published in November 1970 and attracted 57 objections. The Public Inquiry opened in June 1972, the arrangements having been complicated and delayed by proposals for a New Town at Llantrisant which were linked with the alignment of the motorway. After still further delay, the line was eventually fixed in January 1974. The Inspector had recommended that a viaduct should be constructed at Pencoed instead of an embankment and that an interchange should be built at Capel Llanilltern instead of at Miskin but these recommendations were not accepted.

The Coryton–Capel Llanilltern scheme was published in April 1972 and this also ran into difficulties with 86 objections being made to it. The Public Inquiry opened in January 1973 and lasted 5 weeks; the line was eventually fixed in January 1974, the Inspector having endorsed the strategy put forward by the Welsh Office.

At the time of these Public Inquiries, others were being held into the line of the Pyle by-pass and the Bridgend northern by-pass, and the Secretary of State decided to consider all four schemes together so as to give the public some reassurance that the route from Coryton and Groes at the western end of the Pyle by-pass was being considered as a whole and not piecemeal.

The division of the Coryton–Pencoed length at Llanilltern at the Inquiries had arisen from the proposed Llantrisant radial, but for construction purposes it was more appropriate to divide the works at Miskin interchange.

Bridgend northern by-pass. The scheme was published in June 1972 and attracted 45 objections, several concerned about the diversion of footpaths. The Public Inquiry opened in December 1972 and lasted 1 week, the line being eventually fixed in January 1974. The scheme was split into four contracts:

—an advance earthworks contract, to investigate problems posed by cavities formed in the underlying limestone, to treat any cavities found and to construct a 13 m high embankment
—construction of a 378 m long viaduct crossing the Ogmore Valley together with a single span overbridge at Pen-y-fai Road with side road diversions and limited earthworks
—construction of the eastern road works from the Ogmore viaduct to the Pencoed interchange
—construction of the western road works from the Ogmore viaduct to the Pyle interchange.

Pyle by-pass. This runs from Stormy Down in the east to Groes in the west. A line for an all-purpose by-pass had been included in the Glamorgan Development Plan and both private and public housing had been built up to the northern boundary. The scheme was published in May 1971 and attracted 79 objections, including one from the District Council. The Public Inquiry opened in October 1972 and lasted 3 weeks.

The Inspector accepted the published line through Groes but recommended that the motorway should be moved further away from the houses at North Cornelly. However, to avoid further delay in view of the urgent need to improve traffic conditions in Pyle and connections with Swansea and West Wales, the Secretary of State decided to adhere to the published line which was formally adopted in January 1974.

The Round Chapel at Groes was carefully dismantled before work on the motorway started and was re-erected on a new site in Port Talbot at the expense of the Welsh Office.

Extensive piling was involved in constructing the motorway over and alongside the main South Wales railway, a total of 544 cast in situ bored piles and 900 driven shell piles being used[9].

Port Talbot by-pass.[10] The by-pass runs from Baglan to Groes. In 1953 Sir Owen Williams and Partners were commissioned by the Minister of Transport to design a by-pass, construction of which was intended to start in 1956. Previous to this a route had been established in 1949 under the Trunk Roads Act. The by-pass was eventually scheduled as a Special Road in 1959. Meanwhile, from 1953 to 1955 design work proceeded to near contract tender stage, but work was stopped to consider an alternative proposal for crossing the railway in the centre of Port Talbot. At the end of 1957 and after a Public Inquiry it was decided to keep to the original proposals, but it was not until 1961 that planning procedures had been cleared and detailed design could begin. The contract for the main work was let in February 1963.

The by-pass falls into three distinct sections. From Baglan to Pentyla, a distance of about 1 mile, the route crosses Baglan Moor on a flat gradient; because of poor subsoil the road is built on a reinforced concrete raft supported on piles. Between Pentyla and Tai-Bach the route passes through the town for 1¾ miles and is constructed mostly on viaduct or between retaining walls; this section includes a bridge over the River Afan. The third section from Tai-bach to Groes is just over 1½ miles long on the steeply sloping hillside at the back of Port Talbot, where serious earthwork problems arose on account of the unstable ground, calling for special drainage measures.

Morriston by-pass. The line for this by-pass was published in May 1967. There were 13 objections and the scheme was adopted without a Public Inquiry in January 1969.

Pontardulais by-pass. This scheme was published in April 1971 and there were 42 objections. The line was fixed in November 1972 without a Public Inquiry.

An interesting construction detail is the use of glass-reinforced cement (GRC) in the permanent parapet forms on the Loughor Bridge to achieve the required line and appearance[11].

Trunk road in North Wales

As stated earlier the M4 is the only motorway in Wales. However, in the north, priority is being given to upgrading the all-purpose trunk roads A55, A550 and A483 which link with the English motorway network in Cheshire (Fig. 8.1). Dual-carriageway connections are to be provided with the M56/M531 north of Chester by routes passing to the west and north of the town and to the south and east, which will give good access to Merseyside and Manchester. Westwards the A55 is to be upgraded to dual carriageway between Chester and Bangor[3].

Scotland

Introduction

About 80% of the population of Scotland is contained within the area of the Central Belt running from the Fife coast and Edinburgh in the east to north Ayrshire and Glasgow in the west. This area also includes most of the manufacturing industry in the country. It is not surprising, therefore, that when road modernisation was regarded by Government in the late 1950s as an essential part of its economic strategy that improvement to the road system in the Central Belt and of its links with the English road system should receive high priority in the Scottish road programme.

The programme of the early 1960s envisaged development of a main trunk road network of dual carriageways by the early 1970s. Some of this network was to be of motorway standard, but motorways as such were to be justified on their merits. A Select Committee[1] in 1969 was told that 37 miles of trunk road motorway were then in use and that it was expected that some 116 miles would be in use by 1974 or 1975. The total length in 1980 had reached 128 miles.

In March 1969 the Government published a White Paper *Scottish roads in the 1970s*[12] dealing with plans for the improvement or construction of trunk roads and principal roads. The Paper noted that by 1971, in relation to traffic volumes between cities and most large towns, a highly efficient basic network would be largely complete; it stated that between 1962/63 and 1969/70, Government expenditure on the main road building programme grew on average at 16% compound per annum compared with an increase of only 7% in traffic volumes. For the 1970s it was proposed that the dual-carriageway programme should be completed but that there would then be a change of emphasis towards the principal road programme which would have a high urban content.

Economic difficulties during the 1970s meant that programmes had to be cut back. Nevertheless the original dual-carriageway programme, including motorways, in the Central Belt appears to have been largely completed by 1980. In a statement on roads in Scotland issued by the Government in 1980[13] it was noted that a road network providing quick and easy access was important in improving the prospects of firms in Scotland and that this applied particularly to the Central Belt and to areas affected by North Sea oil developments. Priority for the increasingly scarce resources for roads would go to important strategic routes and new trunk roads would be built only where there were pressing current problems. The Secretary of State attached great importance to the development of local road systems as complementing the motorway and trunk road network.

Motorway schemes

Table 8.2 gives a summary of trunk road motorway contracts which have been completed in Scotland and Fig. 8.2 shows where the trunk roads are located. Plans for other motorways in the years up to 1985 include[13]: extension of the M74 southwards to by-pass Lesmahagow and extension northward up to the former Glasgow city boundary; upgrading the A8 from Baillieston to Newhouse to motorway standards; extending the M8 and M9 from Newbridge in Midlothian to the former Edinburgh city boundary; and a Stepps by-pass as the first section of the M80 from Glasgow to Haggs. These schemes will probably complete the trunk road network envisaged at present for central Scotland.

In giving evidence to the Select Committee in 1969[1] about choice of road improvements R.A.H. Allen, then Deputy Chief Road Engineer in the Scottish Development Department (SDD), said that in Scotland the same design capacities were adopted as in England and on that basis it was expected that "only a few miles of dual three-lane carriageways will be needed". As regards the choice between all-purpose dual carriageways and motorways Allen said that "the motorway was the most efficient way of taking traffic between two points". On the other hand he did not want to build short lengths of motorway which would restrict the mileage of new road which could be built. He clearly saw a strong case for building a "reasonable length" of brand new road as a motorway.

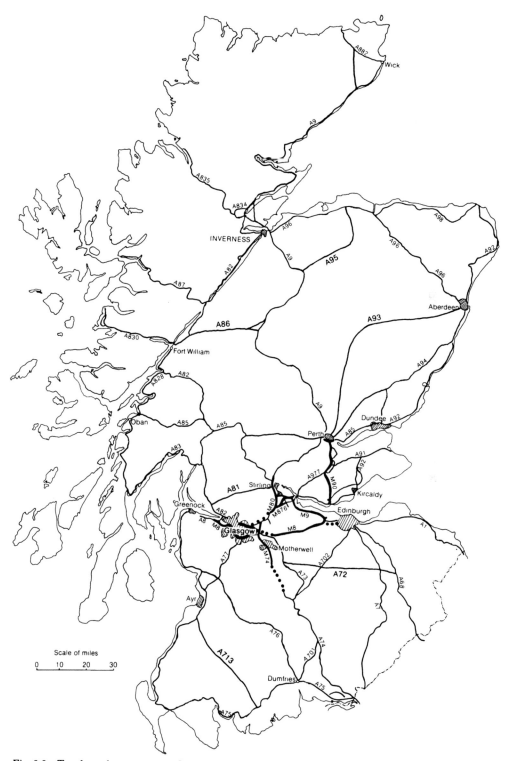

Fig. 8.2   Trunk road motorways in Scotland, 1980 (Crown copyright)

169

Table 8.2. Trunk road motorways in use in Scotland 1980

Scheme	Length: miles	Engineer	Contractor	Contract let	Opened	Standard	Cost: £million
M8 East of Glasgow							
Newbridge–Dechmont		Sir Alexander Gibb	A.M. Carmichael, completed by Tarmac Construction	Nov. 1968	Nov. 1970	D2	4.3
Dechmont–Whitburn		Sir Alexander Gibb	Whatlings	Sept. 1967	Sept. 1969	D2	5.1
Harthill by-pass		Sir Alexander Gibb	Whatlings	Sept. 1963	Nov. 1965	D2	2.1
W. of Harthill–Newhouse		Lanark CC	Whatlings	May 1965	Aug. 1967	D2	3.4
Baillieston interchange		Babtie Shaw and Morton	Cementation Construction	Mar. 1973	Apr. 1980		8.9
M8 West of Glasgow							
Renfrew by-pass		Crouch and Hogg	Marples Ridgway and Peter Lind and Co.	Oct. 1965	Mar. 1968	Part D2 Part D3	6.0
Bishopton by-pass I	37.5	Freeman Fox	Whatlings	Aug. 1968	Dec. 1970	D2	1.2
Bishopton by-pass II		Freeman Fox	Tarmac Construction	Oct. 1973	Nov. 1975	D2	4.4
M9 Edinburgh–Stirling							
Newbridge–Kirkliston (including spur)		W.A. Fairhurst	A.M. Carmichael and Tarmac Construction	Part Oct. 1968 Part Sept. 1971	Nov. 1970	D3	3.2
Kirkliston–Lathallan		W.A. Fairhurst	Tarmac Construction	May 1971	Dec. 1972	D2	7.7
Polmont and Falkirk by-pass		Stirling CC	Logan	Jan. 1966	Aug. 1968	D2	5.0
Stirling by-pass I		Stirling CC	Murdoch MacKenzie	Mar. 1969	Apr. 1971	D2	3.6

Section	Length	Consulting engineer	Contractor			Class	Length
Stirling by-pass II		Stirling CC	F. Drysdale and Balfour Beatty and Co.	Part Apr. 1971 Part Oct. 1971	Dec. 1973	D2	4.5
Bannockburn interchange–Hill of Kinaird	29.4	Stirling CC	Balfour Beatty Construction (Scotland)	Mar. 1978	Feb. 1980	D2	7.6
M73 Maryville–Baillieston	6.2	Babtie Shaw and Morton	Balfour Beatty and Co.	Mar. 1969	May 1971	D3	10.7
Baillieston–Mollinsburn					Apr. 1972		
M74 Hamilton by-pass I	9	Babtie Shaw and Morton	Christiani Shand	May 1974	Dec. 1966	D2	9.0
II	4.4		Tarmac Construction	Sept. 1965			8.5
Hamilton–Bothwell					Aug. 1968	D2	
Bothwell–Maryville					May 1968		
M80 Haggs–Pirnhall	7.4	Stirling CC	Balfour Beatty and Co.	Jan. 1972 July1972 Oct. 1971	May 1974	D2	3.3
M90 Edinburgh–Perth Admiralty Road (Inverkeithing)–Duloch		Mott Hay and Anderson and Fife CC	Whatlings	Dec. 1960	Aug. 1964	D2	1.4
Dunfermline spur					Aug. 1964		
Cowdenbeath and Kelty by-pass		Fife CC and W.A. Fairhurst	Tarmac Construction	Dec. 1967	Dec. 1969	D2	4.6
Kinross and Milnathort by-pass		Babtie Shaw and Morton	Fitzpatrick and Son	Dec. 1969	Dec. 1971	D2	5.7
Arlary–Arngask		Babtie Shaw and Morton	Whatlings	Nov. 1974	Mar. 1977	D2	5.1
Arngask–Muirmont		Babtie Shaw and Morton	Tarmac National Construction	Dec. 1977	Oct. 1980	D2	8.2
Muirmont–Moncrieffe Hill		Babtie Shaw and Morton	Whatlings	July 1975	Nov. 1977	D2	10.1
Craigend–Broxden	30.7	Tayside Regional Council	William Tawse	Feb. 1976	May 1978	D2	3.7

continued overleaf

Table 8.2 (Contd)

Scheme	Length. miles	Engineer	Contractor	Contract let	Opened	Standard	Cost: £million
M90/M85							
Craigend interchange		Babtie Shaw and Morton	Whatlings	Nov. 1973	Aug. 1978		5.4
Friarton Bridge		Freeman Fox	Cleveland Bridge Engineering Co.	Feb. 1975	Aug. 1978	D2	9.1
Friarton Bridge north approach roads	1.8	Freeman Fox	Shellabear Price (Scotland)	Apr. 1974	Aug. 1978	D2	0.6
M876							
Bankhead–Broomage	3.9	Stirling CC	F. Drysdale	Apr. 1973	May 1974	D2	1.1
M876/M9							
North Broomage–Bowtrees	5.1	Stirling CC	Tarmac Construction	Apr. 1977	Feb. 1980	D2	11.0
M898							
Craigton-toll plaza	0.7	Freeman Fox	Whatlings	Aug. 1968	Feb. 1971	D2	1.4

Also in evidence to the Select Committee, E.L. Gillett, then an Assistant Secretary in the Trunk Roads and Motorways Division in the SDD, said that in selecting schemes great account was taken of "fostering industrial development". In some cases regional development had been the most important factor; he cited the M8 between Glasgow and Edinburgh as a case in point. An analysis which had been made of potential savings in accidents and increase in speed from building a motorway there had come "to a very low figure, much lower than was necessary to justify its construction"; but its advantage as a link between Edinburgh and Glasgow was an "essential feature of the economic plan for Scotland" and construction was not, therefore, delayed.

A8/M8, Edinburgh–Glasgow. This route links the two largest cities in Scotland and provides connections to other towns in the Forth/Clyde Valley, including the New Town of Livingston. At its western end there are connections with the M74 leading south to the A74 and Carlisle and thence to the English motorway system via the M6. The route at present is of motorway standard between Newbridge and Newhouse but between Newhouse and Edinburgh and between Newbridge and Glasgow is all-purpose dual carriageway road. Consideration is being given to upgrading these sections to motorway standard at the Glasgow end and the Edinburgh end in the late 1980s.[13]

Poor soil conditions along the route meant that a great deal of excavation and importation of fill was required during construction. In some places, such as the Harthill–Newhouse section, there were dangers of subsidence from old mine workings not far below the level of the road and those workings had to be filled; pulverised fuel ash was used for this purpose.

The Newbridge–Dechmont section involved not only extensive excavation but also the diversion of the Union Canal and the River Almond.

The A8/M8 joins the Glasgow motorway at the Baillieston interchange. This extensive four-level structure incorporates two interchanges and provides links between the M73 and M8 (Monkland motorway), the M73 and A8 and the M8 and A89. The whole interchange covers some 55 hectares and includes 21 concrete bridges. It was officially opened in April 1980 by the Rt Hon. George Younger.

M8 in Glasgow. After World War II plans began to be formulated in Glasgow for major new roads including urban motorways. One of the first steps in implementing improvements was the construction of the Clyde Tunnel and its approaches, both tubes of which were opened to traffic in 1964. To provide a systematic and comprehensive approach to road planning the Glasgow City Corporation in 1960 appointed consultants Scott Wilson Kirkpatrick and Co. (Scotland) to prepare a Highway Plan for Glasgow; William Holford and Associates (Glasgow) architects and planning consultants were appointed as part of the design team. A plan which set out a network of roads required for traffic growth to 1990 and beyond was adopted by the Corporation in 1965 and 3 years

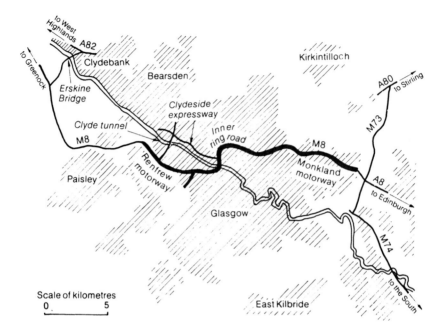

Fig. 8.3   Glasgow motorways and expressways, 1980 (copyright Scott Wilson Kirkpatrick)

later was incorporated into the Greater Glasgow Transportation Study Forecast and Plan.[14] Implementation of the plan was put in hand in 5 year stages and the main objective of the programme up to 1980 was to establish an east–west motorway route across the city connecting the western section of the M8 to the A8 and M73/M74. The route is shown in Fig. 8.3 and consists of the Monkland motorway, the north and west flanks of the inner ring road and the Renfrew motorway. Construction of the last section of this motorway route was completed in 1980 and opened officially by the Secretary of State for Scotland in April that year.

The Monkland motorway was designed and supervised by the Strathclyde Regional Council Department of Roads (Glasgow Division). Construction was in stages the first being from Townhead interchange on the inner ring road to Cumbernauld Road (A80), the second from the A80 to Stepps Road and the third from Stepps Road to the city boundary where the motorway joined the trunk road section leading to the Baillieston interchange. That section of trunk road and the interchange were constructed for the Scottish Development Department. Contractors engaged in various stages were Costain Civil Engineering Ltd, GKN Foundations Ltd, and Whatlings Ltd.

The line chosen for the motorway follows fairly closely that of the old Monkland Canal which had to be drained. The existence of the canal had created a boundary to areas for over a century and severance problems arising from building the motorway were thus minimised.

174

Considerable engineering problems were met on the second stage of the motorway because of poor ground conditions. Sixteen old mine shafts had to be secured and some 320,000 cubic metres of peat were removed where the line of the motorway crossed a peat bed of up to 7 m in thickness.

The north flank of the inner ring road (designer, Scott Wilson Kirkpatrick and Co. (Scotland)) and the west flank (designer, W.A. Fairhurst and Partners) were opened to traffic in 1972 and it is proposed to add the remainder of the inner ring during the 1980s. Some 4,400 houses, mostly sub-standard, were demolished to make way for north and west flanks.

The Renfrew motorway continues the M8 westwards from the inner ring road at the Kingston Bridge to the former city boundary at Shieldhall Road. A main purpose of this section of the M8 was to provide a fast route to the Abbotsinch Glasgow Airport and also to serve industrial developments at Linwood. Construction was carried out in two stages and the motorway has dual three- and four-lane sections in places. Much of the route is elevated above the surrounding countryside and in a westerly direction gives views of distant mountains. Poor ground conditions meant that structures had to be supported on piles. A particular problem arose when it was found not to be possible to drain the motorway into the existing drainage system and a new outfall sewer from the motorway to the River Clyde had to be constructed[15].

Parallel to the Renfrew motorway on the north side of the Clyde is the Clyde expressway which connects the north end of Kingston Bridge to the north approaches to the Clyde Tunnel; the southern end of the tunnel connects with the Renfrew motorway at Cardonald interchange. The expressway is mainly grade-separated but is not built to full motorway standards. It was designed by Sir William Halcrow and Partners, built by Balfour Beatty Construction (Scotland) and opened in April 1973.

In the 1960s Glasgow City Corporation had collaborated with the Road Research Laboratory in the development of an area traffic control system based on central computer control, and as the motorway system took shape it became necessary to consider wider aspects of control embracing not only the ordinary streets but also motorways and expressways. In 1975 the Transport Operations Group of the University of Newcastle upon Tyne were appointed to advise on a central integrated control system for Glasgow. As a first step it was decided to install an interim motorway control and television surveillance system centred on Strathclyde police headquarters, and this was commissioned during 1980[16].

Construction of the motorway system in Glasgow has involved major capital investment and it is important to know what impact that has had on the city. Cullen[17] has attempted to make an assessment of certain of the impacts and he concludes that some of the effects of the motorway in 1980 are

—reduction in total travel time within the city of about 18%

—fuel saving of about 9%
—reduction of 812 injury accidents
—first year rate of return on investment of 15.6%
—a ratio of discounted present value of economic benefits to discounted present value of costs of about 2.5
—environmental benefits arising from transfer of traffic from old roads to the motorway routes
—pedestrianisation of principal shopping streets
—improvements to bus operations.

Bishopton by-pass. This by-pass continues the M8 westwards from the Renfrew by-pass to Westferry Lodge some 6 miles away. From thereon to Port Glasgow the route is all-purpose dual carriageway.

The by-pass was built in two stages; the first included the approach roads to the southern end of the Erskine Bridge A898(M) across the Clyde which at its northern end links with the A82 Glasgow–Inverness trunk road. This first stage was opened in December 1970, a few months in advance of the official opening of the bridge. The 3½ mile second stage was delayed by procedural and other difficulties, e.g. statutory procedures fixing the line of route were held up until the report of the Clyde Estuary Working Group was available. After the completion of the by-pass residents in Bishopton complained that they were cut off from direct access to the motorway and had to make an appreciable detour to reach it. The SDD pointed out that side road closures had been made in the interests of safety and traffic. The by-pass reduced traffic on the A8 through Bishopton by 80%.

M9, Edinburgh–north of Stirling. This route starts in the east at the M8 interchange at Newbridge and the first short section had to be aligned so as to provide a route clear of proposed developments at Turnhouse Airport. A mile-long motorway spur was built from this section to the southern approaches to the Forth Road Bridge. Continuing westwards the route by-passes the ancient town of Linlithgow, where Mary Queen of Scots was born, and then joins the Polmont and Falkirk by-pass. That by-pass was the first section of this motorway to be completed and was opened by Lord Hughes in 1968. At this point the route provides good access to the developing port and industrial area of Grangemouth which lies just to the north.

The next section of the route leading to the Stirling by-pass was the last to be completed as construction was deferred during the economic problems of the mid-1970s. Completion of the M876 link from this section to the M80 was also delayed and the two lengths of motorway were not open to traffic until 1980. The M9 and M80 are linked directly at the southern end of the Stirling by-pass at the Bannockburn interchange.

The Stirling by-pass was built in two stages, the northern stage being built first.

The motorway passes to the west of Stirling and ends in the north at a roundabout junction with the all-purpose dual carriageway A9 south of Dunblane. At the planning stage objections were raised by the Stirling Town Council to the proposed line of the by-pass as being too near the town. The objections were not accepted by the Secretary of State because to move the line further away would be less satisfactory and more expensive. Moreover, the Town Council had accepted the proposed line in the County Development Plan not long before.

For the most part the M9 is dual two-lane motorway but dual three-lane is provided at the eastern end between Newbridge and Kirkliston.

M73, Maryville link road. This 6 mile section of motorway provided an eastern by-pass of Glasgow linking the Glasgow−Carlisle route, M74/A74, to the Edinburgh−Glasgow route, A8/M8, and the Monkland motorway and also to the Glasgow−Stirling route, A80/M80.

M74, Maryville−Draffan. This relatively short (13 miles) stretch of motorway forms the start of the M74/A74 route from Glasgow to Carlisle. It was constructed in stages and the Hamilton by-pass was one of the early motorways to be built in Scotland. Proposals have been put forward by the Secretary of State for an extension southwards from Draffan for about 10 miles. Objections were made to the proposals by the Scottish Association for Public Transport on the grounds that the money could be better spent on other projects. Objections were also made by the Lanark District Council to the original proposals and to modifications to the plans made by the Scottish Development Department. The whole scheme is included in the trunk road programme between 1983 and 1986.

The M74/A74 is one of the most important trunk routes in Scotland and the A74 section is dual carriageway to the English border. It has been said from time to time that such an important route should have been built to full motorway standards throughout its length. Apart from the upgrading to motorway standard of the section south of Draffan the SDD in their report on roads in Scotland in 1980[13] said "on other sections of this road south to the Border there is continuing improvement of the dual carriageway with the addition of 1 metre hard strips and the installation in appropriate places of central reservation barriers".

M80, Haggs−Pirnhall. This short length of motorway of about 7½ miles is part of the trunk route from Glasgow to Stirling. The all-purpose A80 road from Glasgow had been converted to dual carriageway up to Ingliston at the northern end of the Denny by-pass by 1970. Authority was sought to extend the route as motorway up to the M9 and powers were also taken to up-grade to motorway standard the dual carriageway between Cumbernauld and Ingliston. Under consideration is an extension to the motorway to Glasgow in the late 1980s starting with a Stepps by-pass.

M90, Inverkeithing−Perth route and M85, Perth by-pass. The M90 provides a fast route between the northern end of the Forth Road Bridge and Perth. The first sections to be built were the approaches to the bridge and were opened at the same

177

time as the bridge in 1964. The next section going north is the Cowdenbeath and Kelty by-pass and because of the likelihood of subsidence from the Central Fife coalfield, extensive underground consolidation works were required in its construction.

The Kinross and Milnathort by-pass carries the motorway north from Kelty and includes a ¾ mile long 35 ft deep cutting. This section of motorway was the first in Britain to be constructed using unreinforced concrete pavements. Paving was carried out to full width in a single pass using a traditional concrete train with a formed longitudinal joint off-set from the centre line[18].

Hard shoulders were omitted from these early sections on the grounds that traffic volumes did not justify them. Instead formations were made sufficiently wide to take shoulders if required later and meanwhile emergency lay-bys were provided at 1 mile intervals. This gave rise to considerable criticism on safety grounds and in 1973 the Secretary of State announced that in view of the rate of growth of traffic due to developments associated with North Sea oil, hard shoulders would be built on these early sections and would be included in future motorways.

In 1972 the Secretary of State announced his decision on the line of the route from Milnathort through to Craigend at the southern end of the Perth by-pass. This decision followed a Public Inquiry on 28 days between September and November 1971. The Reporter recommended adoption of the line proposed by the Secretary of State with some concessions to objectors which were accepted by the Secretary of State.

Progress with construction was delayed by the oil crisis in 1973 but the final section through Glen Farg between Arngask and Muirmont near the Bridge of Earn was opened in August 1980.

The M90 terminates at the Craighill interchange with the M85 southern by-pass to Perth. The M85 runs as far as the A85 Perth–Dundee road and is one of the shortest motorways in Scotland. Construction of the Craighill interchange involved deep rock cutting and particular care had to be taken during blasting operations to protect a 125 year old railway tunnel.[19]

The M85 includes the Friarton Bridge over the River Tay. The bridge is of twin box girder sections and the start of construction was delayed because of the need to check designs against the Merrison standards.

References
1. SELECT COMMITTEE ON ESTIMATES OF THE HOUSE OF COMMONS. *Sixth report 1968–69. Motorways and trunk roads.* HMSO, London, 1969.
2. BRUNNER C.T. *Traffic problems with particular relation to South Wales.* Institution of Highway Engineers, London, 1949.
3. WELSH OFFICE. *Roads in Wales.* HMSO, Cardiff, 1978.
4. MINISTRY OF TRANSPORT. *The Ross motorway.* HMSO, London, 1960.
5. DEPARTMENT OF TRANSPORT, SCOTTISH DEVELOPMENT DEPART-

MENT and WELSH OFFICE. *Transport statistics. Great Britain 1968–1978.* HMSO, London, 1979.

6. SECRETARY OF STATE FOR WALES. *Wales 1966.* HMSO, London, 1967.
7. SIR OWEN WILLIAMS AND PARTNERS. *Newport by-pass (M4).* Sir Owen Williams and Partners, London, 1970.
8. SECRETARY OF STATE FOR WALES. *Wales 1968.* HMSO, London, 1969.
9. GROUND ENGINEERING FOUNDATION PUBLICATIONS. *Piling on the M4.* Ground Engineering Foundation Publications, Brentwood, 1976.
10. SIR OWEN WILLIAMS AND PARTNERS. *Port Talbot by-pass.* Sir Owen Williams and Partners, London, 1966.
11. PARKINSON J. GRC crosses the Loughor. *New Civil Engineer,* 11 November 1976, No. 218.
12. SCOTTISH DEVELOPMENT DEPARTMENT. *Scottish roads in the 1970s.* HMSO, Edinburgh, 1969.
13. SCOTTISH DEVELOPMENT DEPARTMENT. *Roads in Scotland 1980.* SDD, Edinburgh, 1980.
14. STRATHCLYDE REGIONAL COUNCIL DEPARTMENT OF ROADS. *Report of visit to works by members of Parliament, June 1979.* Strathclyde Regional Council, 1979.
15. McLEAN R.D. Renfrew motorway sewer. *Tunnels and tunnelling,* 1974, **6**, No. 6.
16. MOWATT A. The development of traffic control systems in Glasgow. *Chartered Mun. Engr,* 1980, **107**, January.
17. CULLEN J.M. *The Glasgow motorway system. Planning, construction and evaluation.* Scott Wilson Kirkpatrick and Co. (Scotland), Glasgow, 1979.
18. Scotland's M90 motorway. *Roads and road construction,* 1972, **50**, No. 589.
19. M90/M85 Perth Southern by-pass and Craigend interchange. *Highways and road construction international,* 1977, **44**, No. 1805.

9

Motorways in urban areas

Introduction

By 1980 the development of the trunk road network of motorways and all-purpose dual carriageways had provided a reasonably efficient, though arguably incomplete, means of travel by road between the major urban centres in the country. However, what provision to make for traffic in those centres had long been a matter for argument and is likely to remain so.

Almost all roads and streets in urban areas of Britain are open to all classes of road user. Pedestrians and cyclists mix with motor cars, motorcycles, public transport vehicles and goods vehicles; some 75% of road casualties occur in built-up areas subject to a 30 mile/h speed limit and 90% of pedestrian casualties occur in built-up areas. On these grounds alone, segregation of motor and non-motor traffic has been advocated for many years.

With the growth of motor traffic, traffic congestion in urban areas has become a serious problem. Although traffic management techniques, i.e. techniques designed to make the best use of existing streets, have been used increasingly over the past 20 years or so, starting particularly with work by the London Traffic Management Unit in 1960[1], urban traffic speeds remain relatively slow. Information on speeds obtained by the Transport and Road Research Laboratory[2] in a number of towns and conurbations in Britain is shown in Table 9.1. The eight towns were Bristol, Chesterfield, Leicester, Luton, Preston, Reading, Sheffield and Watford; the five towns in conurbations were Birmingham, Leeds, Liverpool, Manchester and Newcastle.

It can be seen from Table 9.1 that some improvement in speeds took place in the areas studied between 1967 and 1976, but the reasons for this cannot be ascribed to any one factor; traffic management schemes, improved vehicle performance, improved roads all no doubt played a part.

In seeking solutions to the congestion problem in towns it seems to be broadly accepted that an understanding is required of the relationship between land use and the demand for transport. It is also accepted that an understanding is required of what the supply of transport should be to meet the demand: whether it should be road or rail, public or private and if a mixture, what sort of mix it should be. Whilst there is agreement about the need to consider and investigate these issues, there is much less evidence of agreement about what actions to take to improve traffic conditions in towns and in particular about the role that new roads, especially urban motorways, should play.

The problems of accidents and congestion on the roads in towns are undoubtedly of great public concern, but possibly of even greater concern has been the impact of urban traffic and roads on the environment. This was discussed at length in 1963 in the Buchanan Report[3], a report which led to the reappraisal of many town plans in the light of its findings.

Some planning issues

A key issue discussed by Buchanan was that of accommodating the motor vehicle in large numbers in towns. Arguing that "the motor vehicle . . . is a beneficial invention with an assured future" Buchanan considered that it would be possible to make better use of the motor vehicle in towns but to do so would involve major physical changes. "In broad principle these changes comprise the canalisation of longer movements onto properly designed networks serving areas within which . . . environments suitable for a civilised urban life can be developed".

Three years before Buchanan, C.T. Brunner[4] had also discussed the use of motor vehicles, particularly cars in cities. He saw ownership of personal transport as a major factor in people's lives and considered that the rapid growth in the use of cars was the main feature shaping urban life in the future. As life in Britain is predominantly urban he believed that urban areas must be adapted to suit the basic needs of living. The motor vehicle had to be accepted and the environment modified to permit motor vehicles to be used in great numbers.

Both Buchanan and Brunner accepted that some restrictions on the use of motor vehicles in towns were unavoidable, particularly in town centres. Brunner identified two alternatives: rationing by price or by some system of priorities; he favoured the former. These matters were the subject of a study of road pricing by

Table 9.1. Car speeds in urban areas of Great Britain in 1976 (figures for 1967 in brackets): km/h

Area	Peak		Off-peak	
	Eight towns	Five towns in conurbations	Eight towns	Five towns in conurbations
Whole towns	34.0 (32.0)	38.0 (31.7)	29.5 (29.8)	33.7 (27.6)
Central areas	25.0 (19.6)	21.4 (17.6)	20.8 (18.2)	20.4 (14.9)

181

a panel set up in 1962 by the Minister of Transport[5] which examined the technical feasibility of various methods for improving the pricing system relating to the use of roads and relevant economic considerations. These studies were concerned with pricing related to the allocation of resources and not to taxation, i.e. to revenue raising, although taxation is a form of pricing. The use of pricing methods to obtain better allocation of traffic in town centres was favoured by several transport economists[6] and a considerable amount of research and development went into devising equipment for charging motorists on the basis of the congestion they caused. Politically the system was not acceptable in Britain where reliance has been placed, in effect, on parking control as a means of limiting traffic in busy urban areas. A road-pricing scheme has been introduced in Singapore[7] where drivers must obtain a special supplementary licence which has to be displayed on cars driven into a restricted zone during the morning commuting hours.

Plans for the redevelopment of urban areas after World War II included road proposals within the general plans and some guidance on road requirements in those areas was included in departmental reports issued soon after the war[8,9]. Criticism was made of some of the plans as being utopian and unpractical; e.g. F.A. Rayfield[10] in commenting on the County of London Plan prepared by Sir Patrick Abercrombie and J.H. Forshaw remarked that the plan had been drawn up on the assumption that new legislation and financial assistance would be forthcoming and that "to engineers such an approach lacks realism".

The importance of a broad approach to the planning of roads and transport has been stressed by many authorities. For example Brunner[4] in 1960 wrote "Any serious effort to reconstitute urban areas demands something more than local traffic plans or local building regulations". Ernest Davies, a former Labour opposition spokesman on transport, in a paper to the London School of Economics in 1962[11], said "Transport is . . . inseparable from town planning and must be dealt with in relation to it, and development plans need to be drawn with full regard to their repercussion on transport . . .". The Buchanan Report[3] in 1963 stated ". . . the ability to command the comprehensive development or redevelopment of large areas is extremely important to the successful handling of motor traffic". These views were restated in 1972 by the Urban Motorways Committee[12] who said "We regard it as essential that the planning of new urban roads should form an integral part of planning the urban area as a whole; and that the indirect costs and benefits of building urban roads should be looked at with the same care as the direct cost and movement benefits . . .".

These various statements were made before the reform of local government took place in 1974 (in Greater London in 1965), that is at a time when statutory responsibility for town planning was spread among a large number of authorities. With the changes that have taken place since 1974 the present County and Metropolitan County Councils have comprehensive powers covering planning and transport and through block grants from Central Government have greater discretion on how their resources are spent. However, although the administrative arrangements covering urban modernisation may have been improved, economic difficulties and consequent cuts in capital investment in the public sector, pressures for the promotion of public transport together with strong environmental arguments against some forms of redevelopment and road building in urban areas, public participation and inquiry procedures, markedly slowed down urban renewal in the 1970s.

Select Committees

In 1972 a detailed review of urban transport planning was carried out by a Select Committee of the House of Commons[13]. After commenting that transport problems particularly in larger cities were the cause of "increasing public concern" they said there were doubts about the direction and efficiency of transport planning adducing as evidence for this: complaints about train and bus services; public demonstrations against urban motorways; dissatisfaction with traffic congestion; and "the swamping of city streets by private motor cars and intrusive heavy lorries". Their wide-ranging recommendations covered policy objectives, the promotion of public transport, traffic restraint, a new grant structure, transportation studies, the organisation of central and local government and local responsibilities.

Of their 38 recommendations, one was that national policy should seek to promote public transport and discourage the journey to work by car in city areas; and another was the urban roads programme should be abolished and replaced by an urban transport programme linked to the comprehensive plans required in the context of the grant proposals then being proposed.

In their observations on the Select Committee's report the Government[14] said that even a considerable increase in levels of restraint and assistance for public transport would still leave much traffic on the roads, including traffic for which public transport did not provide a suitable alternative. They pointed out that much of the existing road network was unsuited to modern traffic and that most of our cities would require "new and improved roads to provide an adequate network and allow environmental improvements in areas from which through traffic should be excluded".

For reasons indicated earlier, plans envisaged for road-building at the beginning of the 1970s were scaled down after the oil crisis of 1973 and Government policy in 1977[15] was for a much lower level of investment in roads than in the early 1970s. The policy document stated "There will be much less large-scale road building in towns than a few years ago. This is in itself welcome."

In December 1980 the Transport Committee of the House of Commons issued a report[16] as a result of their examination of the Government's White Paper on roads in England issued in 1980[17]. The Committee supported the main objectives and priorities in the White Paper. They believed that there was "a real need for roads policy to be formulated in the context of an overall national transport policy and to be fully and publicly debated and scrutinised at a national level"; they discussed the roles of the Department of Transport and local authorities in this regard and recommended that the local authority associations should look into the possibility of the shire and metropolitan counties taking over responsibility for all road construction and maintenance. They foresaw the Department of Transport's responsibilities eventually being those of overall strategic road planning, co-ordination of the individual counties' programmes and the allocation of national resources to those programmes. These suggestions could have important conse-quences for transport planning in urban areas and it would appear pertinent for a careful assessment to be made of the changes brought about in road planning, in particular as a result of the creation of the Metropolitan County Councils.

The Committee did not discuss specifically roads in urban areas but they did express surprise at the absence in the White Paper of "constructive discussion of matters such as urban traffic management." They also remarked that "The general road system in London is, and will remain, a national scandal" and indicated that they expected to examine the problems of transportation in London during the "lifetime of the present Parliament".

The role of urban motorways

The preceding brief review of some of the complexities of the urban transport problem has shown that improvements to transport have to be considered within the wider context of urban planning and renewal and that various options such as better public transport systems, traffic restraint and new and improved roads have to be taken into account. It is now of interest to consider to what extent motorways can contribute to better transport conditions in urban areas.

There seems to be some uncertainty about what is meant by an urban motor-way. The Buchanan Report[3] defined it as "a motorway in an urban area". The Urban Motorways Committee[12] referred to it as an urban road designed for and restricted to certain classes of traffic. In a written answer to a Parliamentary Ques-tion on 21 April 1980, the Parliamentary Secretary to the Department of Transport stated "There is no precise definition of the term 'urban motorway'. About 100 miles of trunk road and 60 miles of principal road motorway pass through urban areas".

Typical standards for urban motorways recommended by the Department of Transport[18] are shown in Table 9.2.

An urban motorway is essentially a dual carriageway road restricted to specified classes of motor vehicle with no intersections on the level, with a layout of a somewhat lower standard than that for a rural motorway and with access points usually at more frequent intervals. It is, nevertheless, capable of handling large volumes of traffic at speeds substantially higher than those on ordinary streets and is thus well suited to serve as a primary distributor in an urban street network. A primary distributor has been defined[19] as a route which allows heavy volumes of traffic to enter or leave a town rapidly, to pass through it if not accommodated on by-passes or outer ring roads, or to circulate within it between the main centres of business, industry or residence.

Motorway interchanges require an appreciable amount of land outside that needed for the main carriageways. In urban areas this can be expensive and can require the acquisition of much extra property. It is clearly important therefore that, in order to keep costs down and to minimise disturbance, the connections between an urban motorway used as a primary distributor and other parts of the urban road network are located and designed with care. Traffic bound for a city centre requires parking space on arrival and it might be appropriate to feed traffic direct from a motorway into off-street parking accommodation thus avoiding the need for connection to the ordinary streets.

Urban motorways offer a means of providing rapid public transport. In a paper to the urban motorways conference in London in 1956, W.H. Glanville and J.F.A. Baker[20] compared the capacity of a tube train with that which might be obtained on a motorway using buses or coaches. They quoted the case of an 8 car tube train operating at a maximum frequency of 35 per hour in one direction as being able to carry 42,000 passengers per hour. This number of people could be carried by 1,000 buses or coaches carrying 42 per vehicle, possibly on a single lane

Table 9.2. Typical standards for urban motorways

Item	Standard
Design speed	80 km/h
Carriageway width	
Dual two-lane	7.3 m
Dual three-lane	11.0 m
Verge (paved, no hard shoulders)	
Normal width	. 2.75 m
Minimum width	2.0 m
Clearance back of verge to safety fence	0.6 m
Central reserve	
Normal width	3.0 m
Desirable minimum width:	
No lighting columns	2.0 m
With lighting columns	2.4 m
Absolute minimum	1.8 m
Clearance edge of carriageway to safety fence	0.6 m
Design flow (peak hour in one direction)	
Dual two-lane	3,600 veh/h
Dual three-lane	5,700 veh/h

of a motorway, and they suggested that the use of a single lane allocated to buses in the peak hours would be well worth examining. It is interesting that this suggestion was being made before any motorways, rural or urban, had been built in Britain and that 20 years later an experimental limited-stop bus service was tried on the M32 in Bristol[21]. These authors also made a preliminary assessment of the feasibility of constructing a motorway, largely urban, from Aldenham to a point near Marble Arch in London, part of which was to be built many years later when the M1 was extended southwards from Berrygrove to the North Circular Road.

Urban Motorways Committee

Brief reference has already been made to the Urban Roads Committee set up by the Minister of Transport in 1969 with the following terms of reference.

"1. To examine present policies used in fitting major roads into urban areas;
 2. To consider what changes would enable urban roads to be related better to their surroundings, physically visually and socially;
 3. To examine the consequences of such changes, particularly from the points of view of:
   (a) limitations on resources both public and private;
   (b) changes in statutory powers and administrative procedures;
   (c) any issues of public policy that the changes would raise;

 4. To recommend what changes, if any, should be made."

The Chairman of the Committee was a Deputy Secretary in the Department of the Environment and membership was drawn from local government, universities and consultants. The Committee had support from a project team of officials and also arranged for several firms of consultants to carry out studies of schemes already built or which were already planned. The report of the Committee was published in 1972[12] and the reports prepared by the project team and consultants in 1973[19]. In their report the Committee emphasised that by their terms of reference they were concerned with major new urban roads and were not confined solely to urban motorways.

The Committee considered that a new approach to urban road planning was needed and that planning of major new urban roads should form an integral part of planning the urban area as a whole. This was not a new idea but the Committee put emphasis on the need to include indirect costs in assessing projects and on the importance of taking fully into account the views and values of people affected by road schemes.

Objections to urban road proposals arise on three main counts; one is cost, another is demolition of houses and the third is the environment. The Committee, the project team and the consultants paid particular attention to the environment and they identified the main environmental effects of major urban road schemes as traffic noise, severance, visual effects and nuisance during the construction period.

The Committee concluded that "ways of reducing the spread of noise are simple" and identified possible measures as sunken roads, barriers alongside the road such as walls, screens, mounds and "barrier" buildings. They recommended that highway authorities should be required to compensate householders adversely affected by noise as a result of new roads; effect was given to this in the Land Compensation Act of 1973 and the Noise Insulation Regulations 1975. Under the Act, any buildings newly exposed to a noise level of 68 dB(A)L_{10} (i.e. noise such that 68 dB(A) is exceeded for 10% of the time during an average 16 hour day) have a right to insulation or compensation. The Regulations require the Department of Transport to provide double glazing or equivalent compensation for properties which, under certain circumstances, become subject to levels greater than 68 dB(A)L_{10} from the traffic on a new road.

The Committee recommended that full account should be taken of the possible severance of communities when major new roads were being located and they placed particular importance on maintaining proper facilities for pedestrians. In some cases there are existing barriers between communities and a motorway can sometimes be located near them to minimise further severance. The use of the old Monktown Canal in Glasgow is an example of this. The design team thought that the sensitivity of route selection processes could be helped by studies of social groupings in areas being considered for new routes.

The visual impact of new roads was found to be difficult to assess and the design team spent some time examining and devising techniques which could be of help in the process. They were of the opinion that problems involving visual effects had to be considered in the broad context of urban planning and design. A serious difficulty about designing an urban motorway is that the full visual impact of the motorway cannot adequately be understood until construction is complete, by which time it is usually too late to correct faults. The techniques evolved for studying visual intrusion have to be used with considerable caution.

The Committee made a number of recommendations relating to legal, procedural and financial matters, some of which have been brought about or have been affected by changes such as those concerning local government since the Committee's report was published in 1972.

Attention was given by the Committee to the problem of evaluating the merits of road schemes in urban areas as an aid to decision making. They recommended that cost/benefit techniques should be further developed to take account of external costs imposed on the affected community and that more research should be carried out to establish quantitative relations between the costs and environmental effects of alternative road designs. These are difficult and contentious matters and at the end of the 1970s no agreed techniques for evaluation had been evolved, although the Department of Transport was working on a standardised method of cost/benefit analysis for use in urban areas to complement that in use in rural areas, known as COBA, although COBA does not take account of non-tangible factors.

The work of the Committee was going on at the same time as that of the Select Committee on Urban Transport Planning. The Select Committee took evidence from the Chairman of the Urban Motorways Committee and said that they welcomed the report of that Committee.

Transport studies in the conurbations

The population of Britain is largely concentrated in urban areas: about four out of five people live in towns. In England and Wales two out of five live in the major aggregation of towns officially defined as conurbations, namely Greater London, South East Lancashire, West Midlands, West Yorkshire, Merseyside and Tyneside. In Scotland one third of the population live within the Central Clydeside conurbation. The area of these conurbations is only about 3% of the total land area in Britain and the population density in them averages some 8,000 people per square mile. The evolution of the conurbations has been described in some detail by Freeman[22]. The allocation of responsibilities for planning and transportation in the major conurbations and the state of transport plans in the late 1960s was investigated by Colin Buchanan and Partners on behalf of the British Road Federation and reported on in 1969[23].

The Federation also sponsored two other studies at about this time. One[24] was a study to compare traffic satisfaction levels implicit in transport plans of Britain's major conurbations; one of the conclusions was that "although restraint is a fundamental element in transport policy, there is almost no information to guide decision-makers on the advantages and disadvantages of different degrees of restraint." The other study[25] was concerned with the local environmental implications of urban motorway development and with ways in which motorways could be satisfactorily integrated into existing urban areas. One of the conclusions reached was that there was "likely to be a need for a primary network of urban motorways in most major cities". It was considered essential to take account of social and economic costs and benefits of alternative methods of motorway corridor development but it was believed that environmental problems arising from urban motorways were capable of solution "given appropriate machinery and adequate resources". Urban motorways had to be conceived as an integral part of comprehensive urban land-use/transport strategy.

Responsibility for road planning in the conurbations rests primarily with the local authorities but the Department of Transport has an important role as highway authority for trunk roads in the conurbations and also in respect of Transport Supplementary Grants to local authorities. Local authority responsibilities changed as a result of the reorganisation of local government, first in London by the Greater London Act 1963 and secondly by the Local Government Act 1972 which established Metropolitan County Councils in the rest of the country whose areas embrace the major conurbations (the areas are not identical). These changes have meant that highway planning in the conurbations is now carried out by these County Councils together with the Department of Transport.

In 1958 the Ministry of Transport invited local authorities in the conurbations where, at that time, several were highway authorities to form area review committees so as to co-ordinate road plans in the conurbations. These committees carried out some traffic studies to help in their work but by the early 1960s it was clear that more extensive studies were needed and the Ministry of Transport began to encourage local authorities to take a comprehensive approach to road and transport policies through the use of land-use/transportation studies; the Department contributed half the cost of these and participated in their technical direction.

The first major transport study was started in London in January 1962. It was sponsored jointly by the Ministry of Transport and the London County Council with a contribution from London Transport. At that time, relatively little experience of carrying out such large-scale surveys was available in Britain and experience from the USA was imported by appointing joint British and American consultants to undertake the work. The firms were Freeman Fox and Partners from Britain in association with the Engineering Service Corporation of Los Angeles and Wilbur Smith and Associates of New Haven, Connecticut. Phase I of the survey was concerned with collecting information about journeys being undertaken at that time. Phase II was an analysis of the data so as to establish relations between traffic patterns and the main factors governing them with the object of forecasting likely traffic patterns in future years in 1971 and 1981. This study had been called "The London Traffic Survey" and the consultants' reports on phases I and II were issued in 1964 and 1966 respectively. However, when the Greater London Council came into being in April 1965 it was decided that the scope of the survey should be broadened. The consultants were, therefore, commissioned to carry out the London Transportation Study using the Traffic Survey data but examining in more depth factors influencing mobility, particularly the urban structure and land use, with a view to developing a transport plan covering roads and public transport for integration into the development plan of the Greater London Council.

In the light of experience with the London Traffic Survey, the Ministry of Transport took the initiative in urging local authorities in the major conurbations to carry out comprehensive land-use transportation studies in which plans would be tested not only for new roads but also for public transport systems. Studies set up in England were: the Merseyside Area Land Use Transportation Study (MALTS); the South East Lancashire North East Cheshire Study (SELNEC); the Tyne and Wear Plan (TWP); the West Midlands Transportation Study (WMTS); the West Yorkshire Transportation Study (WYTS); and in Scotland the Greater Glasgow Transportation Study. Reports on all these studies had been prepared by 1970 and further studies in the areas have been carried out since then.

There was criticism of some of the studies particularly by academics in evidence to the Select Committee on Urban Transport Planning[13]. J.M. Thomson, then Rees Jeffreys Fellow in the Economics and Administration of Transport at the London School of Economics, thought that the Department of the Environment were placing too much reliance on the results of the studies because the techniques were still inadequate for the purposes to which they were put. However, he added "I think they are absolutely right to encourage these studies and certainly to encourage fundamental research into the techniques". Professor A.G. Wilson of the Department of Urban and Regional Geography in the University of Leeds thought the studies had been "grossly inadequate in some areas" and instanced the WYTS in this respect which he said was essentially an inter-urban study. He thought, however, that the transportation studies carried out up to that time had added substantially to knowledge and he hoped the information obtained would be maintained and updated. He thought there had been inadequacies in the way techniques such as mathematical modelling had been used and he thought that social factors could and should be included in transport planning.

Professor Peter Hall of the Department of Geography in Reading University was critical of the London study as being inadequate to compare investment in public transport and in motorways. He thought that transportation studies tended to be highway oriented. Professor C.D. Foster, then Head of the Centre for Urban Economics at the London School of Economics, said that the early London survey was motorway biassed because American methods had been used. He considered that attempts to reflect the importance of public transport in the London Transportation Study were "extremely unsatisfactory". In his opinion evaluations of public transport systems in that study "were very bad—useless—but so far as it looked at motorways it produced results which were quite meaningful". He said that when he joined the Ministry of Transport in 1966, one of his priorities was to carry out a transportation study which would make it possible to compare the return on highway investment with that on public transport investment. He thought that the SELNEC, MALTS and TWP studies did that.

What these various comments amounted to was that land-use/transportation studies were an essential tool in planning urban roads, especially motorways and public transport systems, but that the techniques then available needed to be developed to include social and environmental factors as well as the more tangible ones. This seems to have been in accord with the view of transport planning consultant J.O. Tresidder, Managing Director of Freeman Fox and Associates, given in written evidence to the Select Committee on Urban Transport. He accepted that it was possible to criticise the detailed methods then used in transportation studies but pointed out that they were the best means available and that they were being progressively improved as experience was gained with them. He thought the techniques were in advance of those concerned with other aspects of the development of conurbations such as mobility of employment and values to be placed on land-use developments which formed part of the quality of life of people living in those areas and which ideally should form part of a land-use/transportation study. "Saying that they are very imperfectly understood and are not readily conducive to the application of analytical techniques immediately places land-use/transportation studies in their correct role of being tools which assist in providing guidance towards an overall judgement rather than something that provides an 'answer' itself".

By 1975 roughly 100 transportation studies had been carried out in towns and conurbations in Britain[26] and many of those were due for up-dating by 1980. With the evolution of modelling techniques and particularly with the developments in computers it has now become relatively cheap and quick to analyse the basic planning and transport data and to test alternative road and transport plans. However, forecasting traffic years ahead must by its nature remain a matter of considerable

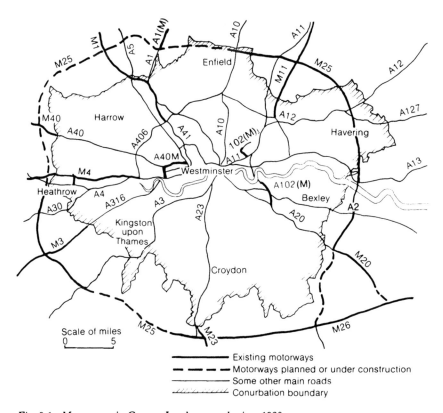

Fig. 9.1 Motorways in Greater London conurbation, 1980

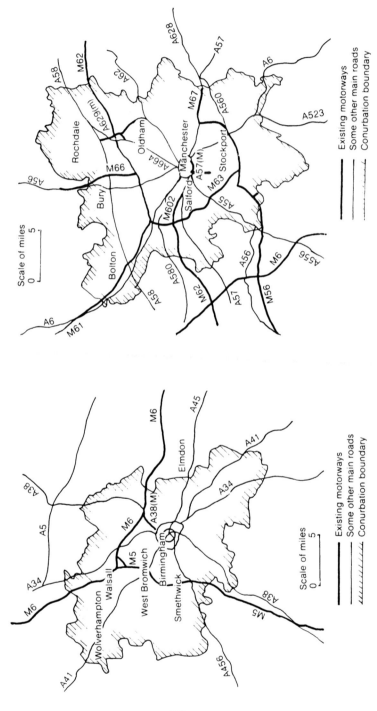

Fig. 9.3 Motorways in South East Lancashire conurbation, 1980

Fig. 9.2 Motorways in West Midlands conurbation, 1980

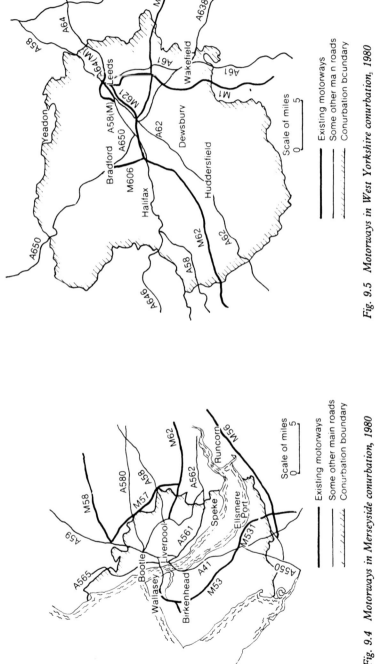

Fig. 9.5 Motorways in West Yorkshire conurbation, 1980

Existing motorways
Some other main roads
Conurbation boundary

Scale of miles
0   5

Fig. 9.4 Motorways in Merseyside conurbation, 1980

Existing motorways
Some other main roads
Conurbation boundary

Scale of miles
0   5

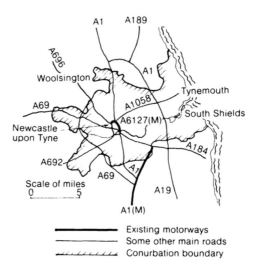

Fig. 9.6 Motorways in Tyneside conurbation, 1980

uncertainty. As J.M. Thomson said to the Select Committee on Urban Transport Planning, "I do not think one would ever expect any great level of accuracy when you are predicting the situation in 20 years' time."

Motorways in the English conurbations

The location of motorways in the major English conurbations in 1980 is illustrated in Figs 9.1 to 9.6. Some are trunk roads for which the Department of Transport is the highway authority and others are principal roads which are a local authority responsibility. Data on road lengths in the conurbations are not readily available and information about roads in the Metropolitan Counties which are now the administrative authorities covering areas approximating to those of the major conurbations is given in Table 9.3.

In these six predominantly urban areas, with high concentrations of traffic and people, only about 1% of the roads are motorways and less than that can be classed as urban motorways.

Planning motorways in the conurbations has often been a contentious matter and their construction has frequently called for considerable ingenuity and skill on the part of design engineers and contractors. In what follows, a brief description is given of the way motorways have evolved in the conurbations against the background of developing ideas about transport in those areas.

Greater London

The conurbation occupies some 700 square miles and has a population of about 7.3 million, but taken together with adjacent built-up areas there is a region, roughly circular with a diameter of some 50 miles, within which are concentrated over a fifth of the population of Britain and over a fifth of the vehicles. There is a noticeable lack of a high standard road network serving these vehicles but, on the other hand, there is a substantial public transport system, particularly by rail, in the area.

Studies of road traffic and planning roads in the capital have a long history and a comprehensive review of road plans between 1900 and 1970 has been made by Buchanan[27]. There are records of speed studies in parts of London in 1905[28]; in 1934[29] a circular letter was sent by the Ministry of Transport to highway authorities in the London Traffic Area saying that the Minister had decided to put in hand "a comprehensive and systematic survey of the highway developments required in the London Traffic Area in order to keep pace with the expansion of traffic." The letter went on to say that C.H. (later Sir Charles) Bressey, who had been Chief Engineer of the Roads Department of the Ministry, was to relinquish that post and devote himself full time to the study. Associated with him was Sir Edwin Lutyens to act as architectural consultant. The terms of reference for the study were "To study and report upon the need for improved communications by road (including the improvement and re-modelling of existing roads) in the area of Greater London and to prepare a highway development plan for that area incorporating so far as is practicable and desirable, schemes already planned or projected".

Among the instructions issued for the study were: that administrative boundaries should be disregarded but that close contact should be maintained with local authorities generally, with town planning committees and with police authorities, and that special attention should be paid to the origin and destination of traffic crossing the area, to the traffic using the main thoroughfares and to the correlation of improvement schemes within the area to the main communications radiating from its circumference. The results of this study were published in 1937[30].

Table 9.3 Lengths of motorways in six Metropolitan Counties in England in April 1979: miles (Source: Department of Transport)

Metropolitan County	Motorways		Total all roads
	Trunk	Principal	
Greater London	21	7	8000
West Midlands	44	2	3970
Greater Manchester	79	10	4790
Merseyside	22	10	2570
West Yorkshire	54	9	4850
Tyne and Wear	2	5	2430

During World War II further plans appeared. Work on a plan for redevelopment of the City of London was begun in 1941 and the plan was published in 1944[31]. Also in 1941 work began on the County of London Plan which was published in 1943[32] and a plan for Greater London was formulated in 1945[33]. The County Plan and the Greater London Plan included major road proposals based on a radial/ring concept. The Greater London Plan had four more or less concentric rings labelled A, B, C and D respectively moving outwards from the centre and these had interconnecting radials linking to trunk routes to Exeter, South Wales, Gloucester, Birmingham, Edinburgh, Cambridge, Ipswich, Canterbury and Eastbourne/Brighton. The County of London Plan included A, B and C rings with some interconnecting radials.

No traffic studies of the kind discussed earlier were carried out in formulating these road proposals; indeed in view of restrictions on traffic in war-time such studies would not have had relevance to peace-time traffic. Some routes were visualised as being motorways but others as all-purpose arterials. The cost of the proposals was clearly very large and in some areas, particularly in the central area, difficult environmental problems would be involved with new roads.

In 1945 the London County Council accepted the concept of three ring roads A, B and C with a series of radials linking them as the basis of their highway plan but without deciding whether these roads would be motorways. In 1950 the A-ring proposal was dropped by the Government in favour of other less ambitious road improvements in London which appeared in the County Development Plan in 1951. By 1955 the A-ring was again under consideration.

At the urban motorways conference in 1956[34] Sir Patrick Abercrombie, who had been responsible for the Greater London Plan and jointly for the County of London Plan which included the ring roads, said that in the Greater London Plan they had come to the conclusion that the A-ring "was impossible as an urban motorway largely on economic grounds". In the same year F.A. Rayfield[10] examined in some detail the case for a ring road in London and came to the conclusion that "on any reasonable assessment of the cost and of the direct and indirect benefits ... the A-ring motorway would be both practicable and justifiable."

In 1959 a committee on London roads under the Chairmanship of Richard (now Lord Richard) Nugent put forward plans for road improvements on a modest scale (some £10 million per year at 1959 prices) which was accepted by the Government. Shortly after this the comprehensive traffic and transport studies mentioned earlier were begun and the Greater London Council came into being. Also about this time several individual planners came forward with schemes for new roads in London[27].

Using the information from the surveys, an analysis was made of various major road systems[35] and as a result in 1966 the Greater London Council put forward proposals for a primary network to motorway standards which incorporated the C-ring and D-ring renamed Ringway 2 and Ringway 3 respectively but which had as the innermost ring Ringway 1, a "motorway box", lying somewhere near the line of the earlier B-ring which had been proposed as a motorway in the early plans. The Government accepted the proposals in principle, pending the outcome of the Public Inquiry into the development plan as a whole.

A Committee of Inquiry under the chairmanship of Sir Frank Layfield was set up by the Department of the Environment and that committee issued its report in 1973[16]. This was a searching and comprehensive inquiry and the committee concluded that "the present state of transport, particularly road transport in London, is unsatisfactory." They were of the opinion that any satisfactory proposals for resolving transport problems should seek to harmonise public transport, the management and restraint of traffic, the improvement of the environment and the provision of roads. They thought that splitting responsibilities for roads in the Greater London area between the Department of Transport, the Greater London Council and the Borough Councils was illogical and that the work of those authorities was not co-ordinated.

As for the proposals for the main road network in the Greater London Plan, the committee endorsed the proposed Ringway 1 (the motorway box) as the inner London motorway. They considered that Ringway 2 would not attract traffic from central and inner London and recommended that the terms of reference of consultants studying Ringway 2 in the south should be reconsidered. Ringway 3 (the D-ring) they rejected as being unnecessary in view of the proposal to go ahead with the orbital route (the M25).

Following the report by the committee, the Secretary of State for the Environment accepted the need for the motorway box but not the full motorway plan in the original proposals. Indeed, in view of the proposal to build the M25, the proposed south circular route was rejected.

In 1973 there was a change from a Conservative to a Labour administration in the GLC; whereas formerly the Labour group had supported the motorway box, the new Council rejected it and motorways were abandoned so far as the GLC was concerned in the Greater London Development Plan of 1976. Four years later with a return to a Conservative administration there was no move to change from that position. The attitude appears to have been that if Central Government was not prepared to provide funds for major roadworks within the GLC area, there was little sense for the GLC once more to go through the whole procedure of producing yet more plans.

The only sections of principal road motorways completed since the GLC came into being are: part of the West Cross route on the western side of the motorway box, an extension of Western Avenue eastwards from the White City, and part of the East Cross route of the motorway box including the Blackwall Tunnel; and these improvements were initiated originally by the London County Council.

From the White City the extension of Western Avenue runs for 2½ miles as an elevated road, Westway, and is part dual three-lane and part dual two-lane. The route is linked to the 0.7 mile length of the West Cross route at Wood Lane. The West Cross route is dual three-lane. Television surveillance and traffic control of signs is carried out by the Metropolitan Police. The roads were opened in 1970.

It was anticipated that these roads might give rise to environmental problems, some of which it had not been possible to resolve in the design stages because of inadequate powers, notably in relation to rehousing people who might be adversely affected. A study was therefore put in hand by the GLC before and after the roads were constructed to assess their impact on the local environment. It was concluded in the report on the studies[37] that the local environmental effects had been dominated by noise and that, in addition, many properties had also suffered visual intrusion of the elevated road, loss of daylight and overshadowing. Many of these difficulties could have been avoided if wider planning powers had been available. The new roads attracted substantial traffic to them from other roads in the area thus improving conditions on those roads.

Although very few principal road motorways have been built in the area, the Department of Transport had by 1980 built a few trunk road motorways, namely the M1 extension from Berrygrove to the North Circular Road, the M11 extension into the North Circular Road, the M20 running east from Swanley, the M3 to Sunbury, the M4 to Chiswick and parts of the M25 round the periphery of the London area. The extension of the M1, which was completed as far as Hendon in 1967 and to Staples Corner in 1977, follows quite closely the line suggested by Glanville and Baker in 1956[20]. The M3 in effect stops at the outer suburbs and the possible continuation towards the centre of London was rejected in the early 1970s by the GLC as part of a policy of discouraging traffic into London. One mile of the innermost section of the M4 is elevated dual two-lane carriageway, completed in 1965. Lack of capacity there and absence of hard shoulders leads to frequent congestion particularly when accidents and breakdowns occur.

The M25, which was given "highest" priority in 1976 and "first" priority in 1978 policy statements, was given "top" priority in the Department of Transport's *Policy for roads: England, 1980.*[17] In a written answer to a Parliamentary Question on 13 November 1980 it was stated that 36 miles had been completed and 21 miles were under construction. These and all other remaining sections, with one exception on the north near South Mimms which would be completed a little later, were expected to be completed by the end of 1984 provided the remaining statutory procedures were completed satisfactorily.

The Department has also been making substantial improvements to the North Circular Road and to the A40 in London as all-purpose routes which approached motorway standard in many places. In 1980 the Department had commissioned consultants to investigate a possible new line for the North Circular Road from South Woodford to Barking with a new river crossing. This route was originally designated as the M15. Another proposal under consideration is an extension of the M11 to connect with the East Cross route motorway and thence to the A2.

Roads on the south side of London are widely regarded as inadequate; the so-called South Circular route and inner ring road have been described as "no more than signposted routes"[38]. As it stands the route appears not to be suitable for terminating radials from the outer areas and as there are no plans for improving the route proposals for new radials are in doubt. Indeed the Department of Transport is abandoning proposals it made in 1968 for the extension of the M23 northwards from Hooley to Mitcham[39] where it would have connected with the erstwhile Ringway 2.

As mentioned earlier, disquiet over London's road system has been expressed by the Committee on Transport in their report in 1980[16] where they described it as a "national scandal". They are proposing to study transport and roads in London as their next priority but what effect yet another study will have is a matter of conjecture. Recent work by Buchanan and others[37] suggests that the missing ingredient in London is a political commitment to a consistent policy for transport in the capital backed by commensurate resources.

The West Midlands

This conurbation includes a population of some 2.5 million in an area of about 270 square miles. Birmingham is the principal urban centre in the area and traffic problems began to arise there in the inter-war years, particularly because of the development of the motor vehicle industry in the Midlands. The possible need for an inner ring road in Birmingham was being considered in 1918, but it was not until 1943 that the City Council approved in principle the layout of an inner ring road and it was not until 1957 that work started on it. The ring road is a three-lane dual carriageway with some grade separation but is not built to full motorway standards. Part of the road is a viaduct and part in tunnel and the road was designed on the principle that radial arterials would finish at the ring.

In 1959 highway proposals were drawn up for the whole West Midlands conurbation by the highway authorities in the conurbation and the Ministry of Transport and these proposals were further developed in the light of the results of a comprehensive transport study in the area in 1964[40]. Motorways proposed in the conurbation included the Midland Links motorway connecting the M5 and M6 and leading to the M1 (some of this lies outside the conurbation proper), the A38(M) Aston Expressway linking the centre of Birmingham north-eastwards to the M6, and the M42 forming a southern and eastern by-pass to the conurbation and ultimately linking to the East Midlands. By 1980 the Midland Links were complete and some widening of the M5 had been necessary, the Aston Expressway and a section of the M42 on the east between the M6 and the A34 and serving the Birmingham Elmdon Airport and the National Exhibition Centre were in use. The Department of Transport in their policy for 1980 saw an urgent need for the completion of orbital routes round Birmingham and the M42 was included in the list of schemes in preparation[32].

The Midland Links motorway came early in the development of the trunk road motorway network. In 1958 consulting engineers Sir Owen Williams and Partners[41] were commissioned by the Ministry of Transport to investigate possible routes for the motorway. They concluded that a direct route through the conurbation giving a close connection to Birmingham was to be preferred even though such a route posed greater problems of land acquisition and construction than one farther out. The route finally agreed by the highway authorities concerned included some 23 miles of urban motorway and work started on it in 1963.

Construction included sections in retained cut, particularly on the M5, and substantial lengths on viaduct; between Gravelly Hill and Castle Bromwich the M6 runs on a 3½ mile long viaduct. The Birmingham Canal was diverted to run underneath the motorway viaduct through Oldbury. Some 300 houses and 70 industrial premises were demolished in the course of construction but many of these would have been cleared as part of normal development.

The Midland Links motorway includes a number of important interchanges, the most complex and spectacular being that at Gravelly Hill. This is a multilevel structure linking the M6 with the A38(M) Aston Expressway and local Birmingham roads. This complex interchange covers 30 acres and includes 0.6 mile of the M6, 1.6 miles of the Aston Expressway together with 2.5 miles of connecting link roads.

Studies were made of the environmental effects of the M6 on houses in a Birmingham Corporation estate near Gravelly Hill before and after the opening of the motorway[42]. Because most of the properties were rented there was no significant loss of property values to the occupiers. Visual degradation and severance were not affected and the chief factors likely to cause annoyance were noise and pollution.

The motorway network is provided with a television surveillance system controlled by the police from a control centre at Perry Barr. Illuminated matrix signs can be brought into use from the centre to advise on speeds, lane restrictions or traffic diversions. By 1980, however, the control system was being stretched to the limit at times because the motorway system did not have the capacity to cope with peak traffic demands and serious congestion was occurring on parts of the system, particularly in the M5/M6 junction area.

Also in 1980, structural problems began to arise with some of the elevated sections where highway slab cracking began to occur. This was ascribed in part to failure of mortar packing under bearings and in part to high friction at some of the bearings themselves.

The Aston Expressway, A38(M), is 1.6 miles long and joins the M6 motorway to Birmingham's inner ring road. It was designed for the former City Council by Sir William Halcrow and Partners. Contractors for the road which was built in two sections were Taylor Woodrow Construction Ltd, and R.M. Douglas Construction Ltd. The expressway, which came into use in 1970, is arranged to take tidal flow on the seven-lane section joining the Gravelly Hill interchange. Surveillance and control of traffic on the expressway and in particular of the tidal flow lane are operated from the traffic control centre at Perry Barr[43].

This is the only principal road motorway in the conurbation and no others are proposed up to 1985/86 in the West Midlands County Council's transport policies and programmes. Instead improvements to all-purpose roads are proposed including a Black Country route, improvements to the eastern side of Birmingham's middle ring road and a ring road in Wolverhampton.

Coventry, which lies at the eastern end of the county has, like Birmingham, a basic radial/ring road system. During the 1960s an inner ring road was built with several grade-separated junctions, but the road is not to motorway standards. In 1981 the Department of Transport laid draft Orders for an eastern by-pass to Coventry between the M6/M69 and A45/A46 junctions.

South East Lancashire

This conurbation is some 380 square miles in extent with a population of 2.5 million. Because of the essentially built-up nature of the conurbation, most of its motorways could be regarded as being urban motorways.

Manchester is the focus of the area and of its roads. Soon after World War II the former Manchester City Corporation published plans for redevelopment which included an inner ring road. The southern section of this road was built as the Mancunian Way, A57(M). In 1962 a highway plan for the area was prepared by the South East Lancashire and North East Cheshire Highway Engineering Committee which comprised essentially the development of a higher capacity radial/ring road system round Manchester with connections to the trunk road motorways in the area.

These trunk road motorways are: the M61 leading in a north-westerly direction from Manchester to the M6; the M62 leading westwards to the M6 and to Merseyside and eastwards to West Yorkshire and constituting a northern outer by-pass to Manchester; the M63 serving as a western outer by-pass to Manchester and linking the M62/M61 to the North Cheshire motorway, M56; the M67 to the south of Manchester, passing through Stockport to Hyde, the last section of which is due for completion in 1981; and on the east of Manchester a projected M66 between the M62 and M67. The M66 runs north from the M62 to Ramsbottom but south from the M62 for only a short distance and its completion to the M67 is unlikely to be before the latter half of the 1980s.

The dual two-lane Stretford–Eccles by-pass, M63, was the first urban motorway to be completed and was built by the Lancashire County Council with a 75% grant from the Ministry of Transport. Six miles long with 1.8 miles of motorway link roads, it was opened in 1961. Variable soil conditions including peat deposits and mining subsidence were encountered in construction and lengths of high embankment for which industrial waste was used had to be provided on the lead up to the Barton High Level Bridge over the Manchester Ship Canal. By 1975 congestion on the bridge was causing difficulties and in 1978 Salford and Trafford Councils were calling for a second bridge over the canal; but a few years later it was decided to widen the existing bridge.

In 1971 the Eccles by-pass M602 was opened. This motorway passes to the north of Eccles and provides a link from the M62/M63 interchange eastwards to Salford. The motorway is some 1¾ miles long with dual three-lane carriageways and in part is routed over semi-derelict land to minimise property acquisition and in part is located near the Manchester–Liverpool railway line so as to reduce severance problems. In all some 353 houses had to be demolished and amongst other buildings knocked down were two churches. The motorway was built by Lancashire County Council with a 75% grant from the Ministry of Transport and the contractor was Leonard Fairclough.

The Government's *Policy for roads: England, 1980*[17] stated that advance work had started on a 2.6 mile extension of the M602 to Salford Docks. This local authority scheme was estimated to cost £13.6 million and would be eligible for a 100% grant.

A little further to the north the M62 and M61 join at the Worsley Braided interchange. This was opened in 1970. This large interchange also provides links with the A580 trunk road and three principal roads, the A666, A572 and A575. The interchange is some 2 miles long in extent and includes the equivalent length of 6 miles of dual three-lane carriageways. Construction involved the excavation of 1,500,000 cubic yards of peat.

In December 1971 the A666(M), a 2 mile long urban motorway, part dual two-lane and part dual three-lane, was opened in Bolton as the eastern limb of the inner relief road. The road was designed by G.F. Read, Borough Engineer and Surveyor, and built by Gleeson (Civil Engineering) Ltd. Emphasis was laid on landscaping and tree planting and the road was conceived as a parkway through the Croal Valley parkland[44].

Moving east, the M66 provides a by-pass to Bury but is only partly in built-up areas. Similarly the 4.6 mile long Rochdale–Oldham motorway, A627(M), and associated Slattocks link, while partly in urban areas, is essentially a connecting link between Rochdale and Oldham with a connection to the M62. This motorway was designed by the Lancashire County Council (acting as agents for those parts within the boundaries of the Rochdale and Oldham Borough Councils) and construction was by a consortium of Sir Alfred McAlpine and Son Ltd with Leonard Fairclough Ltd; the road was opened in 1972.

To the south of Manchester there were local objections by the Greater Manchester Transport Action Group to the east–west route through Stockport between Cheadle and Portwood. This scheme went to Public Inquiry in 1977 and work started in 1979. The line chosen for the 2.6 mile long dual three-lane motorway follows an old railway line so as to avoid introducing a new line of severance.

To the west of this section of the M63 lie the Sharston by-pass, M63, and then the Sale Eastern and Northenden by-pass which connects to the Stretford–Eccles by-pass. To the east, the line of route from Portwood to Denton, M63/M66, was announced by the Department of Transport in February 1977 and this 5 mile motorway, part dual two-lane and part dual three-lane, was included in the Department's programme for 1982 and 1983. The 11 mile long M66 link between Denton and Middleton, the "missing link" in the Manchester outer ring road, is included in the Department's schemes in preparation for their main programme from 1984 onwards. This scheme raised considerable opposition mainly because of the effects of the motorway on housing.

The M67 Denton relief motorway is 1.3 miles long with dual three-lane carriageways and is built mainly below ground level in cutting to make it less conspicuous and to reduce noise from traffic. It was opened in 1981. The M67 is continued eastwards for 3.3 miles by the Hyde by-pass, also a dual three-lane motorway which was opened in 1978.

As for the future of motorways in the conurbation, the Greater Manchester County Structure Plan of 1979 commented "the management and development of the trunk road and motorway system of Greater Manchester is under the control of the Department of Transport and the programming of major extensions to the regional road network such as the Manchester Outer Ring Road's eastern section is therefore not the responsibility of the GMC." The Council had apparently no plans for motorways of their own.

Merseyside

This conurbation with an area of 150 square miles includes the Liverpool and Bootle areas on the north side of the Mersey together with the Wirral peninsular on the south. The population is rather less than 1.5 million (it is a little more in the Merseyside Metropolitan County).

In 1961 a conurbation highways committee carried out traffic surveys on which to base a 20 year highways plan. Results of those surveys and the proposals for a new road network were published in 1965[45]. These proposals included a motorway network round the inner urban areas to connect with the national motorway network in the region, the M53, along the Wirral peninsular to the second tunnel being constructed under the Mersey[46] and the Lancashire/Yorkshire motorway, M62.

In 1965 a plan was prepared jointly by consultant planners and the Liverpool City Planning Department for the centre of Liverpool. The plan included proposals for an inner ring motorway connecting five radial motorways with direct connections to car parks and selected access to local streets. The motorways were to be carefully designed to minimise environmental disturbance. The proposals which have been described as "imaginative"[23] were adopted in principle by the then City Council.

The inner motorway and an extension of the M62 to join it were included in the 1969 list of conurbation schemes, but by 1970 most of the inner motorway plan was rephased. After the oil crisis the plan was shelved and was abandoned by the newly formed Merseyside County Council in 1976. However, in 1977, the Council revived the inner ring road idea but as an all-purpose road at ground level. In 1978 the Minister of Transport announced his decision to give the County Council a grant to assist with the construction of their modified scheme. There has been profound disagreement between the Merseyside County Council and the Liverpool City Council over the scheme. The Liverpool Council are against the proposal primarily on the grounds that public funds would, in their view, be better spent on housing in Liverpool rather than on road improvements which they regard as being largely unnecessary. The arguments have been taken to the House of Commons in an adjournment debate in July 1979 and again in February 1980 on a County of Merseyside Bill. The Government view was that the matter was one for Merseyside County Council to decide, not the Government.

It is interesting to record the approach of the Merseyside County Council to road planning in 1977 as expressed by Audrey Lees, then the County Planning Officer. She wrote[47] "New highways should be constructed only in cases where they are required to:

Improve the movement of buses;

Improve access for goods vehicles;

Reduce or eliminate traffic in sensitive locations such as residential and shopping areas;

Provide access to new development.

Within these criteria emphasis should be placed on the completion of a primary strategic highway network."

Transport planning in Merseyside has been based since about 1970 on the Merseyside Area Land Use and Transportation Study (MALTS). The initial study was carried out in the latter half of the 1960s and has been up-dated since. The first stage of the Liverpool outer ring road M57 was programmed before MALTS. This section which was opened in 1972 is 3½ miles long, mostly dual three-lane, between the A59 and the A580 and was planned primarily for industrial traffic. Only part of it passes through urban areas and 70% is on embankment. The second stage between the A580 and the M62 is 6 miles long and also dual three-lane. The M57 which was built as a local authority road has been made into a trunk road.

To the north of the conurbation, the M58 opened in 1980 provides a link from the Royal Seaforth Dock eastwards to the M6.

The mid-Wirral motorway M53 runs from the second Mersey tunnel to Hooton near Ellesmere Port. It is routed mostly through rural areas and was opened in 1972. In 1975 the Department of Transport had a scheme in preparation for an extension of the M53 from Hooton to Lea-by-Backford but in 1976 this was cut, presumably because the construction of the Ellesmere Port motorway M531 made it unnecessary. The M531, which is dual two-lane, runs from the M53 through the industrial and residential areas of Ellesmere Port to the M56 at Stoak and thence to the A56 at Hoole. The M531 was built in stages, the first section from the M53 to the A5117 being opened in 1976 and the remainder was under construction in 1980.

The North Cheshire motorway M56 is mostly in open country except at its eastern end where it passes through Galley and joins the M63 at Cheadle. The sections from Hapsford to Cheadle were opened in the early 1970s and the westward extensions from Hapsford to Powey Lane in 1980.

Motorways in the Merseyside conurbation are thus more rural than urban in character but they do provide a high capacity network between the main urban centres in the area and also connections to the national network. Within the City of Liverpool the inner ring road remains a contentious issue and it seems unlikely that the earlier proposal for a motorway will be revived in the foreseeable future.

West Yorkshire

This conurbation has a population of some 2 million and an area of 485 square miles. It includes two major centres, Leeds and Bradford, and several other important urban areas such as Wakefield, Huddersfield, Halifax and Dewsbury. There are two important trunk road motorways in the conurbation. The M62 provides an east–west link across the area with connections to Manchester and Liverpool in the west and to Hull in the east. The M1 has its northern terminus in Leeds and provides the conurbation with a good connection to the south of the country. The M1 also links to the M62 to the south of Leeds. To the east of the conurbation is the A1 trunk road and although this is not a motorway, except in parts, it is a dual carriageway road providing access to the north as well as an alternative route to the south. The M62 is joined to the A1 at Ferrybridge.

In 1958 a committee composed of representatives of the principal highway authorities was set up to assess the long-term highway needs of the conurbation. A report[48] was issued by the committee in 1964; it proposed that urban motorways should be built in Leeds and in Bradford to link up with the trunk road motorways in the area.

In 1965 the Ministries of Transport and of Housing and Local Government, jointly with the Leeds City Council, undertook a study of the application of integrated parking, traffic management and public transport policies within a framework of land-use planning in Leeds. The study also considered the design and improvement of environmental areas from which traffic could be excluded as a result of those policies. A report[49] was published in 1969 and as regards roads it was concluded that the development and improvement of a primary road network in the area was essential. It was proposed that a system of urban motorways connecting with the national trunk road and motorway network should be built.

A start was made on the first stage of the Leeds inner ring motorway, A58(M), in 1964. This was the north-west sector of the ring and was opened in 1967. The dual two-lane road is mostly in cutting with a 1,200 ft cut-and-cover tunnel through the University and Hospital precinct. The tunnel relies on natural ventilation and carbon monoxide levels are monitored continuously. There is also television monitoring of traffic in the tunnel.

The second stage of the ring was the north-east sector which was begun in 1967 and opened in 1971. This sector is also mostly in cutting with a design speed of 40 mile/h on the main carriageways and of 20 mile/h on ramps.

By 1980 some 2½ miles of inner ring motorway were in use and the West Yorkshire County Council had programmes for further work to be started in 1982 and 1983[50].

It is believed that improvement of the central area environment, commercial benefits of pedestrianisation with advantages to the shopper, the increased accessibility and reliability of the bus services are considerable and are mainly due to the inner ring road construction.

To the south of Leeds, the M1 had initially ended at Stourton in 1967. The route was extended northwards to the city boundary in 1972 and the route was carried 2½ miles into the city on an urban motorway to join with the main road network in Leeds. The Leeds southern ring road was started in 1979 but is an all-purpose dual carriageway.

The M62 is linked to the south-west of Leeds by the M621, a 4 mile long dual two-lane motorway. This scheme went to Public Inquiry in 1970 and a contract for the work was let in 1971; the road was opened to traffic in 1973.

In 1972 a scheme for the Leeds south-west urban motorway to link the M621 to the M1 and the inner ring road went to Public Inquiry. A contract was awarded for the construction of the road in 1974 and the road opened in 1976. Large areas of the route have been landscaped and particular attention has been paid to noise reduction by the use of earth mounds and acoustic walls, and at one point, near a school, the road is in tunnel.

The only other motorway in the conurbation is the Bradford south radial motorway, M606. This is 2½ miles long and runs from the M62 at Chain Bar to the Bradford outer ring road at Staygate. It was started in 1970 and is part dual two-lane and part dual three-lane. In 1979 an old mine shaft capping collapsed leaving a hole in the central reservation and requiring the motorway to be closed until repairs were carried out. Many miles of new motorway had been constructed in West Yorkshire which successfully allowed for mining subsidence as well as faults and mine shafts and this was the first occasion that the problem had not been detected at construction stage.

Plans to carry this motorway spur in a north-westerly direction from Bradford towards Skipton, the Airedale motorway, were wrecked by the militant disruption of the Public Inquiry in the 1970s. The Department of Transport *Policy for roads:*

England, 1980[17] noted that the Airedale route "is still heavily congested" and they hoped to start on a new road by-passing the more congested urban areas after 1984.

An inner ring road, not a motorway, has been partially built in Bradford and the West Yorkshire County Council has plans to continue with this in the latter half of the 1980s.

In 1966, the Regional Economic Planning Council identified a need for a motorway to link the M1 to the A1 north of Leeds. In *Policy for roads: England, 1980* the Department of Transport recorded that "There is a pressing need for a good link between the A1 north of Leeds and the M1 to the south". Proposals for such a link were being prepared and the West Yorkshire County Council gave particular support to them in the context of county schemes in Leeds. The County Council were hoping to start schemes to improve the road network to the east of Leeds.

In Huddersfield an inner ring road, not a motorway but with some restriction on access, was completed in 1974 and the first stage of an inner ring road in Halifax was opened in 1973. This latter is partly in cutting and partly on elevated viaducts and embankments. A ring road for Dewsbury, also not a motorway, was scheduled to start in 1981/82.

Tyneside

The Tyneside conurbation has an area of 90 square miles and a population of between ¾ and 1 million people. The only motorways through the area are the 1 mile section of the A6127(M) running north-south through the centre of Newcastle-upon-Tyne and the A1(M) to the south of Newcastle, in particular the 4 mile length between Blackfell near Birtley service area and White Mare Pool which was originally the A194(M) linking the A1 at Blackfell to roads leading to the Tyne Tunnel. The A1 is now routed through the tunnel northwards and in effect provides an eastern by-pass to the area round Newcastle. The A194(M) was opened in 1970.

In the early 1960s proposals were put forward by W. (now Sir Wilfred) Burns for a system of motorways in central Newcastle and reaching across the River Tyne to Gateshead[51]. The motorway network enclosed the central business district and there was included a motorway link in tunnel across the central area. Extra traffic capacity was required across the river and a new bridge was envisaged in place of the existing Redheugh Bridge, now under construction; another new bridge was also proposed but this was not proceeded with. Burns's idea was that the whole inner area was to be redeveloped as a modern shopping and commercial centre, the shopping area being pedestrianised; the motorway ring and associated long-term car parks were included as the best way of removing traffic from the area. Considerable attention was given to the motorway environment. Burns considered that where the motorway could enhance the atmosphere of the area it should be designed as a piece of civic or traffic architecture, but where the motorway was unlikely to make a positive contribution to civic design it should be integrated with building development so as not to intrude on people in the city centre.

In 1972 a start was made on a section of motorway leading from the northern side of the central area round by the east to the Tyne Bridge. This motorway, originally designated Central Motorway East, was opened to traffic in 1975 and is now the Great North Road, A6157(M). Less than 1 mile long, the motorway is partly in cutting and partly on two levels and there are eight pedestrian crossings by overbridges and subways. It is the only part of the inner motorway network to be built because, although there were plans to build more of the motorway system, the downturn of the economy and policy changes in favour of public transport resulted in those plans being abandoned. A substantial amount of funds available for transport development has been allocated to the new Metro system of rapid rail transit in the area.

The Structure Plan 1979 for the Tyne and Wear County recorded that in the previous 15 years there had been a substantial development of the county's road network with nearly 100 miles of dual carriageway roads constructed. For future new roads priority would be given to those which improved operating conditions for buses, improved access to and within older industrial areas or to new industrial land, and improved the environment and safety in areas adversely affected by heavy traffic flows. The Transport Policies and Programmes 1981/82 noted that capital programmes were still dominated by the Metro and replacement of Redheugh Bridge until 1983/84.

As to trunk road schemes, the Department of Transport *Policy for roads: England, 1980* included a Newcastle western by-pass A69 in the list of schemes in preparation for the main programme 1984 onwards. This will link the A69 to the A1(M) to the south. The by-pass will also link the A69 to the A696 and the A1 to the north via an extension proposed by the County Council.

Conclusion

There are relatively few miles of motorway in urban areas in Britain and even fewer within the heavily congested inner areas of cities. There seem to have been various reasons why they were built. Some, such as the M5 and M6 near Birmingham, are part of the national strategic network and routed near to major sources of traffic; others, such as the M621 in Leeds, link national routes to terminal areas in cities, and still others have been built to provide relief to congested areas, e.g. the Mancunian Way in Manchester. However, opinions about them are sharply divided and facts about their benefits and disbenefits are scarce. Evidence from Glasgow suggests that despite their high cost they can yield large economic benefits. Some of the early motorways in towns have been shown to have serious environmental faults but experience now suggests that many of these can be reduced or eliminated by better design, at a cost. Many objections to new roads, not just motorways, have been based on arguments about loss of housing but there are doubts about validity of some of the arguments, particularly where redevelopment is scheduled anyway.

There is a very clear awareness that motorways in urban areas should not be planned in isolation but should be part of the overall planning of land use and transport. Over the past 15 to 20 years planners and engineers have developed techniques of locating, designing and constructing motorways in complex urban conditions within the broader transport planning framework. They have also applied traffic management methods to make better use of the existing streets. However, there is a limit to what can be done by these means and in many areas that limit has been reached. In those cases traffic congestion and road accidents will only be eased by the construction of new roads and/or greater restraint of traffic using the roads.

In a prize-winning essay on transport and inner city areas Poulton[52] observed that lane capacity is generally low on mixed-use urban roads, whereas motorways can operate much more efficiently. He suggested that one motorway lane can replace three primary road lanes and that it might be expected that motorways would be attractive by draining traffic from parallel roads and by cutting down noise, danger and filtering traffic. He suggests that they are not being built because of their "oppressiveness" and as a result "journeys to and from the inner city take three times as long as they need do."

He proposes that motorways are needed that connect the central areas to the primary network beyond the inner suburbs and that offer demonstrable environmental benefits. These motorways would be designed to move traffic only between central areas and outer suburbs and would, therefore, not have frequent access points.

Whatever view is taken about the place of motorways in urban areas, it is evident that they can be designed and built so as to minimise many of the objections to them on environmental grounds, but that this will be more costly. In some cases, motorway construction can, indeed, improve the environment. It is a matter for political decision as to what resources should be made available for roads and other forms of transport dependent on public funds. In view of the relatively long time-scale involved in the planning, design and construction of transport facilities there are obvious advantages to be gained if policy is directed to providing a consistent long-term strategy for transport in towns.

References

1. CHARLESWORTH G. London traffic management. *Traffic engineering and control*, 1962, **4**, No. 2.
2. MARLOW M. and EVANS R. *Urban congestion survey 1976. Traffic flows and speeds in eight towns and five conurbations.* Digest SR 438. TRRL, Crowthorne, 1978.

3. BUCHANAN C.D. *et al. Traffic in towns. Report of the Working Group.* HMSO, London, 1963.
4. BRUNNER C.T. *Cities—living with the motor vehicle.* British Road Federation, London, 1960.
5. MINISTRY OF TRANSPORT *Road pricing: the economic and technical possibilities.* HMSO, London, 1964.
6. ROTH G.J. The equilibrium of traffic on congested streets. *Rev. Int. Statistical Inst.*, 1963, **31**, No. 3.
7. WATSON P.L. and HOLLAND E.P. *Relieving traffic congestion: the Singapore Area Licence Scheme.* Staff working paper no. 281. World Bank, Washington DC, 1978.
8. DEPARTMENTAL COMMITTEE OF THE MINISTER OF WAR TRANSPORT. *Design and layout of roads in built-up areas.* HMSO, London, 1946.
9. MINISTRY OF TOWN AND COUNTRY PLANNING. *The redevelopment of central areas.* HMSO, London, 1947.
10. RAYFIELD F.A. The planning of ring roads with special reference to London. *Proc. Instn Civ. Engrs, Part 2,* 1956, **5**, 99–135.
11. DAVIES E. *Transport in Greater London.* Greater London papers no. 6. London School of Economics and Political Science, London, 1962.
12. URBAN MOTORWAYS COMMITTEE *New roads in towns.* Report to the Secretary of State for the Environment. HMSO, London, 1972.
13. SELECT COMMITTEE OF THE HOUSE OF COMMONS. *Second report: Urban transport planning.* HMSO, London, 1972.
14. DEPARTMENT OF THE ENVIRONMENT. *Government observations on the second report of the Expenditure Committee.* HMSO, London, 1973.
15. DEPARTMENT OF TRANSPORT, SCOTTISH DEVELOPMENT DEPARTMENT and WELSH OFFICE. *Transport policy.* HMSO, London, 1977.
16. TRANSPORT COMMITTEE OF THE HOUSE OF COMMONS. *1st report 1980–81. The roads programme.* HMSO, London, 1980.
17. DEPARTMENT OF TRANSPORT. *Policy for roads: England, 1980.* HMSO, London, 1980.
18. DEPARTMENT OF THE ENVIRONMENT. *Cross-section design of road verges and central reserves on or under bridges.* Highways Directorate technical memorandum H9/71. Department of Transport, London, 1971.
19. URBAN MOTORWAYS PROJECT TEAM. *Report of the Urban Motorways Committee of the Department of the Environment.* HMSO, London, 1973.
20. GLANVILLE W.H. and BAKER J.F.A. Urban motorways in Great Britain? *Proceedings of the urban motorways conference.* British Road Federation, London, 1956.
21. AVON COUNTY COUNCIL DEPARTMENT OF HIGHWAYS AND ENGINEERING. *Rapidride 62. Final report.* Avon CC, Bristol, 1977.
22. FREEMAN T.W. *The conurbations of Great Britain.* Manchester University Press, Manchester, 1959.
23. COLIN BUCHANAN AND PARTNERS. *The conurbations.* British Road Federation, London, 1969.
24. ALAN M. VOORHEES AND ASSOCIATES. *Traffic in the conurbations.* British Road Federation, London, 1971.

25. LLEWELYN-DAVIES, WEEKS, FORESTIER-WALKER AND BOR. *Motorways in the urban environment.* British Road Federation, London, 1971.
26. ATKINS S.T. Transportation planning: is there a road ahead? *Traffic engineering and control,* 1977, **18**, No. 2.
27. BUCHANAN C.M. *London road plans 1900–1970.* Greater London Research Intelligence Unit research report no. 11. GLC, London, 1970.
28. STANDING JOINT COMMITTEE OF THE RAC, AA and RSAC. *The case for a revised road policy.* London, 1952.
29. MINISTRY OF TRANSPORT. *Report on the Road Fund for the year 1934–35.* HMSO, London, 1935.
30. BRESSEY C.H. and LUTYENS E. *Highway development survey 1937 (Greater London).* HMSO, London, 1938.
31. *Post-war reconstruction in the City of London.* Batsford, London, 1944.
32. FORSHAW J.H. and ABERCROMBIE P. *County of London Plan.* Macmillan, London, 1943.
33. ABERCROMBIE P. *Greater London Plan 1944.* HMSO, London, 1945.
34. BRITISH ROAD FEDERATION. *Proceedings of the urban motorways conference.* British Road Federation, London, 1956.
35. TRESIDDER J.O. *et al.* The London Transportation Study: methods and techniques. *Proc. Instn Civ. Engrs,* 1968, **39**, 433–464.
36. DEPARTMENT OF THE ENVIRONMENT. *Report on the Panel of Inquiry into the Greater London Development Plan.* HMSO, London, 1973.
37. GREATER LONDON COUNCIL. *Westway: an environmental and traffic appraisal.* GLDP Inquiry: background paper no. 494. GLC, London, 1971.
38. BUCHANAN M. *et al. Transport planning for Greater London.* Saxon House, Farnborough, 1980.
39. RIDOUT G. DTp sets out to defend its U-turn on the M23. *New Civil Engineer,* 1/8 January 1981.
40. FREEMAN FOX, WILBUR SMITH AND ASSOCIATES. *The West Midlands Transport Study.* Birmingham, 1968.
41. SIR OWEN WILLIAMS AND PARTNERS. *Midland Links motorway.* Sir Owen Williams and Partners, London, 1972.
42. LAWSON B.R. and WALTERS D. The effects of a new motorway on an established residential area. *Psychology and the built environment.* Architectural Press, London, 1974.
43. WALL J.S. and BURR M.A. Aston Expressway signing and signalling system. *Traffic engineering and control,* 1972, **14**, No. 8.
44. READ G.F. Parkway concept for Bolton's first motorway. *Surveyor,* 1971, **38**, No. 4150.
45. STEERING COMMITTEE ON MERSEYSIDE TRAFFIC AND TRANSPORT. *Merseyside conurbation traffic survey 1962.* Liverpool, 1965.
46. CAIRNCROSS A.A. and EVANS A.J.R. The Liverpool–Wallasey tunnel—traffic investigation, choice of location and layout of approaches. *J. Instn Highway Engrs,* 1968, **5**, No. 12.
47. LEES A. The relationship of road strategy to economic development and industrial

activity in the Merseyside Region. *Proceeding of the sixth British regional congress on a road network and its effects.* British Road Federation, London, 1977.

48. REVIEW AREA COMMITTEE. *A report on the long-term highway needs of the West Riding Special Review Area.* Leeds, 1964.

49. LEEDS CITY COUNCIL, MINISTRY OF TRANSPORT and MINISTRY OF HOUSING AND GOVERNMENT. *Planning and transport: the Leeds approach.* HMSO, London, 1969.

50. WEST YORKSHIRE COUNTY COUNCIL. *Transport policies and programmes 1981–86.* Wakefield, 1980.

51. BURNS W. and BRADSHAW D.T. Planning for movement in Newcastle-upon-Tyne. *Proceedings of the International Road Federation 5th world meeting.* International Road Federation, London, 1966.

52. POULTON M.C. Transport and the viability of central and inner urban areas. *J. transport economics and policy,* 1980, **14**, No. 3.

10

Planning, design and maintenance

Introduction

The evolution of the motorway system has involved the development of techniques for determining where motorways are needed and where their construction can be justified on economic grounds. It has also been necessary to evolve standards of road layout and of construction and various other design issues have arisen, for example, relating to the use and safety of the motorways.

The Ministry (now the Department) of Transport as highway authority for trunk road motorways has been responsible for laying down standards and for generally advising on techniques and other matters relating to motorways. In so doing they have drawn on research, particularly that carried out by the Transport and Road Research Laboratory, on development work in the Department and on the experience gained by designers and contractors working on motorway projects. The standards which have emerged from this process have been issued by the Department, e.g. the *Specification for road and bridge works*,[1] various technical memoranda etc., with periodic revisions in the light of experience gained with them.

The results of the research carried out at the Transport and Road Research Laboratory relating to motorways have been described in various papers and publications by the research staff. In particular three successive directors of the Laboratory have described some aspects of that work in papers to the Institution of Civil Engineers. Glanville[2] in 1960 described traffic and economic studies carried out on the London–Birmingham motorway; Lyons[3] discussed trends in research on motorway design and use in 1971; and Silverleaf[4] considered the contribution of research at the conference on 20 years of British motorways in 1980. Silverleaf drew attention to "the close and growing interaction between those engaged in the planning, design, construction, operation and maintenance of the motorway network and research workers in government laboratories, universities and other organizations." He considered that the contribution from research had led to a saving in time and cost in the building of the motorway network.

213

When, in the 1950s, it was decided to start on the construction of motorways in Britain "many, if not most highway engineers were faced for the first time with the practical as opposed to the theoretical problems of major highway design and construction".[5] Many standards had to be determined as the motorways were built "and there has been a continuing evolution to take account of changes in traffic and experience gained during the period".[5]

Some technical aspects of the planning, design and maintenance of motorways in Britain will now be briefly considered; administrative aspects (e.g., consultation of the public and Public Inquiries) were covered in chapters 5 and 6.

Traffic surveys

A first step in planning a motorway route or network is to assess the amount of traffic the motorway will attract. This information is needed in deciding on the size of the motorway and is one of the factors of importance in choosing the line of route to be followed. Early techniques used for traffic planning were the origin-destination surveys evolved in the USA in the 1940s[6] which were originally concerned with planning roads in urban areas but which also had application to inter-urban roads.

The usual method of carrying out these surveys was to stop traffic using the existing roads in the area concerned and to ask a sample of drivers about the origin and destination of their journeys. An estimate of the amount of traffic which might transfer to the proposed motorway was made on some assumption about whether drivers would save time by so doing. Examples of this kind of survey carried out in England in the 1950s are described in *Research on road traffic.*[7]

Information about origins and destinations of journeys can also be obtained by interviewing people in their homes. The "home interview" has become an important item in transport planning because not only can information be obtained about journeys but other socio-economic information can be obtained of relevance to assessing potential future traffic.

With the advent of electronic computers and as a result of theoretical developments, traffic survey methods became more sophisticated and current techniques take a broader view of transport demand. Modelling techniques are widely used and are commonly based on four steps: trip generation and trip attraction; trip distribution; modal split; and trip assignment.[8] The models attempt to identify and develop relations between various factors which are assumed to determine what trips travellers will make. The models are calibrated against observed data and are used to forecast future traffic demand. Some of the processes have been described in the Leitch report[9] with particular reference to the Regional Highway Traffic Model (RHTM) which was started by the Department of the Environment in 1975 and to which brief reference was made in chapter 6. The Department had not been wholly satisfied with the methods of traffic modelling which had been evolving and some of the problems with which the RHTM project were concerned have been described in a private communication by R.J. Bridle who was Chief Highway Engineer in the Department of Transport at the time and in charge of the project. According to Bridle, the key problems which RHTM policy set out to solve were as follows.

Planning data. The data input into traffic modelling were highly variable and there was a need for national consistency between areas. A base year for the country was agreed as part of the RHTM project, future predictions were made "mechanistically" and Regional Directors in the Department were to agree departures from the material. In this way it was hoped to avoid the major problem of overforecasting and Bridle says this was achieved.

Making use of all surveys. Previously surveys had been carried out to variable standards and data collected were not generally compatible. In the RHTM standards using common definitions were set and rigorously followed so that there was a good degree of consistency in the data collected thus making it more widely usable.

Common description of the network. This was also necessary for consistency and according to Bridle has been achieved. The network has commercial value to firms wishing to solve transport problems and is being used by the Department in connection with the Trunk Road Inventory and the formation of maintenance programmes.

Standardisation forecasting methodology. The idea was to provide a robust national data bank of zones, with good planning data, and a network with a common specification, a calibrated matrix of flows in various planning years and common traffic assignment techniques as a background from which regions could develop models to solve particular problems with local infilling data.

Calibration and validation. There were initial problems in the work "because the police prevented interviewing on motorways" and a large slice of robust data was lost since the framework of surveys which could be adopted was then less than the best. The problems which followed concerned unexplainable differences between household and roadside data and there were large differences between predicted and observed data in validation.

The difficulties which arose with the project were referred to SACTRA, the Standing Advisory Committee on Trunk Road Assessment, and on the recommendation of the Committee further work on the project was abandoned in 1980. Bridle believes that all the original policy aims of the project were met and that the uncertainties arising in the transport modelling process had been brought out. As he has pointed out, the project produced a valuable collection of data which are being made available by the Department, although some are now several years out of date. The experience with the project suggests that possibly some aspects could with advantage have been studied beforehand by research on a pilot scale. But perhaps in the end the political and economic climate was not conducive to continuing work related to the further development of a national road network.

Route location

In broad principle, the methods used for selecting the line of a motorway have not changed during the period of the motorway programme. Many factors are involved in selecting a route, such as traffic demand, engineering problems, environmental questions, public acceptability; a pragmatic approach seems to have been followed in reconciling these many factors. Goldstein[10] has outlined the fundamental approach as first defining the area within which the motorway is likely to be routed, then determining by survey without reference to any particular route the problems and obstacles likely to be encountered within the whole area, and finally selecting routes for study which from the outset recognise the difficulties which might be met. Hutton[11] recommended a walking reconnaissance at an early stage to assess the general nature of the area where a route might pass and considered that authorities such as the Ministry of Agriculture, National Parks and Forestry Commission should be sounded out before any detailed surveys were made.

Once preliminary lines have been identified, the public are consulted for their views. As Goldstein pointed out[10] "the chance of any motorway route being implemented is slight unless it is accepted by the community." A preliminary report is prepared which summarises facts and opinions about possible routes and indicates which appears to be the preferred route on which detailed work should proceed. That work leads to a firm programme report after which draft Orders are published and the various statutory procedures take place, including Public Inquiries.

The engineering surveys cover topography, geology, water sources and levels and weather. Topographical surveys are carried out on the ground, or in some situations from the air, and topographical cost models have been developed using data mainly from ordnance sheets for use at the earlier planning stage. The models provide a quick evaluation and are not for use in optimising arguments. Soil conditions can be very variable and a balance has to be struck in making soil surveys between obtaining great detail which is expensive and sufficient detail to avoid costly errors in subsequent design. Geological survey maps and information from the Institute of Geological Sciences is usually available to help in deciding on soil types and the Institute must be consulted for all schemes involving large earthworks, major structures and tunnels or where geological problems are believed to exist.

In rural areas about a quarter of the construction costs of motorways is typically spent on earthworks. In looking at possible alignments of a route it is clearly desirable to select those within the broad constraints of alignment which minimise earthworks. Research has been carried out[3] which has resulted in the production of a number of computer programs which can be of considerable assistance in optimising the line of a route taking into account earthworks and other factors.

Weather conditions such as snow, ice, wind and fog which might be encountered on a route need to be established and the importance of those conditions in selecting the line of route for the M6 near Shap and the M62 across the Pennines have been referred to in chapter 7.

Economic assessment

The justification for building motorways involves decisions about many issues such as relief from traffic congestion, reduction of accidents, savings in operating costs, environmental effects, road construction and maintenance costs, and political expediency. Whether or not it is justified to build any particular motorway can in large measure be looked upon as an economic investment question although the other factors mentioned have also to be taken into account. Investment in a motorway yields a number of direct economic benefits to the users and, although the cost of the investment is not charged specifically to those road users, it is possible to relate the benefits to costs so as to assess whether the investment is worth while and also to make comparisons between schemes and so provide a standard by which to judge priorities.

During the 1950s, when the decision to start a motorway programme was taken, research was being carried out into developing methods for assessing the economic returns from road works[12,13]. These methods were not immediately taken up by the Ministry of Transport but in 1963 they used a measure of traffic congestion and accident rate called Travel and Accident Loss (TAL) to effect a measure of economic assessment of schemes. However, following further development of the methods devised in earlier research, the Ministry, in 1967, adopted a more sophisticated method of taking account of benefits, and this in turn was superseded by the current procedures which are applied in some form to all trunk road schemes. For schemes costing more than £½ million a computerised system, COBA, is used for making the assessments.

Benefits to road users are counted as savings in time, savings in vehicle operating costs and savings in accidents. Typically time savings are about 70–80% of the total benefits, and accident savings about 20%; savings in vehicle operating costs are usually small.[14] Included in costs are capital and maintenance items and the major element is the capital cost which includes construction and land costs and compensation payments associated with the land costs. A net benefit figure is calculated by aggregating time savings, vehicle-operating cost savings and accident savings less maintenance costs and subtracting from that total the land and construction costs. It is necessary to define the period over which benefits and costs are counted and in COBA a period of 30 years is used. Benefits and costs are discounted over this period to give "net present values" (NPV) related to a fixed base year. A scheme is justified in economic terms if its NPV is greater than zero, i.e. if its discounted benefits are greater than its discounted costs. If more than one scheme is justified the best scheme is that with the highest NPV. However, where there is an explicit budget constraint, schemes with a positive NPV are ranked in order of declining values of the ratio of net present value to cost. These procedures are set out in detail in the Department of Transport's COBA 9 manual[15] issued in 1981.

The benefits included in the COBA scheme are essentially the more tangible elements of cost savings although a notional item is included in accident costs to reflect "pain, grief and suffering". The absence of non-monetary factors in the assessment was criticised by the Leitch committee[9] who, whilst accepting that assessments based on COBA were "sound as far as they go", considered that those assessments were unbalanced because they were dominated by those factors susceptible to valuation in money terms. Instead they thought that the right approach was "through a comprehensive framework, relying on judgment, which embraces all the factors involved in scheme assessment."

Following the Leitch recommendations, the Department of Transport adopted a form of environmental impact statement setting out the significant impacts of a scheme and identifying the people and policies affected. The framework includes the COBA elements and items such as noise, severance, land-use planning, environmental conservation and effect on transport operators.[14]

Standards of road layout

Motorway carriageways are either dual two-lane, dual three-lane or dual four-lane; they are mostly dual three-lane. The width is selected on the basis of the traffic predicted to occur over the period being designed for, e.g. 15 years after opening, in relation to certain standards laid down by the Department of Transport. Originally those standards were referred to as traffic capacities and were expressed in passenger car equivalents. The values of passenger car equivalents were also prescribed by the Department, e.g. one heavy commercial vehicle was adjudged to have the same effect on traffic speed as three passenger cars. In 1961 the standards of capacity of rural roads[16] expressed in passenger car units per 16 hour day were:

Dual two-lane carriageway	9,000–25,000
Dual three-lane carriageway	over 25,000

In 1968[17] the Ministry standards for rural motorways in passenger car units per 16 hour day were:

Dual two-lane carriageway	33,000
Dual three-lane carriageway	50,000
Dual four-lane carriageway	66,000

Currently the Department has discontinued the use of passenger car units because of difficulty in using them in practice and does not use traffic capacity in a quantitative sense for design purposes. Instead the Department has laid down recommended flow levels as shown in Table 10.1[18].

The cross-section recommended for motorways has changed over the years as can be seen from Table 10.2. The change from lay-bys to hard shoulders took place before the first motorways were built and the use of 12 ft lanes was an early innovation. When standards were being formulated during the 1950s there was a proposal to use 4 ft 6 in wide hard shoulders so constructed that grass would grow on them. Shoulders of that width had, however, been found to be dangerous on the German *Autobahnen* and initially it was decided by the Ministry to adopt an 8 ft width. However, this was increased to 10 ft in the light of experience on the Preston by-pass and the southern sections of the M1. The early standard of 11 ft for the width of a lane was also brought into question, particularly by the possibility then under consideration of permitting goods vehicles and buses to be built up to 8 ft in width. There was very little firm evidence available from experience in other countries as to desirable lane widths but there seems to have been a consensus among highway engineers that 12 ft was probably about right and that was adopted in Ministry standards.

The design speed for rural motorways is 70 mile/h and for urban motorways 50 mile/h.

Considerable importance has been attached to achieving a "flowing alignment" when locating motorways and ways of achieving this were put forward by Spencer[23] in 1948. Whilst paying attention to basic engineering principles such as

Table 10.1. DTp recommended flow levels for various carriageway layouts

Road type	Peak hourly flows: vehicle/hour/carriageways*		16 hour average daily flow (both directions)	
	Standard	Max.working	Min.	Absolute max.
Urban motorways				
Dual 2 lane	3,600	3,600	—	—
Dual 3 lane	5,700	5,700	—	—
Dual 4 lane	†7,600	†7,600	—	—
Rural motorways				
Dual 2 lane	2,400	3,200	35,000	56,000
Dual 3 lane	3,600	4,800	45,000	85,000
Dual 4 lane	4,800	6,400	70,000	115,000

*Where heavy vehicles form more than 15% of the traffic, lane flows at both standard and maximum working hourly level shall be reduced as follows

    15–20%   100 vehicles/hour/lane
    20–25%   150 vehicles/hour/lane

† Where centres of interchanges are more than 3 km apart add 400 vehicles per hour.

Table 10.2. Rural motorway cross-sections

Item	1948	1963	1968/69	1980
Verge	15 ft	10 ft	5 ft	1.5 m (4.9 ft)
Hard shoulder	4 ft 6 in with lay-bys 100 ft long 10 ft wide	10 ft	9 ft 6 in	3.3 m (10.8 ft)
Nearside marginal strip	1 ft	1 ft	1 ft	0.2 m (0.6 ft) on shoulder
Carriageways	Normally 22 ft	D2 : 24 ft D3 : 36 ft	Normally 36 ft 24 ft for dual 2 lane	3 lane : 11.0 m (36 ft) 2 lane : 7.3 m (23.9 ft)
Offside marginal strip	1 ft	1 ft	6–8 in wide edge strip on carriageway surface	0.2 m (0.6 ft) on carriageway
Central reservation (half width)	7 ft 6 in	6 ft 6 in	6 ft 6 in	2 m (6.5 ft)
Formation width dual 3 lane	109 ft	129 ft	116 ft	35.6 m (117 ft)
Formation width dual 2 lane	93 ft	105 ft	92 ft	28.2 m (92.5 ft)
Source	Aldington[19]	Smith[20]	Select Committee[21]	DTp[22]

balancing cut and fill he proposed that there should be a correct phasing of horizontal and vertical curvature so as to present a pleasing appearance of the road ahead by "obviating the appearance of kinks or optical malalignments." The objectives of flowing alignment were later set out in the Ministry of Transport's memorandum on the layout of roads in rural areas,[14] and one of the important principles recommended was that short curves and straights should not be used but instead horizontal and vertical curves should be as long as possible. It seems that straights were not favoured and one of the reasons for that was the fear that they would be monotonous and would lead to loss of concentration by drivers. Probably most drivers on British motorways would agree that the alignments adopted are usually attractive to travel along, but there does not seem to have been any critical assessment made of the general principles followed; it could be that long straights would be equally acceptable.

On rural motorways horizontal curves have an absolute minimum radius of 510 m and a desirable minimum of 960 m. Transition curves are desirable on curves with a radius less than 3,000 m and are regarded as essential on curves with a radius less than 1,500 m.

Vertical curves are provided at all changes of gradient and the curvature has to be large enough to provide safe stopping sight distances. At intersections, horizontal and vertical curves are made so as to give as generous sight distances as possible.

Gradients are normally not more than 3% but in hilly country 4% is acceptable.

Motorway interchanges are of several designs, the most common being the two-level kind with a roundabout over the motorway. This type gives good visibility to drivers on the side roads and helps to slow up traffic leaving the motorway. One of the most economical types is the diamond arrangement where the slip roads to and from the motorway make simple junctions with the side road; this type of junction is not regarded as being suitable for side roads carrying appreciable volumes of traffic.

In the case of motorway to motorway interchanges, designers are recommended[24] to consider non-free flow solutions first as they are likely to be cheaper. This type of interchange should be designed to allow the through movements to travel on the main route at the design speed; links for turning movements should normally be designed to a lower speed than through routes.

Research has been carried out by several workers[25-28] on the capacity of interchanges, particularly the areas where merging takes place and design guide lines have been drawn up. In some areas, e.g. near Birmingham, traffic volumes have reached levels that result in congestion at the interchanges. The solution to the problems in these areas could well involve major new road works although some temporary relief might be achieved by traffic control. Traffic signals are used in some cases in peak hours on the side roads so as to reduce the risk of traffic backing-up on off-ramps on to the carriageways of the motorway. There is a need for further study of ways of coping with these problems; and if traffic growth continues major road works will almost certainly be required to provide the needed extra traffic capacity.

The motorway environment

The environment of a motorway has been defined by Williams[29] as "everything touching the lives of the people on it or in its vicinity" and this could be extended to include fauna and flora as well as people. The principal factors to be taken into account in assessing the environment associated with a motorway are appearance, weather, noise and pollution.

The landscaping of motorways and the concept of "flowing alignment" have figured in the layout of motorways from the start. The Ministry of Transport, besides setting up the Advisory Committee on the Landscape Treatment of Trunk Roads in 1956, a little later also appointed landscape architects and horticulturalists to take part in the design and layout of trunk roads.[5] Prior to this, in 1954, a committee drawn from representatives of motoring organisations and several conservation societies had issued a report on the landscape treatment of roads[30] in which were set out principles and methods of "treating land acquired for present and future road purposes and land adjacent to it." In a foreword to the report the Minister of Transport and Civil Aviation, the late the Rt Hon. Alan Lennox-Boyd (later Lord Boyd), commended the report and hoped that the new road programme which he had just announced would give an opportunity for the principles in the report to be put into practice.

Practical aspects of landscaping roads were described by Rose[31]. He identified four main factors affecting the appearance of a road in the countryside, namely the surroundings; the overall size and scale of the road; the contrast between the firm parallel lines of construction and the irregular pattern of the countryside; and the appearance of bridges. Flattened slopes, rounded at shoulders and toes, smooth the road into the countryside, although this may be at the expense of more land-take. Flatter slopes also can make maintenance, e.g. mowing, easier and they can sometimes be used for agriculture. The treatment of slag heaps where motorways have been built in mining areas has led to a general improvement in the environment.

Planting of trees and shrubs has been used extensively in landscaping motorways and well over 20 million trees and shrubs have been planted on trunk roads and motorways since the motorway programme began.[5]

The treatment of motorways in urban areas is more complex and brings in particularly questions of noise and pollution as well as appearance and severance, and these issues were discussed in some detail by the Urban Motorways Committee[32] and their Project Team. Nuisance from noise can be reduced by sound insulation of properties affected and by noise barriers, although these can be visually intrusive. Earth-mounding has been found to be effective in some cases and to be less objectionable visually. There are cases, however, where a satisfactory solution can only be achieved by expensive tunnel or cut-and-cover techniques.

Pollution arises from airborne fumes and dust created by motor traffic and from chemicals dissolved in water which runs off the road surface. The view of the Urban Motorways Committee Project Team writing in 1973 was that the "... consensus of opinion in Britain is that although the effects of vehicle emissions must be very closely watched, particularly as traffic volumes increase, these do not at present constitute a general health hazard".

An interesting feature, particularly of rural motorways, is the protected habitat provided for plants and wild life by the banks and verges alongside the carriageways. Long-term studies are being carried out by the Nature Conservancy into these matters[33] and Dame Sylvia Crowe[34] has observed that many motorways have "linear Nature Reserves along their verges" and that their flanking trees form a background to the landscape on each side.

Earthworks

Earthworks can account for a substantial part of the cost of building a motorway. To achieve a satisfactory quality in the finished road it is essential that the earthworks on which the road is founded are properly compacted and consolidated. In the early days of road construction reliance was placed on compaction by traffic and by allowing relatively long periods for earthworks to settle. When the first sections of the M1 were built the passage of construction traffic over the fill was relied on to a large extent to consolidate embankments to acceptable densities[35]. With the motorway programme it has been important to complete contracts within 2 to 3 years and the necessary compaction therefore had to be achieved at the time of construction. A considerable amount of research was carried out on the performance of plant used for compaction[36] and into the rate of settlement of embankments[37].

Before 1969 earthwork compaction was covered by an end result specification clause relating to air voids,[5] but after that date a method specification was introduced instead whereby the minimum number of passes of various roller types and weights were defined for various thicknesses and classes of soil; this specification was based on the research at the Road Research Laboratory to which reference has just been made. The reason for the change was said to be to speed up approval of earthworks, but difficulties have been found in applying the procedure in practice[38] because of problems relating to the responsibilities of the Engineer and the Contractor.

The quality of material suitable for use as fill has been changed as a result of research and experience and it is possible to use lower grade material, though this may be at the cost of slower construction[35]. Waste materials such as slag and pulverised fuel ash have been used extensively in a number of contracts, but their use on environmental rather than economic grounds has not been successful because of the difficulty over assessing the value of environmental benefits.

It is inevitable during the actual construction of motorways that there is a degree of disturbance caused by the noise from construction plant and lorries and by the dust and dirt stirred up by earthworks. Although exempt from the provisions of the Control of Pollution Act of 1974, the Crown has given an undertaking to abide by the spirit of the Act. This means that a degree of control can be exercised over the type of plant or machinery which may be used, the hours that it may be used, and the noise level coming from the site. A study was carried out on the M27 to assess the usefulness of belt conveyors for earthmoving in road construction[39] and it appeared that where material had to be moved more than 1.5 km a belt conveyor system could be more economical than scrapers and dump trucks and could eliminate construction traffic on existing roads and streets thus providing environmental advantages as well.

Drainage

The basic design requirements for motorway drainage have been defined[40] as motorway cross drainage, which is that needed to maintain the natural drainage pattern of the country through which the route passes, and motorway surface water drainage. The precise arrangements for drainage are a matter for detailed design in specific cases but it seems that the main motorway drainage system being used is in the form of a combined surface water-French drain. Pipes of steel or concrete or precast forms are preferred for culverts to in situ construction[38]. The design of drainage systems to cope with storm water on motorways has been the subject of research[41,42] from which two methods of hydrological design were evolved.

In 1967 full-scale experiments were started on the M40 High Wycombe by-pass to compare the ability of a wide range of bituminous surfacings to retain a non-skid performance when wet. Included in the trials was a section with a pervious overlay to see to what extent the spray thrown up by vehicles on wet roads could be reduced. Rain-water could percolate through the pervious layer and flow laterally across the impervious surface layer below to the side drains. Spray was reduced substantially by this arrangement.[3] Further extensive trials have confirmed this finding but the effect is reduced as the overlay becomes clogged by compaction and debris. The long-term economic value of the technique is still being assessed.

Pavement design and construction

In describing the specifications relating to pavement design at the time the London–Birmingham motorway was built, Baker[43] wrote that the Ministry of Transport standard specification covered both rigid and flexible forms of construction and included alternatives in the case of flexible pavements depending on the materials locally available and site conditions. The decision between the rigid and flexible forms depended mainly on comparative costs. For rigid forms, the design was based on recommendations in the Road Research Laboratory's Road note 19[44] on the design thickness of concrete roads; this had been issued in 1955 with an addendum in 1957. For flexible forms design was based on layered construction with a total thickness determined by the Californian Bearing Ratio (CBR) of the subgrade which was measured during the initial soil survey and also during the course of construction.

As Silverleaf[2] has pointed out, pavement design problems were revealed by early failures on the London–Birmingham motorway which were attributable to unsatisfactory surfacing materials, inadequate base materials and construction processes, and a substantially heavier traffic loading than anticipated. Mainly as a result of experience with the early motorways the Ministry of Transport and the Road Research Laboratory, in collaboration with representatives of the County Surveyors' Society, the Association of Consulting Engineers and certain trade organisations, drew up a guide to the structural design of flexible and rigid pavements for new roads, the first edition of which was published as Road note 29 in 1960 with revisions in 1965 and in 1970.[45] This guide brought together the results of many years of research and of practical experience.

Some of the early surfacings on flexible pavements were specified to have a high stone content (55%) as it was thought that this would give good skidding resistance and riding quality and would obviate the need for hand-spreading of chippings which led to lack of uniformity. These surfacings, however, proved to be pervious to water, and this led to stripping of the base course binder and failure of the surfacing. The development at the Road Research Laboratory of a mechanised chipping spreader which gave a uniform and controllable rate of spread enabled a lower stone content (30%) asphalt to be used into which could be rolled precoated chippings. This process has proved highly successful and continues to be used today.

Problems arose with the measurement of CBR values of wet cohesive soils because of the influence on them of the method of sample preparation and compaction. To overcome some of these difficulties Road note 29 provides values of estimated CBR values for various British soil types which can be used in place of measured values if necessary.

The earlier editions of Road note 29 used design criteria based on the number of commercial vehicles per day expected 20 years after construction. The latest edition has changed this approach and designs are now based on the cumulative total of "standard" axles expected to be carried during the "design life" of the road. The standard axle load chosen is 8,200 kg (1,800 lb); in terms of numbers and damaging power it represents the most damaging class of axle load in Britain. The equivalent number of standard axles is that number that has the same damaging power as the actual traffic on the road.

During 1969 the political decision was taken to build some motorways with concrete pavements. A requirement was introduced by the Ministry to seek tenders for rigid as well as flexible pavements for new roads and unreinforced of the same thickness as reinforced pavements were permitted on heavily trafficked roads[5]. Since 1971 concrete pavements have been designed on the basis of the third edition of Road note 29 for a cumulative axle load calculated over a period of 40 years. Standard concrete paving plant used in early years has been to a large extent replaced by slipform equipment. Slipform pavers originated in the USA and were adapted to use under British conditions as a result of joint research and practical experience.[46]

Although the design procedures have been the subject of much investigation and refinement there are problems to be overcome in the actual processes of construction. It has been pointed out[35] that the pavement has to be built in a series of discrete operations spread over appreciable periods of time during which weather and construction traffic can cause serious damage to the pavement layers, particularly to the formation. The Department of Transport's current design standards include a capping layer over the formation as a specific element of the pavement and this can provide the contractor with a working platform giving access through the site for the completion of earthworks and drainage.

The use of a concrete haunch between pavement and hard shoulder proved to be a source of weakness because of water becoming trapped at the haunch. The use of wire-controlled paving machines led to the haunch being dispensed with in many cases, but this in turn had the disadvantage of removing what contractors found to be a firm datum line along the motorway.

Structures

Motorways, being limited access highways, have to pass over or under a great many other roads besides having to cross other obstacles such as rivers, canals or railways. In 1966[47] it was estimated that on the 384 miles of motorway then completed there were some 2.65 structures per mile on the motorways. The cost of those structures was some 25% of the total cost of motorways in rural areas and 30% in urban areas. Motorway structures are of several kinds, built of steel and/or concrete and include: interchanges, ranging from the relatively simple diamond type to the complex structures such as at Almondsbury where the M4 and M5 join and at the junction of the M8 and A8 at Baillieston in Glasgow; bridges, ranging from farm-access bridges to the Severn Bridge; viaducts, such as at Tinsley on the M1 and at Chiswick on the M4; and tunnels, as in Leeds and on the M4 in Newport. A brief description of some of these has been given in chapters 7, 8 and 9 and Drake[48] has described interchange and bridge design with examples taken from motorways in Lancashire.

Motorway bridges have to be designed to meet Department of Transport standards and specifications for road and bridge works. These have evolved during the years during which motorways have been built and the Department has issued technical memoranda and other guidance notes to keep practice up to date. In doing this the Department has worked closely with British Standards committees in preparing the British Standard-code of practice covering steel, concrete and composite bridges.[49] Some aspects of design according to earlier Ministry guidance have been described by Hall[50].

As mentioned in chapter 6, the design and construction of steel box girder bridges was brought into question by the accidents on the Milford Haven Bridge in Wales and the Yarra Bridge in Melbourne, and this led to the setting up of a committee under Sir Alec Merrison to inquire into the basis of design and the method of erection of steel box girder bridges. That committee issued "rules" covering these aspects, based on the limit state design concept, which were adopted by the Department of Transport. Pending the results of the inquiry, restrictions were placed on traffic crossing existing steel box girder bridges which remained in force until any necessary strengthening needed to comply with the Merrison rules had been carried out.

Basically bridges must be structurally sound in performance and service and they are required to be of an acceptable standard of appearance within limits of overall economy. In this connection proposed designs of major structures are submitted by the Department of Transport to the Royal Fine Art Commission for acceptance.

In 1973 the Department of Transport introduced a Technical Approval and Certification System to unify the approach to structural standards of bridges with the object of guarding against serious errors in design. The system has been described by Bridle[51] and all Department of Environment bridge designs of any significance have to be formally approved in principle. Each case has to be referred to a Technical Approval Authority (TAA) which may be the Bridge Engineering Division of the Department of the Environment or a Road Construction Unit headquarters. The TAA can agree proposals by the designer for deletions from the Technical Approval (TA) list of general codes, standards and bridges engineering technical memoranda as well as including extra requirements needed for any particular structure. The design office must then issue certificates of design and check to the TAA. Three categories of check have been established.

Category I. A certificate is required stating that the design conforms to the TA list and to TAA instructions, that the design has been accurately translated into contract drawings and that a check has been made within the design team by someone other than the originator.

Category II. Two certificates are required, one as for category I and the other stating that the design has been checked by an independent team in the design office.

Category III. As for category II but the independent check must be made by a different design organisation.

The procedures also require new certificates where conditions arise during construction which have not been allowed for in design.

This system has been described by Sriskandan[52] as being needed to overcome the problem of coping with checking the large number of designs being submitted to the Department. He thought that it was not true that the system stifled innovation. He also referred to the steps taken by the Department to introduce quality control during construction, making reference to failures that had occurred with falsework and to the certification system for falsework introduced by the Department. Yeadon and Stevens[38] have also remarked on the problems at site level regarding responsibility for falsework as a result of the Health and Safety at Work Act; they queried to what extent statutory requirements under the Act related to the supply of individual certification for falsework.

Research to aid in the design of bridges and other structures has been carried out in Government laboratories, universities and trade associations, and some of this has been briefly described by Silverleaf.[4] Some of the research undertaken by the Transport and Road Research Laboratory has been concerned with fatigue in steel bridges. The design life of British bridges is 120 years, during which time there may be up to a billion (10^9) cycles of potentially damaging stress produced by goods vehicles. Early research indicated that fatigue-cracking was likely to occur under traffic loading in orthotropic bridge decks then being designed. According to Silverleaf[4] this was not given sufficient attention at the time, with the result that fatigue-cracking began to appear within a relatively short time in the life of some steel structures, particularly in welded joints. These failures have been on main girders of short and medium span bridges having concrete decks as well as in welded joints of orthotropic steel decks. A notable example is the cracking which occurred in some of the welds on the Severn Bridge which required to be repaired some 10 years after the bridge was opened.

Besides traffic stresses, fatigue can also be caused by resonant stresses arising from vibration of structures. Vibrations of this kind were developing in the inclined hangers of the Severn Bridge and it was necessary to fit dampers to avoid possible problems.

Research has also been carried out into a number of other aspects of design and maintenance, including bearings, joints, deck surfacings, waterproofing, corrosion and paint systems.

Traffic guidance and control

The advent of motorways with their restrictions on access and high speed traffic meant that a fresh appraisal had to be made of existing means of communicating with drivers and with exercising control over them. Soon after the motorway programme was launched, the Minister of Transport appointed a committee under the Chairmanship of Sir Colin Anderson "To consider and advise the Minister of Transport and Civil Aviation what traffic signs should be provided on the new motorways". The committee sought views of a wide cross-section of organisations who might be interested and had technical support in their work from the Road Research Laboratory[53]. Their initial proposals were first tried experimentally on the Preston by-pass and, after slight modification to some direction signs, were then tried on the London–Birmingham motorway. The committee issued a final report[54] in 1962 and the signs currently in use on motorways are essentially those they recommended.

Some direction signs on unlit motorways have had individual illumination provided but as this has proved expensive the policy now is to use the new high intensity reflective material on these signs instead. Where motorways are lit, however, all major signs are lit individually.

To assist drivers at some of the more complex interchanges, especially where there are heavy flows of weaving traffic, overhead gantry type signs have been introduced.

In addition to the normal traffic lane markings, motorways have been provided with a light coloured marginal strip along the edges of the carriageways and in some places coloured reflecting studs have been added to assist drivers at night to identify the edge of the carriageway and exit and entry lanes at interchanges. On some motorways hard shoulders of a colour contrasting with that of the carriageway have been used to help delineate the edge of the carriageway.

Emergency telephones, separate from the national telephone network, are provided at 1 mile intervals for use in the case of breakdown or accident. These telephones are connected to centres under police control. In the light of experience it became clear that some means of communicating with drivers other than by the static signs was needed, e.g. to warn of fog or accidents, and in 1966 a signal system was introduced to advise drivers what action they should take in such circumstances. Late in 1969 work began on the installation of a standard national motorway communications system[5] based on a small number of regionally based computers from which police could monitor both motorway signals and telephones. These systems are still undergoing development and may eventually lead to the introduction of automatic detection of incidents and bad weather and to a more sophisticated display of information on the signals.

Television surveillance is in use in some areas, e.g. on the Midland Links, and it seems likely that this will be extended in future as an aid to better traffic control.[55]

Safety fences were not used on the early motorways except on the approaches to bridges and where the motorway was on an embankment more than 20 ft high. The occurrence of an increasing number of cross-over accidents led to a change of policy towards the use of safety fences on the central reservation. At the request of the Ministry of Transport, the Road Research Laboratory undertook a programme of research into a suitable design of fence for this purpose and also into a design for use on bridges, and this work resulted in the adoption of a tensioned beam guard rail on central reservations and of steel and aluminium parapets on bridges. More recently work was carried out on concrete safety fences.[4]

Lighting of motorways has been somewhat controversial, in part because evidence of its effects has not been decisive. In the beginning the only lighting provided was at terminal roundabouts but gradually a number of individual sites were lit, e.g. the London end of the M4 and an urban section of the M1 at its southern end. Accidents on some uphill gradients at night and accidents in fog on busy motorways led to further lengths being lit and currently all rural motorways carrying more than 55,000 vehicles/16 hour day are lit.[5] Lighting systems on motorways usually use double bracketed 12 m high columns located in the central reserve, but catenary-supported lanterns suspended from columns with a frangible base in the central reserve have also been used.

Anti-dazzle screens on the central reservation were tried experimentally on a short length of the London–Birmingham motorway and other trials have been made but no conclusive result as to their effectiveness seems to have been reached.[4]

Service areas

Service areas where drivers can stop for a rest, refuel and obtain refreshments are provided at varying intervals, averaging some 25 miles, along the motorways. The size of the areas is also variable, some of those on the "London–Birmingham" section of the M1 being about 12 acres in extent whilst later ones ranged up to 20 acres. The use of service areas is discussed further in chapter 11.

Maintenance

The Marshall Committee on Highway Maintenance[56] identified three main groups of activities under the heading of maintenance: structure; aids to movement and safety; and amenity. Structure included items such as reconstruction, resurfacing, maintenance of bridges and embankments. Movement and safety included snow and ice clearance and the repair and maintenance of traffic signs, road markings and lighting; and amenity included grass cutting and maintenance of hedges and trees.

Although the Secretary of State for Transport in England and the Secretaries of State for Scotland and for Wales are the highway authorities for trunk roads in England, Scotland and Wales respectively, they do not employ direct labour organisations and maintenance of the motorways is in the hands of County Councils as agent authorities for their Departments. Maintenance programmes are drawn up by the counties after discussion with the Departments and the counties carry out agreed programmes within financial limits approved by the Departments.

County Councils carry out routine maintenance and small jobs using either their own direct labour organisations where they exist or term contractors; major repairs are normally carried out by contractors. For winter maintenance the Departments own and maintain fleets of vehicles especially designed for snow ploughing and salt spreading, which are operated by the County Councils from depots located alongside the motorways and which are supplemented by County Council owned vehicles in certain authorities.

Reference has been made to the structural failures of some of the earlier motorways, particularly as a result of the higher wheel loads imposed on them than had been forecast at the time they were designed. Severe problems of rutting in nearside wheeltracks were caused by the intense canalisation of commercial traffic in the 1970s on some motorways. These problems were largely solved, partly by improved pavement design and partly by specially designed asphalt wearing courses.

It is clearly important that designers pay particular attention to future maintenance problems, e.g. by providing access to vulnerable parts of structures and by anticipating future traffic problems which arise during maintenance. The Department of Transport's *Policy for roads: England, 1980*[57] drew attention to the growing importance of structural maintenance of the motorway network and to the disruption of traffic that major roadworks can cause. To reduce this, it has become necessary to phase the timing of major repairs and to pay particular attention to the traffic arrangements at the sites where repairs are taking place. Measures which have been used include the avoidance of peak periods such as holiday weekends, night-time working, the ready availability of recovery vehicles for dealing with breakdowns and accidents, and the use of the hard shoulder as an extra lane (this has underlined the importance of constructing shoulders capable of being used in this way). The use of the hard shoulder has been necessary where contra-flow arrangements have been used, as in the case of some major carriageway reconstruction works.

Following recommendations of the Marshall Committee, a systematic approach to maintenance needs has been developed and computerised methods of data handling and analysis have been evolved for roads in general, not only motorways.[58] Among data collected are those on the strength of flexible pavements and of skidding resistance which are obtained, respectively, by the use of the deflectograph and SCRIM, the Sideway force Coefficient Routine Investigation Machine. The design of overlays for strengthening pavements using data from the deflectograph has been described by Lister and Kennedy.[59]

Repairs to surfaces have sometimes been effected using surface dressings but there are problems with loose chippings if proper control is not exercised over the work. In the case of concrete roads, skid resistance which has been lost by the polishing action of traffic has been restored by cutting grooves in the concrete surface; care has to be taken (e.g. by randomising the groove spacing) to avoid excessive and unpleasant noise caused by tyre-road interaction.

The more routine type of maintenance of motorways includes cleansing and maintenance of the drainage system, white-lining and renewing reflecting road studs, cleaning and repairing traffic signs and signals, maintenance of street lighting, maintenance of the verge and central reservation and of fencing, painting steel bridges and maintenance of joints and bearings on bridges[35].

Because of the strategic importance of the motorway network it is essential that so far as possible the motorways are kept free from snow and ice in the winter months. This work has been carried out by County Councils, and strikes by council workers in the winter of 1978/79 meant that some motorways were not cleared of snow of ice on occasion. The cost of winter maintenance had been rising towards the end of the 1970s and in March 1981 the Minister of Transport set up a committee to look into the use of private contractors to carry out winter maintenance. The committee was to examine methods of improving efficiency and economy consistent with safety for the travelling public and with ensuring effective control over expenditure. A report[60] was issued in November 1981 by the Department of Transport setting out a statement of service and code of practice for winter maintenance of motorways and trunk roads.

References

1. MINISTRY OF TRANSPORT, SCOTTISH DEVELOPMENT DEPARTMENT and WELSH OFFICE. *Specification for road and bridge works.* HMSO, London, 1976; supplement no. 1, 1978.
2. GLANVILLE SIR W.H. The London–Birmingham motorway. Economic and traffic studies. *Proc Instn Civ. Engrs*, 1969, **25**, 333–352.
3. LYONS D.J. Trends in research on motorway design and use. *Proceedings of the conference on motorways in Britain.* Institution of Civil Engineers, London, 1971.
4. SILVERLEAF A. The contribution of research. *Proceedings of the conference on 20 years of British motorways.* Institution of Civil Engineers, London, 1980.
5. WILLIAMS H. *et al.* Standards, specifications and design. *Proceedings of the conference on 20 years of British motorways.* Institution of Civil Engineers, London, 1980.
6. MATSON T.M. *et al. Traffic engineering.* McGraw-Hill, New York, 1955.
7. DEPARTMENT OF SCIENTIFIC AND INDUSTRIAL RESEARCH, and ROAD RESEARCH LABORATORY. *Research on road traffic.* HMSO, London, 1965.
8. DICK A.C. and WOOTTON H.J. *Transport planning and modelling teach-in.* Institution of Civil Engineers, London, 1977.
9. DEPARTMENT OF TRANSPORT. *Report of the Advisory Committee on Trunk Road Assessment.* HMSO, London, 1977.
10. GOLDSTEIN A. *Motorway route location studies.* RTPI, Keele, 1966.
11. HUTTON T.E. The design of motorways. *Proc. Instn Civ. Engrs*, Part 2, 1953, **2**, 711–737.
12. COBURN T.M. *et al. The London–Birmingham motorway. Traffic and economics.* Department of Scientific and Industrial Research Road Research technical paper no. 46. HMSO, London, 1960.

13. CHARLESWORTH G. and PAISLEY J.L. The economic assessment of returns from road works. *Proc. Instn Civ. Engrs*, 1959, **14**, 229–254.
14. PARKINSON M. *Economic aspects.* PTRC, 1980.
15. DEPARTMENT OF TRANSPORT. *COBA 9 manual: a method of economic appraisal of highway schemes.* Department of Transport, London, 1981.
16. MINISTRY OF TRANSPORT. *Memorandum on the design of roads in rural areas.* Memorandum 780. HMSO, London, 1961.
17. MINISTRY OF TRANSPORT, SCOTTISH DEVELOPMENT DEPARTMENT and WELSH OFFICE. *Layout of roads in rural areas.* HMSO, London, 1968.
18. DEPARTMENT OF TRANSPORT. *Design flows for motorways and all-purpose roads.* Directorate General Highways technical memorandum H6/74. Department of Transport, London, 1974.
19. ALDINGTON H.E. *Design and layout of motorways.* Institution of Highway Engineers, London, 1948.
20. SMITH J.G. Motorway progress. *Traffic engineering and control,* 1963, **5**, No. 3.
21. SELECT COMMITTEE OF THE HOUSE OF COMMONS. *Sixth report session 1968–69. Motorways and trunk roads.* HMSO, London, 1969.
22. DEPARTMENT OF TRANSPORT. *Manual of standard highway designs.* Rural motorways: typical cross sections: verge and central reserve treatment. Department of Transport, London, 1972, Technical memo H1/72, Drawings RM/B/1, RM/B/2.
23. SPENCER W.H. The co-ordination of horizontal and vertical alignment of high speed roads. *Instn Civ. Engrs road paper no. 27.* ICE, London, 1949.
24. DEPARTMENT OF TRANSPORT. *Design of rural motorway to motorway interchanges: general guide lines.* Technical memorandum H6/75. Department of Transport, London, 1975.
25. SALTER R.J. and EL-HANNA F. *Investigation into the merging action of vehicles entering limited access highways.* Postgraduate School of Studies in Civil and Structural Engineering, University of Bradford, 1978.
26. ACKROYD L.W. and MADDEN A.J. Vehicle behaviour during entering and leaving motorways. *Symposium on geometric road design standards, Helsingor.* OECD, 1976.
27. SEDDON P.A. *et al. Merging on urban motorways.* Department of Civil Engineering, University of Salford, 1974.
28. BURROW I.J. *The capacity of motorway merges.* TRRL report no. LR 679. Transport and Road Research Laboratory, Crowthorne, 1976.
29. WILLIAMS SIR E.O. The motorway and its environment. *Jl R. Inst. Br. Archit.,* 3rd series, 1956, **63**, No. 4.
30. CPRE. *The landscape treatment of roads.* Report by a joint committee representing the Council for the Preservation of Rural England, the Institute of Landscape Architects, the Roads Beautifying Association, the Royal Forestry Society of England and Wales and the Standing Joint Committee of the RAC, AA and RSAC. CPRE, London, 1954.
31. ROSE R.W. Landscape engineering. *Proceedings of the conference on landscaping of motorways.* British Road Federation, London, 1962.

32. DEPARTMENT OF THE ENVIRONMENT. *New roads in towns.* Report of the Urban Motorways Committee. HMSO, London, 1972.

33. WAY J.M. Further observations on the management of road verges for amenity and wild life. *Road verges in Scotland,* 1–13. Monks Wood Experimental Station, Abbots Ripton, Huntingdon, 1970.

34. CROWE DAME S. Conservation in a changing landscape. *J. Royal Soc. Arts,* 1981, **129**, No. 5295.

35. LAING W.K. *et al.* The London–Birmingham motorway. Luton–Dunchurch: construction. *Proc. Instn Civ. Engrs,* 1960, **15**, 387–400.

36. LEWIS W.A. Full-scale studies of the performance of plant in the compaction of soils and granular base materials. *Proc. Instn Mech. Engrs,* 1966, **181**, Part 2A, No. 3.

37. MURRAY R.J. *Embankments constructed on soft foundations: settlement study of Avonmouth.* Report LR419. Road Research Laboratory, Crowthorne, 1971.

38. YEADON H.L. and STEVENS H.J. Construction and maintenance. *Proceedings of the conference on 20 years of British motorways.* Institution of Civil Engineers, London, 1980.

39. LEWIS W.A. and PARSONS A.W. The application of belt conveyors in road earthworks. *Proc. Instn Civ. Engrs,* Part 1, 1973, **54**, 425–450.

40. SIR OWEN WILLIAMS AND PARTNERS. *London–Yorkshire motorway.* Sir Owen Williams and Partners, London, 1973.

41. SWINNERTON C.J. *et al.* Conceptual model design for motorway stormwater drainage. *Civ. Engng,* 1973, Feb., 123–132.

42. SWINNERTON C.J. *et al.* A dimensionless hydrograph design method for motorway stormwater drainage systems. *J. Instn Highw. Engrs,* 1972, **19**, Nov., 2.

43. BAKER J.F.A. The London–Birmingham motorway: the general motorway plan. *Proc. Instn Civ. Engrs,* 1960, **15**, 317–332.

44. ROAD RESEARCH LABORATORY. *The design thickness of concrete roads.* HMSO, London, 1955, Road note 19.

45. ROAD RESEARCH LABORATORY. *A guide to the structural design of flexible and rigid pavements for new roads.* Road note 29. HMSO, London, 1st edition 1960; 2nd edition 1965; 3rd edition 1970.

46. BURKS A.E. Application of the slip-form paver to British road construction. *Cement lime gravel,* 1965, **40**, No. 5, 173–178.

47. MINISTRY OF TRANSPORT. *Roads in England 1965–1966.* HMSO, London.

48. DRAKE J. *Motorways.* Faber and Faber, London, 1969.

49. BRITISH STANDARDS INSTITUTION. *Steel, concrete and composite bridges.* British Standards Institution, London, 1978–82, BS 5400.

50. HALL H.A. Motorway bridge design. *J. Instn Mun. Engrs,* 1969, **96**, 86–90.

51. BRIDLE R.J. Structural safety and the Department of the Environment. *Proceedings of the 4th international safety conference.* Institution of Civil Engineers, London, 1975.

52. SRISKANDAN K. Discussion on standards, specifications and design. *Proceedings of the conference on 20 years of British motorways.* Institution of Civil Engineers, London, 1980.

53. MOORE R.L. and CHRISTIE A.W. Direction signs for motorways, *The Engineer,* 13 May 1960.

54. MINISTRY OF TRANSPORT ADVISORY COMMITTEE ON TRAFFIC SIGNS FOR MOTORWAYS. *Motorway signs.* HMSO, London, 1962.
55. BRIDLE R.J. Lessons for the future. *Proceedings of the conference on 20 years of British motorways.* Institution of Civil Engineers, London, 1980.
56. COMMITTEE ON HIGHWAY MAINTENANCE. *Report.* HMSO, London, 1970.
57. DEPARTMENT OF TRANSPORT. *Policy for roads: England, 1980.* HMSO, London, 1980.
58. NICHOLAS J.H. Management and control of highway construction and maintenance in Great Britain. *Australian Road Research Board Proc.*, 1976, 8, 25–39.
59. LISTER N.W. and KENNEDY C.K. A system for the prediction of pavement life and design of pavement strengthening. *Proceedings of the 4th international conference on structural design of asphalt pavements.* University of Michigan, Ann Arbor, 1977.
60. DEPARTMENT OF TRANSPORT. *Winter maintenance of motorways and trunk roads.* Department of Transport, London, 1981.

11

The usage of motorways

Introduction

By 1980 motorways accounted for about 10% of the total mileage run on roads in the country and the proportion was higher still, at some 16% of the total mileage run, on trunk and principal roads; about 15% of all goods traffic travelled on motorways. It is very likely that a high proportion of the population has used motorways at some time or other and that a high proportion of the goods they use have also been transported on motorways.

The higher speeds which can be sustained on motorways have made it possible for changes to take place in the kinds of journeys to be undertaken. For example, trips which might have taken 2 days to complete before motorways were available may well become achievable in half the time; and commuters can live farther away from their place of work. Drivers have had to learn new skills in driving at high speed for long periods and motor vehicle manufacturers have had to design vehicles suitable for motorway use.

Motorways have proved safer than all-purpose roads, but there is a continuing need to seek ways of reducing the risk of those accidents which occur since they tend to involve serious injury. Particularly hazardous conditions can arise from adverse weather, such as fog, and from lane closures and a great deal of attention is being paid to ways of controlling traffic under those conditions. Controlling traffic and enforcing the law at the high speeds which occur on motorways have created new problems for the police.

It was recognised from the outset that the travelling public would need facilities on the motorways where they could stop for refreshments and for fuel, and where toilets were available. These facilities are provided in service areas, the standards of which have come in for a certain amount of criticism over the years.

Provision has also had to be made for dealing with emergencies on the motorways such as are occasioned by vehicle breakdowns and accidents; the telephone system linked to the police is the means whereby the appropriate service can be called to the scene.

236

Some of these aspects of motorway usage will now be considered in a little more detail.

Traffic volumes

In 1979 the average annual daily traffic flow over the whole motorway network was some 30,000 vehicles per 24 hour day[1] but there was a wide variation about the mean at different points on the motorway network; for example, a daily flow of 6,000 vehicles was recorded on the M45 compared with a figure of over 90,000 vehicles on the M4 near London. Williams and Laugharne[2] have given some data on the growth of traffic on motorways from which it may be deduced that the average daily flow on the motorway network approximately doubled between 1960 and 1977; during this time the network increased 15-fold in length and the vehicle-mileage increased 30-fold. This is a growth rate in traffic volume of between 4 and 5% compound and is not very different for the growth rate on the rest of the road system. However, substantially greater growth rates have been recorded, e.g. total 24 hour weekday traffic on the M4 Slough by-pass from mid-1964 to mid-1969 traffic increased 2.8 times[3]. On the dual two-lane M4 Chiswick flyover some 12 miles east of Slough weekday traffic volumes between mid-1969 and mid-1974 increased by only 15%[4]; the traffic volumes in 1974 were high, about 80,000 vehicles/day, and the low growth was almost certainly a result of capacity restraints imposed by the flyover.

As the mileage of motorways has increased an increasing proportion of the total vehicle-mileage on the road system has been run on motorways. Thus in 1968,[1] when motorways comprised some 0.3% of the total road system, they carried 4% of the total vehicle-mileage; by 1978, when they constituted about 0.7% of the total length, they were carrying about 10% of the total vehicle-mileage and almost 20% of the total vehicle-mileage run in non-built-up areas. Thus it appears that the motorway system has attracted to it an amount of traffic about in proportion to its increase in length.

In 1978 the composition of motorway traffic was as shown in Table 11.1[1]. About three quarters of the traffic was cars and taxis. Goods vehicles accounted for most of the remainder; the heavier goods vehicles amounted to some 18% of the total. On roads other than motorways in non-built-up areas, these heavier vehicles constituted less than 9% of the total; since motorways are located for the

Table 11.1. Composition of motorway traffic in 1979: %

Cars and taxis	73.7
Motorcycles etc.	0.5
Buses and coaches	0.9
Light vans	6.3
Other goods vehicles	18.6

most part in those areas they can be seen to be acting as important "freight-ways" in the more rural parts of the country.

The amount of traffic on motorways varies somewhat from month to month, being least in the winter months and most in the summer. The nature of this variation is illustrated by data for 1979 shown in Table 11.2 which has been compiled from *Transport statistics. Great Britain 1969–1979*[1]. There is a greater variation between months in the case of cars and taxis than in the case of goods vehicles and the variation of the total motorway traffic is not very dissimilar to that on all non-built-up roads.

The daily variation of motorway traffic in 1979, averaged over the year, is shown in Table 11.3. On motorways the average weekday had about 15% of the total traffic during the week and the traffic on Saturday and Sunday combined was about a quarter of the total. Somewhat similar proportions applied to trunk and principal roads in non-built-up areas.

Some studies have been made of the distribution of traffic between the lanes of motorway carriageways. Hollis and Evans[4] analysed data obtained on the M1, M4 and M6 and found that the distribution of heavy vehicle flows between the left-hand and middle lanes could be related to the total flow of heavy vehicles by two simple expressions, namely

$$\text{Flow in nearside lane} = 1200Q/(1200+Q)$$
$$\text{Flow in middle lane} = Q^2/(1200+Q)$$

where Q = total flow of heavy vehicles/hour. No similar relations could be established for the total flow of vehicles.

Table 11.2. Monthly variation of traffic in 1979 as percentage of total

Month	Motorways			Non-built-up roads: all vehicles
	Cars and taxis	Goods	Total	
January	5.3	6.6	5.6	6.1
February	5.9	7.6	6.3	6.4
March	7.5	9.0	7.8	8.0
April	8.5	8.1	8.4	8.4
May	8.8	8.9	8.8	9.1
June	8.6	8.7	8.7	9.1
July	10.1	8.9	9.9	9.5
August	10.8	8.0	10.1	9.8
September	9.6	8.4	9.3	9.5
October	9.2	9.4	9.3	8.7
November	7.9	9.3	8.2	7.9
December	7.8	7.1	7.6	7.5
Average month	8.33	8.33	8.33	8.33

Williams and Laugharne[2] have reported work by Ackroyd and Bettison on the distribution of traffic in the three lanes of the M1 in Nottinghamshire in 1974/78 which found that about four fifths of medium and heavy goods vehicles used the nearside lanes. The composition of traffic in the various lanes was also studied and the results showed that in the left-hand, nearside lane some 30% of the traffic was cars and 70% was goods vehicles; in the centre lane about 80% was cars and 20% was goods vehicles; and in the right-hand, off-side lane about 99% of the traffic was cars.

Silverleaf[5] has commented on the lack of information on the distribution of journeys between different locations using motorways. He drew attention to the difficulty of obtaining origin-destination data by stopping drivers: it is not practically possible, for safety reasons, to stop traffic for that purpose on motorways. He referred to registration number matching techniques which had been used in limited surveys by the Transport and Road Research Laboratory and which had shown that only a very small proportion of cars travel a long distance on motorways in the course of a journey. This is clearly an area where more work is required as information about the nature of journeys being undertaken now and forecast for the future is vital to the planning of future roads and to the management of the existing road network not only of motorways but of roads in general. Moves in this direction were being taken in the data being collected in connection with the now abandoned Regional Highway Traffic Model, but that information is now several years out of date.

Traffic speeds

When motorways first came into use there was no restriction on the speed at which drivers could travel, except that vehicles towing a caravan or trailer with fewer than four wheels could not be driven at more than 40 mile/h. In 1965 an experimental 70 mile/h limit was introduced and this was confirmed some 2 years later as described in chapter 5. Goods vehicles other than light vans have a limit of 60 mile/h. In chapter 6 reference is made to the 50 mile/h limit imposed at the time of the oil crisis in 1973/74.

Whereas the Department of Transport has established a continuing and systematic series of counts of traffic on motorways, no similar collection of infor-

Table 11.3. Daily variation of traffic in 1979

Day	Motorways	Trunk and principal non-built-up roads
Monday–Friday	75.8	73.5
Saturday	11.9	14.1
Sunday	12.3	12.4

mation on speeds has been undertaken, although speed measurements have been made from time to time for various research studies undertaken by the Transport and Road Research Laboratory and by some other workers, e.g. at universities.

Some of the earliest speed measurements on motorways were made on the M1 in clear fine weather between 1959 and 1965[6]. In 1959 the average spot speed of cars was a little under 60 mile/h; that of light goods vehicles was about 50 mile/h; that of medium goods vehicles was a little over 40 mile/h; and that of heavy goods vehicles was about 36 mile/h. Between 1959 and 1965 there was a steady upward trend in the average speed of all classes of vehicle as shown in Table 11.4.

Studies on the M1 were also made by Ackroyd and Bettison[7] between 1968 and 1973 which indicated that the percentage of cars exceeding the 70 mile/h limit increased from 15% in 1968/69 to 25% in 1972/73. Later work on the M1 by these authors between 1974 and 1978 was quoted by Williams and Laugharne[2] who gave mean speeds of traffic in the three lanes as: nearside lane 50−53 mile/h; centre lane 60−62 mile/h; and off-side lane 71−73 mile/h.

A series of observations of car speeds since 1970 has been reported by the Transport and Road Research Laboratory. Studies between 1970 and 1976[8] on sections of the A1(M), M1, M3, M4, M5, M50, M56, M6 and M62 gave the results in Table 11.5. The proportion exceeding the 70 mile/h limit at 36% in 1973 and 1976 was appreciably higher than that of 25% observed by Ackroyd and Bettison on the M1.

Other data collected by the Transport and Road Research Laboratory at two points, one on the M3 and one on the M4 between 1973 and 1979,[9] are given in Table 11.6.

Table 11.4. Rate of increase of mean speeds on the M1, 1959/65

Vehicle type	Mile/h/year
Cars	0.70
Light goods	0.71
Medium goods	0.98
Heavy goods	1.24

Table 11.5. Car speeds on selected motorways, 1970/76

	1970	1973	1976
Mean spot speed (mile/h)	63½	66½	66½
Per cent exceeding			
60 mile/h	62	75	75
70 mile/h	27	36	36
80 mile/h	7	9	8

From this somewhat fragmentary evidence it appears that the mean speed of cars and other light vehicles, which was increasing steadily in the earlier years, has probably stabilised at around the 70 mile/h level; but that means that a substantial proportion, perhaps a third or more, are exceeding the 70 mile/h legal speed limit.

Data for the speeds of goods vehicles are much more limited. The rapid increase in speed noted in the early years on the M1 almost certainly resulted from a major improvement in the performance and quality of goods vehicles, particularly the heavy vehicles, and it is probable that the heavier goods vehicles are travelling near to their 60 mile/h limit. It is likely also that the increase in fuel prices makes drivers aware of the need to drive at speeds giving economical fuel consumption.

Fuel consumption

The effects of road and traffic conditions on fuel consumption were studied at the time the M1 was opened in 1959[10]. Comparisons were made using two cars and two lorries of journey times and fuel consumption on a round trip of 125 to 130 miles between Park Street and Dunchurch using the A5/A45 and the M1. By using the motorway cars saved some 35 to 40% of time on the round trip on the A5/A45 before the motorway opened but they used between 18 and 25% more fuel. A 5 ton petrol lorry saved both time and fuel and a 5 ton diesel lorry also saved time but used slightly more fuel.

Later studies of the effect of road and traffic conditions on fuel consumption were carried out by Everall[11] on six vehicles ranging from a small saloon car (Vauxhall Viva) to a heavy goods vehicle (AEC Matador 22 ton articulated truck). At a given traffic speed, fuel consumption was less on motorways than on all-purpose roads because constant driving speed is possible on motorways. At the same average speed, 10 to 20% less fuel was used by cars on motorways than on all-purpose roads but, because the average speed on motorways was higher than

Table 11.6. Mean spot car speeds on M3 and M4: mile/h

Month	1973	1974	1975	1976	1977	1978	1979
January		57	66				
February		60	65				
March		60		69	68	69	69
April		66					69
May			66				
June							
July			67	67	68	68	
August							
September	70	69		67			
October			70		68	70	
November	58						
December	56, 53						

on all-purpose roads, the actual fuel consumption was about the same on the two classes of road. The gradients on motorways did not significantly affect the fuel consumption of cars.

The fuel consumption of goods vehicles was affected by gradient and by load. The effect of gradient rose steadily with gradient, particularly with the heavy lorry, and the effect of load was greater at lower speeds due to the extra work which had to be done during each acceleration period. Because gradients on motorways are limited to 3 to 4% and because constant speeds can be achieved under motorway conditions, fuel consumption of goods vehicles at a given speed will be less on motorways than on all-purpose roads.

More recent work has been reported by Waters,[12] who gave a break-down of the energy consumed in the UK in 1977. Petroleum accounted for 43% of the total energy supplied and 25% of the energy from petroleum was consumed by road transport, i.e. about 11% of the total energy produced. Of the total energy used by road transport 63% was taken up by cars, 11% by light goods vehicles and 20% by heavy goods vehicles, while other vehicles such as motorcycles used the remaining 6%. Waters discussed ways of economising in fuel consumption and gave data from which it could be shown that on a motorway a small car could save some 25% of its fuel by driving at an average speed of 80 km/h (50 mile/h) compared with a speed of 110 km/h (70 mile/h). Other data for fuel consumption and gross vehicle weight indicate that on a motorway a vehicle with a gross weight of 32,000 kg would save some 17% of its fuel compared with that on an all-purpose rural road; for a gross vehicle weight of 14,000 kg the saving would be about 13%.

Other savings can be achieved by reducing the air drag on a vehicle and its load. In the case of goods vehicles travelling on motorways the shape of the load carried can be an important factor affecting air drag and hence fuel consumption.

Vehicle design

There does not seem to be much published information about the influence of motorways on vehicle design. It has been suggested[13] that, whilst the development of the motorway network has resulted in major changes both in the pattern of operations of goods vehicles and in their design and construction, British-based goods vehicle manufacturers were already accustomed to exporting vehicles to markets with better road systems before the Preston by-pass was opened. (Leyland used that by-pass before it was open to traffic to test their "Comet" range of vehicles at speeds of up to 70 mile/h fully laden.) Furthermore, since motorway systems have evolved more rapidly in other developed countries the effect of Britain lagging in terms of road system development and, in particular, in vehicle gross combination weight has been serious for British-based manufacturers.

An indication of some of the developments in vehicle design was given by Webster[14] in 1965. Although he considered that the driver was the main accident risk on motorways he thought that many accidents were caused by failures of various components of a motor car which should have been noticed or checked by the driver before he set out.

Among specific improvement in vehicles and vehicle components for high speed travel Webster referred to tyres and brakes. In tyre design he instanced greater reliability, reduced wear rate and increased steering power, radial tyres and improved rubber-mix and tread patterns for high speed travel. Disc brakes were more widely used and these were safer than drum brakes on motorways in the wet.

The shape of the car body or lorry cab was important, particularly the view to the rear, since good visibility all round was essential on motorways. He noted that many safety features incorporated into body design were of value generally and not just on motorways and listed among those features anti-burst door locks, interior soft padding, avoidance of sharp projections, strong seat-belt anchorages, collapsible steering wheels and columns and locating fuel tanks away from engines to reduce fire risk.

Engine development was based on bench-testing representing sustained high speed operation. For petrol engines this would typically involve cycling engine speeds between 4,000 and 5,000 rev/min continuously under high power output for some 500 hours, representing 30,000 miles of severe motorway running. Diesel engines for commercial vehicles would be run 1,000 hours under power interspersed with rest periods totalling another 500 hours.

Accidents on the M1, London–Birmingham motorway

One of the principal arguments put forward in favour of motorways was that they were safer than all-purpose roads, and it was therefore of particular interest when the first motorways were built to see whether this was in fact the case under British conditions.

Early figures for the M1 London–Birmingham motorway were quoted by Glanville.[15] For the period from November 1959 to February 1960 the number of casualties per million vehicle-miles was 1.4 and this could be compared with a rate on the parallel A5 in 1956 of 3.4 per million vehicle-miles. Glanville, in commenting that the casualty rate had been considerably better than halved, suggested that since the motorway was only just beginning it might be that time would show that the initial figures would be improved with experience. At the time Glanville did not have sufficient reliable data available to separate out various categories of injury, but this was done later by Coburn,[16] some of whose results are shown in Table 11.7. These more complete results confirmed Glanville's predictions that an improvement in the accident rate might be expected as experience was gained with using the motorway. However Table 11.7 shows that while the accident rate and number of fatalities per vehicle-mile were appreciably lower on the motorway than on the all-purpose trunk route the number of fatalities per accident were somewhat higher on the motorway; for every 100 in-

Table 11.7. Accident rates on London–Birmingham motorway, M1/M10/M45 and trunk route A5/A45: accidents/million vehicle-miles

	Trunk route	Motorway	
	1958/59	1959/60	1960/61
All injury accidents	2.1	0.7	0.5
Fatalities	0.14	0.07	0.04
All casualties	3.2	1.2	0.9

jury accidents on the trunk route there were about 7 fatalities, compared with between 8 and 10 on the motorway.

On the basis of the results in Table 11.7 Coburn concluded that the motorway saved about 20 to 30 fatalities and about 600 to 800 casualties in its first year of operation. An analysis of the changes in numbers of accidents on main roads near the motorway was made by Newby and Johnson;[17] they concluded that on roads within approximately 5 miles of the motorway injury accidents were about 20% fewer in the 12 months after the motorway came into use, but that at greater distances the reductions were much smaller.

Newby and Johnson[18] also carried out a detailed analysis of accidents on the motorway during the first 2 years after it was opened and Adams[19] used early experience on the M1 in considering safety aspects of motorway design. Some of the conclusions reached were as follows.

—Of the total vehicles involved in accidents about one fifth were involved at terminals, junctions or interchanges.

—None of the fatal accidents occurred at terminals and less than a tenth at junctions or interchanges.

—Nearly all the accidents at terminals were due to drivers approaching too fast along the motorway (large "Reduce Speed Now" notices were fixed in February 1960).

—The junctions of motorways, interchange roundabouts and diamond type interchanges had proved to be satisfactory.

—Casualty and accident rates in dark hours were about twice those in daylight.

—At the terminals, which had street lighting, 15% of accidents occurred in the dark compared with 40% at junctions and interchanges where there was no lighting.

—On a section with an anti-dazzle screen along the central reservation, glare from approaching headlights was abolished and the screened section showed no significant change in accidents overall although there was a significant increase in accidents involving vehicles over-running the central reserve and striking the fence (in later work on the M6[20] it was concluded that an anti-dazzle screen was effective in reducing glare, was acceptable in appearance, had no adverse effect on traffic and was marginally beneficial in terms of accident reduction).

—Excluding accidents at terminals, junctions and interchanges, a total of 29% involved either a vehicle running partly or wholly on to the central reservation but not encroaching on the opposing carriageway (17%) or a vehicle crossing into the opposing carriageway (12%) (at that time crash barriers were not installed on the central reservation: Minstry of Transport policy changed in 1970).

One other study of early accident experience on the M1 was made by Hillier and Wardrop[21]. They observed that accidents in 1963 at the southern end of the southbound carriageway, particularly on two-lane sections, was relatively high and as a result of their investigations concluded that this was largely attributable to the effect of gradient, which was predominantly down hill to the south.

Accidents on the national motorway network

Accident statistics on motorways are currently included in official publications and Table 11.8 gives details about accidents and casualties taken from published data for 1979[22]. Three of the longest motorways, the M1, M4 and M6, had over 500 accidents each in the year, the accidents per km per year being highest on the M1 at 2.62, compared with the average for all M roads of 1.58. Among the other roads there were exceptionally high figures of about 15 accidents/km in the year on the 1 km length of the M41 and on the 4 km length of the A40(M) and there was another high figure of 8.0 on the 7 km of the M63, all of which warrant a more detailed study by the authorities.

There are no published statistics of traffic flows on all the motorways so that a comparison of the individual roads on the basis of the amount of traffic carried is not possible. Information is available[22], however, about accident rates on different classes of road and some data are given in Table 11.9.

These figures show that there was an overall fall in accident rates between 1969 and 1979 and that the fall was most marked in the case of fatal accidents on motorways and A(M) roads. The figures also confirm that motorways are much safer per unit distance travelled than all-purpose roads.

The numbers of accidents, especially fatalities, on most of the roads in Table 11.8 are small and comparisons between individual roads have, on that account, to be made with care. In Table 11.10 data for the roads with over 100 injury accidents in the year are shown and it appears that on the major motorways in 1979 if an injury accident did occur the chances of being killed in it ranged between about 3 and 7%, with an average figure of about 5; this was about the same as that for all-purpose roads in non-built-up areas. Table 11.11 shows how accidents were divided between daylight and darkness.

The number of accidents in the dark was about half that during the hours of daylight and, although traffic data are not available for hours of daylight and

Table 11.8. *Injury accidents and casualties in 1979 on M and A(M) roads*

Motorway	Length (km) on 31 Dec. 1979	Accidents	Accidents/km	Casualties	Fatalities
M1	305	800	2.62	1,465	31
M2	41	89	2.2	146	8
M3	65	109	1.68	186	3
M4	277	540	1.95	931	35
M5	280	303	1.08	520	19
M6	370	678	1.83	1,134	26
M8	75	182	2.43	305	6
M9	40	32	0.8	37	—
M10	5	7	1.4	12	1
M11	61	42	0.7	53	—
M18	44	30	0.7	54	1
M20	32	23	0.7	29	2
M23	27	37	1.4	73	3
M25	28	25	0.9	30	3
M27	40	32	0.8	48	2
M32	6	10	1.7	17	—
M40	51	65	1.3	111	5
M41	1	15	15	16	1
M42	13	5	0.4	5	1
M45	13	2	0.2	3	—
M50	34	15	0.4	24	1
M53	17	23	1.4	29	1
M54	9	3	0.3	5	—
M55	20	23	1.2	40	1
M56	48	45	0.9	59	2
M57	16	30	0.2	43	2
M58	5	3	0.6	3	—
M61	36	59	1.6	152	4
M62	168	286	1.70	417	15
M63	7	56	8.0	69	3
M66	17	10	0.6	11	1
M67	5	1	0.2	1	—
M69	26	10	0.4	17	1
M73	10	15	1.5	21	—
M74	25	25	1.0	43	—
M80	12	12	1.0	28	4
M85	3	2	0.7	3	—
M90	42	33	0.8	51	5
M180	39	15	0.4	28	1
M181	4	4	1	4	2

continued on facing page

Table 11.8 (contd)

M271	4	3	0.8	3	1
M275	3	3	1	4	—
M531	8	1	0.1	1	—
M602	4	3	0.8	3	—
M606	4	7	1.8	9	—
M621	9	8	0.9	10	—
M876	6	5	0.8	13	2
M898	1	2	2.	2	—
Total M	2,356	3,728	1.58	6,273	193
A1(M)	115	141	1.23	219	6
A3(M)	8	—	0	—	—
A38(M)	3	8	2.7	14	—
A40(M)	4	59	14.8	83	—
A41(M)	4	6	1.5	9	—
A48(M)	4	—	0	—	—
A57(M)	3	19	6.3	26	—
A58(M)	4	12	3	20	—
A66(M)	3	2	0.7	2	—
A102(M)	6	46	7.7	63	—
A194(M)	6	—	0	—	—
A308(M)	1	3	3	4	—
A329(M)	12	8	0.7	14	1
A423(M)	4	1	0.2	1	—
A627(M)	7	11	1.6	17	1
Total A(M)	184	316	1.72	472	8

Table 11.9. Accident rates per 10^8 vehicle-km

Road type	1969	1974	1979
M and A(M)			
Fatal	1.9	0.7	0.6
All severities	22	15	15
Built-up areas (non-motorway)			
Fatal	3.6	3.0	2.3
All severities	183	153	142
Non-built-up areas (non-motorway)			
Fatal	3.1	2.5	2.2
All severities	67	51	50

Table 11.10. *Motorways with over 100 injury accidents in 1979*

Road	Length: km	Accidents	Fatalities	Fatalities/ accident
M1	305	800	31	0.04
M3	65	109	3	0.03
M4	277	540	35	0.07
M5	280	303	19	0.06
M6	370	678	26	0.04
M8	75	182	6	0.03
M62	168	286	15	0.05
A1(M)	115	141	6	0.04
All M and A(M)	2,540	4,044	201	0.05

darkness over the motorway network, the vehicle-kilometrage run in the dark is almost certainly appreciably less than half that in daylight, so that accident rates in the dark hours are likely to be appreciably higher than in daylight. The number of fatalities in the dark was only about 10% less than the number in daylight, so that the fatality rate per vehicle-km is likely to be substantially higher at night than by day. These figures indicate that there is a prima facie case for introducing street lighting, at least on the busier motorways. However, Silverleaf[3] has commented that the limited experience of lighting short sections of motorway has given conflicting results about the effect on accident rates, partly because other changes had taken place besides lighting. It is worth noting that the ratios of day to night accidents and fatalities on motorways are rather similar to those for all-purpose roads in non-built-up areas.

Speeds and accidents

As mentioned earlier, there was no speed limit on most vehicles when motorways first came into use in Britain, but as time went on concern began to be expressed about dangers from high speeds which were occurring on the motorways and in 1965 a 70 mile/h limit was introduced on all roads, not just motor-

Table 11.11. *Accidents and fatalities in 1979 on motorways in daylight and darkness*

	All injury accidents		Fatalities	
	Daylight	Darkness	Daylight	Darkness
All M roads	2,481	1,247	102	91
All A(M) roads	210	106	6	2
Total M and A(M) roads	2,691	1,353	108	93

ways, except those already subject to a lower limit. As described in chapter 5, the Road Research Laboratory was asked to evaluate the effect and their report showed that there was a marked reduction in the speeds of cars on motorways and in the number of casualties.

The effect of the 50 mile/h speed limit imposed during the oil crisis of 1973/74 was also studied by the Transport and Road Research Laboratory and, as described in chapter 6, the reduced speeds of traffic were associated with a reduction in accidents.

Other workers[23] also made a study of the effects of the 50 mile/h limit on motorway traffic and they concluded that a 1% rise in average speed resulted in a 2.85% increase in all accidents. Their results also showed that the effect of reduced traffic volume during the period of the 50 mile/h limit was of roughly equal importance to the reduction in speed in reducing accidents.

A detailed analysis[24] of accident rates between November 1973 and July 1975 showed highly significant reductions in injury accident rates on motorways and all-purpose roads. The opinion was expressed that from a public health standpoint it was important to appreciate that the effect of speed restrictions is most apparent in the more serious accidents.

Vehicular breakdowns

Vehicular breakdowns are a potential source of danger to other drivers and, if they occur at places such as road works where flow is restricted, they can cause serious delay as well. For this reason special arrangements for clearing breakdowns and accidents are in operation in critical areas such as the Severn Bridge. This has been discussed by Maclean[25] in relation to the time required to clear an obstruction caused by a breakdown; he gives evidence which suggests that the average duration of a breakdown where there are full surveillance and recovery facilities is probably about 10 min, but that the average probably reaches 40 min where there are no special facilities other than emergency telephones available for calling for assistance.

Maclean quotes breakdown rates on motorways per million vehicle-kilometres of 30 for light vehicles and nearly 100 for heavy vehicles. Coburn[26] estimated the breakdown rate on the London–Birmingham motorway in 1959/60 as some 60 per million vehicle-miles, i.e. about 37 per million vehicle-km, a figure in reasonable accord with the more recent data given by Maclean.

Other data for breakdowns have been given by Ferguson and Jenkins[27]. For disablements they quote rates varying between 2 and 30 per million vehicle-km and refer to figures obtained by Salter and Jadaan on the M62 for disablements reported over the emergency telephones of between 22 and 31 per million vehicle-km. The average duration of a breakdown was given by Ferguson and Jenkins as about 30 min.

Coburn[26] showed that if b = number of breakdowns per million vehicle-km, n

Table 11.12. Types of breakdown on M6, 1978/79: per cent

Type of breakdown	Police involved	Total
Engine failure	35	50
Tyre failure	11	15
Fuel shortage	13	17
Other and unknown	14	18
Total	73	100

= number of broken down vehicles at any given instant, t = average duration of breakdown (hours) and q = traffic flow (vehicles/hour), then

$$n = bqt \, 10^{-6}$$

Thus taking a rounded figure of b as 40 per million vehicle-km and a figure of 30 min for the average duration of a breakdown on a busy motorway carrying say 5,000 vehicles/h, then n would be 1.0, i.e. there would be one stopped vehicle for every kilometre of road at any time.

Some idea of the nature of breakdowns on motorways can be obtained from records of recovery vehicles operating on a section of the M6 in Warwickshire during maintenance work. Table 11.12 has been compiled from data kindly made available by the Transport and Road Research Laboratory on 1,000 breakdowns (excluding accidents) which occurred between November 1978 and October 1979.

The police were involved in about three quarters of the incidents and about half the total breakdowns were identified as being engine or other mechanical faults. Most of the "other and unknown" category were cases where the recovery team were unable to identify a fault because the vehicles had moved away. Tyre failures and running out of fuel figured prominently in the list of causes for breakdowns. During the period concerned there were also some 67 accidents involving 112 vehicles.

Manktelow and Salter[28] carried out a study of breakdowns reported by the emergency telephone system on the motorways in the West Riding of Yorkshire between October 1970 and October 1971. The distribution of faults which they found is reproduced in Table 11.13. Mechanical faults, fuel problems and tyre failures also featured prominently in these breakdowns.

Tyre failures

Tyre failures have been shown to be a serious cause of breakdowns. An investigation[29] of accidents reported to the police during 1961 and 1962 on the M1 London–Birmingham motorway showed that in some 17% of those accidents loss of control of the vehicle was attributable to tyre failure. A more detailed study of all accidents during 1962/63 on a 17 mile section of the M1 of tyre failures (but only those mentioned in police reports) showed that about half the tyre failures occurred on commercial vehicles, and 60% of those were bursts. Punctures accounted for about 90% of the failure in cars and of these the risk of failure for tubed tyres was 5 times as great as that for tubeless tyres. The risk of a burst by using remoulded tyres on cars was about 20 times as great as the risk by using tubeless tyres. For commercial vehicles the risk of a puncture using a remould was about twice that for a normal tyre and of a burst about 4 times as great.

Further studies[30] of the incidence of burst tyres immediately prior to an accident were made between 1968 and 1970 on the M1 London–Birmingham motorway and the M4 between Chiswick and Maidenhead. In broad agreement with the results of the earlier study, about 16% of personal injury accidents were preceded by one of the vehicles involved sustaining a burst tyre. Where two-wheeled vehicles were involved in accidents, 36% had a tyre burst beforehand; with medium or heavy goods vehicles the percentage was only about 3%.

Another investigation[31] on part of the M5 during the autumn of 1971 confirmed that about one sixth of all injury accidents have tyre failure as a major contributory factor. In this investigation an attempt was made to obtain data on all tyre failures, and it was estimated that about 2% of all tyre failures led to injury accidents and 3% to accidents of all kinds reported to the police.

It is of interest to note that on the M1 London–Birmingham motorway in 1970 out of the total cases reported for process or given verbal cautions by the police some 5% were in respect of defective tyres[32].

Fog on motorways

Driving on any road in fog can be difficult and dangerous and on motorways, where speeds tend to be high and where there is a large proportion of heavy

Table 11.13. Breakdowns on Yorkshire motorways, 1970/71

Fault	Percentage of reported faults	
	Cars	Commercial vehicles
Illness	0.2	0.1
Lack of fuel	13.1	10.6
Fuel/mechanical	6.0	10.9
Tyre failure	6.8	15.3
Cooling system	1.1	1.3
Mechanical	53.2	50.8
Mechanical/electrical	10.6	5.6
Electrical	7.1	2.5
Braking system	0.3	1.3
Lack of oil	1.6	1.6

vehicles in the traffic, serious accidents can and do occur involving large numbers of vehicles. In 1979 about 3% of all injury accidents on M and A(M) roads occurred in fog. The proportion which were fatal or serious was just over 30% and was about the same for all injury accidents. However the number of fatalities per accident was nearly twice as great overall in fog and 3 times as great at night.

An analysis was carried out by Johnson[33] of accidents in fog over the period 1969/71 on the five main motorways then in use, i.e. M1, M2, M4, M5 and M6. These motorways had about 80% of all motorway accidents at the time. Fog accidents made up some 4% of the total and of this total some two thirds occurred in daylight hours, which was about the same proportion of non-fog accidents occurring in daylight. However, fog accidents were more serious and some 58% involved fatal or serious injury compared with 40% of non-fog accidents. Results obtained by Codling[34] and quoted by Johnson showed that in 1969/70, 36% of fog accidents on motorways involved four or more vehicles compared with 4% of non-fog accidents, and 11% of fog accidents involved at least nine vehicles compared with 0.3% of non-fog accidents.

There was a considerable difference between the numbers of fog accidents in 1969 and 1970 (50% more in 1969) although the incidence of fog averaged over a number of sites was much the same in the 2 years; the incidence at individual sites differed by as much as 3 to 1 between the 2 years, indicating that fog and fog accidents might be a local phenomenon. In June 1972 it was announced in the House of Commons that lighting was to be installed on 86 miles of motorway in areas particularly prone to fog; these comprise six sections, two on the M1, one on the M5, two on the M6 and one on the M62 and they had been selected by analysing accidents in fog over a 3 year period. From an analysis of accidents at five of these sites Johnson confirmed that they were more prone to fog accidents and he estimated that about 45% of fog accidents and 22% of non-fog accidents occurred on about one seventh of the motorway network.

Grime[35] made a study of two groups of rear-end chain accidents: one, all serious accidents on the M1 in 1971, and the other all accidents on a section of the M4 between 1965 and 1971. He found that a third of the serious chain accidents occurred in fog and that the number of serious chain accidents in fog was about 10 times that to be expected if fog created no extra hazard. He concluded from his analysis that consideration should be given to diverting heavy vehicles from motorways in foggy weather, to the compulsory wearing of seat belts, and to the use of a brighter rear lamp for use in fog (such lamps are now in use).

In addition to accident studies, investigations have also been made into driver behaviour in fog. One investigation[36] of drivers on the M4 in 1975/76 showed that drivers' safety margins decreased with decreasing visibility, and at a visibility of 50 m or less more than half the drivers were exceeding the speed at which they could stop within this visibility distance. In a later study on the M4 in the winter of 1977/78,[37] it was concluded that in conditions where the visibility does not fall below about 150 m drivers tend to adopt speeds so that most could stop well within their visibility distances. A reduction in speed with falling visibility was, however, accompanied by a marked reduction in the time gap between vehicles and an increased tendency to form platoons, with the result that drivers were considerably more at risk from following too closely behind one another.

It may be remarked that drivers have a tendency to travel at time headways less than those recommended in the *Highway Code* in good, clear conditions. It has been observed[38] that there is a greater involvement of heavy vehicles than light vehicles in close following and platoon formation, and since heavy vehicles in general require longer stopping distances than light vehicles, this is a matter of some concern particularly where hazards such as fog are concerned.

Other driving hazards

Fog, although a serious hazard to motorists driving on motorways, is, as has been seen, a relatively rare event; thick fog only occurs on about 10 days in the year and has a tendency to occur most frequently in a relatively small number of places. There are many other hazards which occur more frequently and these include such things as: severe congestion, which occurs regularly in some locations such as on the M1, the M4 and the M6; accidents which can block the carriageway; wet roads which reduce skidding resistance and which lead to spray being thrown up, particularly by heavy vehicles; and road works, which are occurring with much greater frequency now that many motorways are reaching the end of their design lives.

In an interview survey[39] of drivers using the M4 near London it appeared that the hazards drivers would most like to have been warned about were fog and accidents, with warnings of congestion and other bad weather being ranked of lower importance. As for information drivers would like about hazards, location was regarded as being the most useful, followed by recommended action, length of delay and recommended maximum speed.

Road works on motorways can be a serious source of delay to traffic and careful attention needs to be paid to planning arrangements for handling traffic in the safest and most economical ways during the period that works take place. Mathews and Maclean[40] have described various methods of organising traffic flows at road works and the factors involved in making a choice in particular circumstances. Methods discussed are: lane closure systems; carriageway closure with two-way operation on the other carriageway; diversion to alternative routes; contra-flow systems where on a three-lane dual carriageway road one lane on the carriageway being repaired is left open for traffic and one lane on the other carriageway is combined with it to give two lanes in one direction, with the remaining two lanes giving two lanes in the other direction; and the use of narrow lanes, for example where one three-lane carriageway is closed completely and the other carriageway and hard shoulder is marked so as to provide four narrow lanes, two in each direction. Trials have been made with various systems[41-43] and it has been found that the use of narrow lanes gives a better through-put of traffic than segregated contra-flow or two-way operation with standard width lanes. The Transport and Road Research Laboratory have developed a computer model QUADRO (QUeues And Delays at ROadworks)[44] to calculate traffic delays and associated road user costs (but excluding accident costs) due to road works for carrying out economic appraisal of delays during future maintenance of a road under the method proposed for managing the traffic.

Road works are also a potential source of accidents and it has been found[25] that personal injury accident rates at road works are some 3 to 4 times the normal accident rate of 15 injury accidents per 10^8 vehicle-km.

Finally, reference should be made to hazards due to weather other than fog. Most frequent is the incidence of rain, which not only reduces skidding resistance but also reduces visibility particularly as a result of the spray thrown up by heavy vehicles. The problem of wet road skids has been studied for many years and is well understood: for drivers it is necessary for safety for them to adjust their speed and following distance to suit the prevailing conditions; and for the highway engineer it is necessary to make regular checks on the wet road skid resistance of the road surface and to take remedial action when necessary.

The problem of spray was investigated by Maycock[45] who concluded that although spray generated by vehicles was a nuisance it was not a serious contributor to accidents. Speed has a marked effect on the spray produced: the higher the speed the worse the spray and the more difficult it is to control it at source. Mudflaps on cars at high speeds are not very effective but improvements to mudguards on commercial vehicles could well be worthwhile. In some trials with a commercial vehicle at 50 mile/h a suitably designed mudflap could reduce the spray 10 yards behind by a factor of 3 to 4.

Another method of reducing spray which has been studied experimentally is by the use of porous surfacings[46]. Neither these nor improvements to commercial vehicles seem to have been followed up by the Department of Transport.

The other main weather hazard is snow and ice, and the Department of Transport and its agents the County Councils pay particular attention to keeping motorways open so far as possible during the wintry weather. Maintenance depots are located near the motorways, from which gritters and other machines can operate and where salt is stored; maintenance staff keep a 24 hour cover from mid-November to March at the depots. Winter maintenance procedures in Lancashire have been described by Drake[47].

Warning of hazards

The various hazards which occur on motorways have brought to the fore the problems of how incidents can be detected and information passed on to motorists in time for them to take avoiding action.

During the 1960s the Ministry of Transport began to install a system of signs for warning motorists of hazards and a remote-controlled system of roadside signs is now in use on the motorway network[48]. Possible developments of this and other systems have been the subject of research and development for a number of years and the possibility of international collaboration in such work in Europe has also been discussed for several years.

Some investigations have been directed towards means of providing automatic detection of incidents. The computer-controlled communications system on motorways can be used to interrogate sensors, and devices for automatically providing information about weather and traffic conditions have been developed and tested experimentally by the Transport and Road Research Laboratory. Wind gauges linked to police control centres are in use in some locations, e.g. on the M62 in the Pennines where there are particular hazards arising from high wind speeds.

Investigations are also being carried out into ways of improving the performance of road-side warning signs, both as regards their visibility and as regards the messages they display. A patent specification for the use of optical fibres in signs was taken out by the Rank Organisation in 1974[49]; a particular feature of this is the use of bundles of optical fibres to form various displays instead of the wiring and switching systems used in the signs in use. Investigations by the Transport and Road Research Laboratory (TRRL) have included the influence of colour and shape of enclosing borders on the perception and understanding of motorway symbols and also the design of suitable symbols for use on changeable message matrix signs for conveying information about motorway hazards. Work has been done in Northern Ireland by the Department of the Environment there into the efficiency of "roller blind" type hazard warning signs controlled from a remote source on a short length of motorway. The University of Aston in Birmingham has been carrying out research into the public understanding of symbols and legends currently in use on standard motorway matrix signs and of a new set of signs and symbols designed in conjunction with the TRRL.

Work at the TRRL has also covered "in-car" systems for communicating with drivers, including studies of area broadcasting as a traffic information system, the feasibility of using mobile transmitters to provide information to a driver via a special radio receiver and the feasibility of communicating with drivers by visual displays of information inside their vehicles.

A sample of drivers using the London end of the M4 in 1973[39] were asked, among other things, about their understanding of standard motorway matrix symbols. Speed restriction signs were well understood, except that the majority of drivers thought that the speed displayed was mandatory. The rural "wicket" signals indicating lane closure were extremely well understood. There was a poor understanding of flashing red "Stop" lights: many drivers did not regard them as mandatory and others did not know whether or not they were to remain waiting

Table 11.14. Offences on the M1 in 1970

Offence	Reported for process	Verbal cautions	Total reported and cautioned	Total: %
Stopping/driving on hard shoulder	1,100	1,784	2,884	32.4
Prohibited traffic				
Pedestrians	843	2,580	3,423	38.5
Pedal cyclists	8	7	15	0.2
Learner drivers	129	10	139	1.6
Crossing/stopping on the central reservation	63	16	79	0.9
Excess speeds				
Trailer	250	371	621	7.0
70 mile/h	855	373	1,228	13.8
Travelling wrong way	46	10	56	0.6
Reversing/turning	69	37	106	1.2
Use of offside lane by heavy goods vehicles	286	53	321	3.6
Failure to control animals	8	9	17	0.2
Total	3,639	5,250	8,889	100

Table 11.15. Motorway offences, England and Wales 1979

Offence	Proceedings	Written warnings	Total proceedings and written warnings	Total: %
Driving a vehicle on part of motorway not carriageway	4,736	1,323	6,059	15.4
Prohibited traffic				
Pedestrians	2,118*	—	2,118	5.4
Pedal cyclists	67	—	67	0.2
Learner drivers	2,857	261	3,118	7.9
Excluded traffic using motorway	449	152	601	1.5
Driving etc. on central reservation	307	23	330	0.8
Excess speeds				
Vehicles subject to 50 mile/h	420	16	436	1.1
Over 70 mile/h	20,093	282	20,375	51.7
Driving vehicle in wrong direction	383	91	474	1.2
Reversing vehicle	546	104	650	1.6
Prohibited vehicle using right-hand or off-side lane	2,469	142	2,611	6.6
Motor user failing to keep animal under control	10	3	13	0.1
Other	2,355	193	2,548	6.5
Total	36,810	2,590	39,400	100.0

* Includes proceedings and oral cautions.

for an indefinite time.

The effect of an advisory 50 mile/h speed signal on speeds was found[50] to reduce mean car speeds by about 5% from a little above to a little below 70 mile/h, and it was concluded that when the reason for the advisory speed was not obvious to drivers it had only a small effect on average speeds; where traffic flows were higher the average speed was reduced more.

Police and emergencies

If an accident or breakdown occurs on a motorway the police are normally informed by the emergency system of telephones installed at 1 mile intervals on all motorways, or the incident is found by police patrols. Depending on the nature of the incident rescue services, ambulance, fire or breakdown, will be brought into operation. If the carriageways are obstructed, the police take action to warn other traffic and to divert traffic away from the obstruction. The technique used by police for this purpose and the equipment carried by police vehicles for use in emergencies have been described by Gott[32].

Besides dealing with emergencies and other incidents, the police also are responsible for enforcing traffic rules and regulations and for maintaining law and order on the motorways generally; as Gott has pointed out this includes dealing with criminals who use the motorways as rapid means of movement to and from the scenes of crimes. Gott referred to the early co-operation between Chief Constables in policing motorways; Williams and Laugharne[2] referred to the continuation of this co-operation in 1980 and to the production of a motorway manual covering all the principles and techniques of motorway policing, which is widely used by police patrols.

To assist police patrols, police observation platforms have been constructed at the side of motorways[51]

"(a) to provide vantage points where police patrol vehicles can stop, off the carriageway and hard shoulder to improve surveillance of traffic flows and behaviour

"(b) to make the police presence more conspicuous to drivers using the motorways and thereby to improve the standard of driving and reduce the likelihood of accidents".

The platforms are normally between 8 and 16 km apart on both carriageways and laid out so that the police vehicles can park at right-angles to the traffic flow.

An indication of the nature of offences against the motorway regulations on the M1 was given by Gott[32] for the first 9 months of 1970 and his data are reproduced in Table 11.14. A surprising feature of this table is the large proportion of offences involving pedestrians on the motorway, many apparently trying to hitch-hike.

Some more recent information about motoring offences on motorways kindly made available by the Home Office is given in Table 11.15. The data in this table are not exactly comparable with those in Table 11.14 as statistics related to oral cautions are not collected centrally.

The high figure for pedestrian offences reported on the M1 by Gott was not repeated in the more recent data covering all motorways in England and Wales. Exceeding the 70 mile/h speed limit accounted for over half the total offences in 1979 and in both Tables 11.14 and 11.15 offences of driving off the carriageway and of speeding were two of the most common offences.

Motorway service areas

Because stopping on motorways is prohibited, except in emergencies, it was necessary from the start to provide places for travellers to rest and to obtain fuel and refreshment and where there were lavatories. The first of these service areas was built alongside the M1 at Newport Pagnell by Forte and Co. Ltd, in 1960; by 1980 there were 42 in use in England and Scotland; there were none in Wales.

Buying sites for service areas is the responsibility of the Department of Transport in England and its counterparts in Scotland and Wales, and the policy followed for the provision of service areas was, until recently, as stated by the Under-Secretary of State for the Environment in an adjournment debate on 12 January 1972 in the House of Commons. Once the line of a motorway was fixed, the Department selected sites for service areas at approximately 25 mile intervals with provision for the possible development of intermediate sites, if necessary. Engineers from the Department and the Advisory Committee on Landscape Treatment of Trunk Roads examined likely sites and once a preferred site was located the local planning authority was consulted about its suitability and, if necessary, a local non-statutory inquiry would be held into the proposal. Once a site had been acquired, the Department then invited tenders in open competition for the commercial development of the site. Tenders had to be offered in two parts, one the financial offer and the other the layout and design of buildings proposed; the Department sought the views of the local planning authority on the way development was to take place and on the designs put forward. The successful tenderers had additionally to seek the views of the Royal Fine Art Commission on their design.

According to Hearn[52] each tenderer was provided with a layout indicating where parking, catering facilities and petrol stations were to be located, together with details of the minimum facilities required and a minimum cost for the project; the intention behind this last item was to establish good standards in design and construction. A 24 hour service had to be provided and sales of alcohol were prohibited. The caterer submitted his tender on the basis of a fixed rent and a rental based on turnover, together with a design for the building. The successful tenderer had to obtain planning permission from the local authority as well as the

Royal Fine Art Commission. The Department provided access roads, parking areas, the original landscaping and services such as water, gas, electricity and drainage. Provision of everything else, including maintenance of the facilities provided by the Department, was the responsibility of the applicant. Sites were rented by the Department on 50 year leases.

Service areas usually include land on both sides of the motorway with a foot-bridge connecting the two sides. Rear access to the areas is provided from the ordinary road system to service areas for the use of staff and suppliers of the areas. The early areas cover about 10 acres but later ones are much larger, up to 30 acres in extent, and on that account are possibly more attractive to users. If service areas are sited on a summit near the motorway, traffic entering the area does so on a rising gradient, which helps deceleration, and traffic leaving does so on a descending gradient, which aids acceleration particularly of the heavier vehicles.

In 1965 the Ministry of Transport commissioned the Bartlett School of Architecture at University College London to study the service provision on British motorways. In a report on this study[53] Nutt showed that catering turnover and fuel turnover on a motorway were linearly related to the amount of travel on the motorway. He also gave some evidence of the usage of service areas based on the amount of motorway traffic turning into those areas. Average percentage turn-ins ranged from 21% on winter weekdays to 33% at weekends in the summer; corresponding figures for the average stops per 1,000 vehicle-miles were 8 and 13. Hearn[52] in 1971 stated that at least one vehicle in every five used a service station during its journey.

Nutt concluded from his investigations that as motorway traffic was increasing year by year the level of demand for service facilities was increasing and therefore the financial risks inolved in opening service facilities on motorways were much less than for an equivalent business venture in a town or city. He observed, however, that many service areas were not proving as profitable as was expected and this he attributed to staff costs, kitchen duplication and over-investment. Among recommendations he put forward which he thought would make service areas more profitable and more pleasant to use were the following.

—Each new service area should be developed to meet statistically predictable demands over the next few years with the possibility of expansion later if demand grew. This he called a policy of "least commitment".

—Buildings should be designed so that those areas not required during slack periods could be shut down.

—Only "nominal" catering was required for one fifth of the year.

—Catering buildings must be readily adapted to changing standards and eating habits.

—Catering facilities should be planned round one centralised kitchen as this would reduce capital building expenditure and staff costs.

Table 11.16. Owners of motorway service areas in England in December 1980

	Service areas in which terms were agreed for disposal to present operators		
Operator	Service area	Operator	Service area
Rank	Farthing Corner M2 Aust M4 Forton M6 Helton Park M6 Knutsford M6	Trust House Forte (Motorchef)	Scratchwood M1 Newport Pagnell M1 Woodall M1 Fleet M3 Gordano M5
Granada	Toddington M1 Trowell M1 Woolley Edge M1 Heston M4		Keele M6 Charnock Richard M6 Corley M6 Burtonwood M62
	Leigh Delamere M4 Exeter M5 Frankley M5 Southwaite M6 Birch M62 Washington Birtley A1(M)	Imperial Foods (Motoross)	Leicester Forest East M1 Membury M4 Michael Wood M5 Hartshead Moor M62

	Other service areas and their present operators		
Operator	Service area	Operator	Service area
Blue Boar	Rothersthorpe M1 Watford Gap M1	Mobil	Burton West M6
BP	Killington Lake M6	Road Chef	Rownhams M27 Taunton Dene M5 Sandbach M6
Kenning Motor Group	Strensham M5 Anderton M61	Westmorland	Tebay West M6

Hearn[52] writing in 1971 commented on the large capital investment by the catering and fuel industries in service areas and discussed some of the problems facing the operators of those areas; such as the need to operate a 24 hour service and the resulting increases in staff costs, vandalism and theft, and high rate assessments. As far as customers were concerned, experience had shown that motorists were selective about the service areas they used and that most were looking for value for money; if they liked the presentation, the service and the food, and if they got good value they would return.

In 1973 the Department of the Environment commissioned an independent research organisation to undertake a survey of users of motorway service areas and from the survey it was concluded that

—most travellers were satisfied with the food provided, the speed with which it was served and the price they paid
—most motorists had a quick drink or snack or both rather than a leisurely full-scale meal.

Criticism of the quality of food and standards at service areas has, however, continued for many years, notably by Egon Ronay who, as a result of a survey conducted in August, September and October 1980[54] commented "The standard of food along the motorways is as awful as it has ever been and worse in some cases. Caterers—with one exception—appear to have ignored nationwide criticism swelling over the last 2 or 3 years." Ronay's criticisms had, in fact, started in 1959 before any service areas were in use, because the Ministry of Transport had not taken catering experts' advice in setting up the arrangements governing service areas. The inspectors who carried out the Ronay survey in 1980 concluded that the quality of food in the restaurants and cafeterias visited was "poor" or "appalling" in just under three quarters of cases, "acceptable" in a quarter and "good" at only one service area.

In 1977 the Secretaries of State for Transport and for Prices and Consumer Protection set up a Committee of Inquiry into motorway service areas under the chairmanship of Peter J. Prior "to consider and report on how far the present facilities available at motorway service areas meet the needs of motorway users having particular regard to price, quality, variety, and effective competition; and on what further provision should be made for the convenience of travellers, bearing in mind road safety and any other relevant factors." The report of the Committee was published in 1978[55] and included the results of two surveys carried out by public opinion consultants on behalf of the Committee. One survey was of motorists in their houses and the other of people at service areas. The following are some of the findings of these surveys.

—The most important reason people stopped at service areas was for food or drink.

—The three most frequently used facilities were, in order, the lavatories, the self-service cafeteria and the petrol services.

—Nearly half of those questioned in their homes who were regular motorway users thought that the service areas were "poor" or "very poor".

—14% of those questioned at the service areas and 32% of those questioned at home thought the food to be "not enjoyable" or "unpleasant".

The Committee concluded from this and other evidence that "some extreme views expressed by the media on the quality of motorway food are unsupported by public or expert opinion" but they went on to express disquiet at the standards being offered and thought that improvements should be made to raise the average level to that of the best.

The Committee made a large number of recommendations ranging from changes in control of the service areas to other facilities which might be provided in the areas, and including suggestions of possible relaxation of some of the terms under which contractors operated.

The Committee's report was to a Labour administration which went out of office not long afterwards. It was followed by a Conservative Government which decided to dispose of leases of the motorway service areas in England to the private sector, a decision announced in October 1979. Just over a year later, on 10 December 1980, the Secretary of State for Transport issued a press release stating that three quarters of the motorway service areas had been sold; a list of the owners of service areas in England at that time is given in Table 11.16. By May 1981 some £42 million had been collected by the Exchequer from the sale of 28 service areas.

Under the new arrangements, companies buying motorway service areas pay premiums for new 50 year leases with only a peppercorn rent payable. The Minister believed that competition between operators would be stimulated through the greater commercial freedom allowed under the new leases and that the removal of adverse lease conditions would encourage operators to undertake further capital investment. It is interesting that in 1971 Hearn[52] considered that because service areas were only 25 miles apart, a distance which would usually be covered in 20–30 min, there was a high degree of competition between operators; if a motorist did not like one place it was not far to go to the next.

The position of the consumer in the new leases is covered by covenants which require operators to continue to provide free short-term parking and free lavatories and to offer a 24 hour fuel and refreshment service. In confirming this in reply to a Parliamentary Question on 10 December 1980 the Minister also said that there was no question of alcohol being served at the motorway service areas.

References

1. DEPARTMENT OF TRANSPORT, WELSH OFFICE and SCOTTISH

DEVELOPMENT DEPARTMENT. *Transport statistics. Great Britain 1969–1979.* HMSO, London, 1980.

2. WILLIAMS T.E.H. and LAUGHARNE A. Motorway usage and operations. *Proceedings of the conference on 20 years of British motorways.* Institution of Civil Engineers, London, 1980.

3. CAPLAN R. and DUNCAN N.C. *Traffic flows on M4 motorway 1961–70.* TRRL report LR 452. Transport and Road Research Laboratory, Crowthorne, 1972.

4. HOLLIS E. and EVANS R. *Motorway traffic patterns.* TRRL report LR 705. Transport and Road Research Laboratory, Crowthorne, 1976.

5. SILVERLEAF A. The contribution of research. *Proceedings of the conference on 20 years of British motorways.* Institution of Civil Engineers, London, 1980.

6. COBURN T.M. Trends in speeds on British main roads. *Proceedings of the third conference of the Australian Road Research Board.* Australian Road Research Board, Melbourne, 1966.

7. ACKROYD L.W. and BETTISON M. Vehicle speeds on the M1 in Nottinghamshire 1969–73. *Traffic engineering and control,* 1974, **15**, No. 9.

8. DUNCAN N.C. *et al. Measurement of the speeds of cars on motorways in 1976.* TRRL digest SR 326. Transport and Road Research Laboratory, Crowthorne, 1977.

9. TRANSPORT AND ROAD RESEARCH LABORATORY. *Car speeds and petrol prices.* TRRL leaflet LF 881. Transport and Road Research Laboratory, Crowthorne, 1979.

10. DAWSON R.F.F. Effect of the M1 on journey time and fuel consumption. *Traffic engineering and control,* 1961, **2**, No. 7.

11. EVERALL P.F. *The effect of road and traffic conditions on fuel consumption.* TRRL report LR226. Transport and Road Research Laboratory, Crowthorne, 1968.

12. WATERS M.H.L. *Research on energy conservation for cars and goods vehicles.* TRRL supplementary report SR 591. Transport and Road Research Laboratory, Crowthorne, 1980.

13. FRYARS R.A. Private communication, 1980.

14. WEBSTER H.G. Developing vehicles for high speed roads. *Financial Times,* 27 September 1965.

15. GLANVILLE SIR WILLIAM. Discussion on the London–Birmingham Motorway. *Proc. Instn Civ. Engrs,* 1961, **19**, 61–119.

16. COBURN T.M. The relation between accidents and layout on rural roads. *Int. Road Safety and Traffic Rev.,* 1962, **10**, No. 4.

17. NEWBY R.F. and JOHNSON H.D. *Changes in the numbers of accidents and casualties on main roads near the London–Birmingham motorway.* Road Research Laboratory note LN/348/RFN.HDJ, April 1983. Unpublished.

18. NEWBY R.F. and JOHNSON H.D. London–Birmingham motorway accidents. *Traffic engineering and control,* 1963, **4**, No. 10.

19. ADAMS W.F. *Safety aspects of motorway design.* Institution of Civil Engineers, Traffic Engineering Study Group, London, 1961.

20. WALKER A.E. and CHAPMAN R.G. *Assessment of anti-dazzle screen on M6.* TRRL report LR 955. Transport and Road Research Laboratory, Crowthorne, 1980.

21. HILLIER J.A. and WARDROP J.G. Effect of gradient and curvature on accidents on London–Birmingham motorway. *Traffic engineering and control,* 1966, **7**, No. 10.

22. DEPARTMENT OF TRANSPORT, SCOTTISH DEVELOPMENT DEPART-
    MENT and WELSH OFFICE. *Road accidents. Great Britain 1979*. HMSO, London,
    1981.
23. GHOSH D. *et al*. Death on the motorway. *New Society*, 1974, **29**, No. 620.
24. ANON. Speed limits and public health. *British Medical Journal*, 1977, **1**, No. 6068.
25. MACLEAN A.D. Facilities for vehicle breakdowns: their effects at roadworks on
    dual carriageways. *Traffic engineering and control*, 1978, **19**, No. 1.
26. COBURN T.M. *Rural motorways*. Road Research Laboratory report LN/787/TMC,
    1965. Unpublished.
27. FERGUSON J.A. and JENKINS I.A. Incidents on high speed roads. *Traffic
    engineering and control*, 1977, **18**, No. 5.
28. MANKTELOW H. and SALTER R.J. Some characteristics of disabled vehicles on
    the Yorkshire motorway system. *Traffic engineering and control*, 1973, **15**, No. 7.
29. STARKS H.J.H. Tyre failures in accidents on the motorway M1 in 1962–63. *J. Inst.
    Auto. Assess.*, 1966, **17**, No. 1.
30. GODLEY M.J. *The incidence of burst tyres prior to injury accidents on M1 and M4
    motorways*. TRRL report LR 498. Transport and Road Research Laboratory,
    Crowthorne, 1972.
31. LOWNE R.W. *Tyre failures on part of the M5 motorway*. TRRL report LR 585.
    Transport and Road Research Laboratory, Crowthorne, 1973.
32. GOTT J. The police and operational systems. *Proceedings of the conference on motor-
    ways in Britain*. Institution of Civil Engineers, London, 1971.
33. JOHNSON H.D. *Motorway accidents in fog and darkness*. TRRL report LR 573.
    Transport and Road Research Laboratory, Crowthorne, 1973.
34. CODLING P.J. Weather and road accidents. *Climatic resources and economic activity*,
    chap. 11. David and Charles, Newton Abbott, 1974.
35. GRIME G. Rear-end 'chain' type accidents on motorways in Great Britain. *Pro-
    ceedings of 12th international study week in traffic engineering, Belgrade, 1974*. World
    Training and Automobile Association.
36. DEPARTMENT OF THE ENVIRONMENT and DEPARTMENT OF
    TRANSPORT. *Transport and road research 1976*. HMSO, London, 1977.
37. WHITE M.E. and JEFFERY D.J. *Some aspects of motorway traffic behaviour in fog*.
    TRRL report LR 958. Transport and Road Research Laboratory, Crowthorne, 1980.
38. SUMNER R. and BAGULEY C. *Close following behaviour at two sites on rural two-
    lane motorways*. TRRL report LR 859. Transport and Road Research Laboratory,
    Crowthorne, 1978.
39. CHARMIAN A. *An interview survey of motorway driver information requirements and
    signal understanding*. TRRL report LR 742. Transport and Road Research
    Laboratory, Crowthorne, 1977.
40. MATHEWS D.H. and MACLEAN A.D. Traffic operation at roadworks on dual car-
    riageways. *Traffic engineering and control*, 1976, **17**, No. 5.
41. MACLEAN A.D. *Traffic delays due to resurfacing of M4 motorway in 1970*. TRRL
    report LR 421. Transport and Road Research Laboratory, Crowthorne, 1971.
42. MACLEAN A.D. and GREENWAY M. *Crawler lane construction on M5: the use of
    narrow lanes*. TRRL report LR 782. Transport and Road Research Laboratory,
    Crowthorne, 1977.

43. MACLEAN A.D. *M6 reconstruction: two-way traffic using narrow lanes*. TRRL report SR 474. Transport and Road Research Laboratory, Crowthorne, 1979.

44. TRANSPORT AND ROAD RESEARCH LABORATORY. *QUADRO—on model for calculating delays and user costs at roadworks*. TRRL leaflet LF 929. Transport and Road Research Laboratory, Crowthorne, 1981.

45. MAYCOCK G. Spray thrown up by vehicles travelling on wet roads. *Road tar*, 1968, **22**, No. 3.

46. BROWN J.R. *Pervious bitumen-macadam surfacings laid tò reduce splash and spray at Stonebridge, Warwickshire*. TRRL report LR 563. Transport and Road Research Laboratory, Crowthorne, 1973.

47. DRAKE J. *Motorways*. Faber and Faber, London, 1969.

48. POOLE P.H. Motorway communications system. *Light*, 1973, **66**, No. 9.

49. RANK ORGANIZATION LTD. *Optical signalling*. Patent specification 1,344,262. The Patent Office, London, 1974.

50. WEBB P.J. *The effect of an advisory signal on motorway traffic speeds*. TRRL report SR 615. Transport and Road Research Laboratory, Crowthorne, 1980.

51. DEPARTMENT OF TRANSPORT. *Police observation platforms on motorways*. Technical memorandum H 4/75. Department of Transport, London, 1975.

52. HEARN D. Motorway service areas. *Proceedings of the conference on motorways in Britain*. Institution of Civil Engineers, London, 1971.

53. NUTT B. Research report on motorway service areas. *Traffic engineering and control*, 1965, **9**, No. 2.

54. RONAY E. *Just a bite*. Lucas guide 1981. Egon Ronay, London, 1981.

55. DEPARTMENT OF TRANSPORT and DEPARTMENT OF PRICES AND CONSUMER PROTECTION. *Report of the Committee of Inquiry into Motorway Service Areas*. HMSO, London, 1978.

12

Some economic and social aspects

Introduction

There can be little doubt that the construction of the motorway system to date has had important economic and social consequences for the community at large and some of these have been touched on in earlier chapters. The total investment from public funds in the motorway programme between 1959 and 1978 was stated by Gwilliam and Wilson[1] to be some £2,775 million at 1976 prices, and they estimated the direct economic benefits from the programme in terms of resource cost and time savings to be between £5,200 million and £6,500 million also at 1976 prices. It has to be noted, however, that these benefits were estimated on the basis that all motorway schemes had to be justified in cost/benefit terms and the savings were deduced assuming a ratio of net present value to discounted cost in the range 0.2 to 0.5. Unfortunately there is very little evidence available from direct observation before and after motorways were built as to what benefits were being achieved.

This question of before and after studies was commented on by the Leitch Committee[2] in respect of the assessment of trunk road schemes. The Committee observed that, while there had probably been a few limited studies made to check traffic flows and user benefits after major road improvements in some regions, the number of published reports was small. They noted that estimates of potential traffic and forecast rates of economic return were common features of major road schemes and found it difficult to understand why similar exercises had not been carried out after construction, particularly as there was a growing trend to carry out before and after studies of environmental issues.

The Committee quoted actual and predicted flows on the London–Birmingham motorway in 1960 obtained in studies by the Road Research Laboratory (RRL), and in referring to predicted rates of return said it was "unfortunate that no official follow-up to those analyses were made to establish 'actuals' in 1960 and 1965." In a report prepared at the RRL in 1965 Coburn[3] stated that the first year rate of return on the motorway was predicted at 10% in 1960, and that experience after the opening of the motorway had shown that traffic flows and time savings had

266

been predicted fairly accurately, savings in fuel consumption had been over-estimated and savings in accidents had been underestimated. On balance actual benefits appeared to be in good agreement with predictions, but because of under-estimation of construction costs the corrected rate of return in 1960 was only about 7%. He believed, however, that because of the high capacity of the motor-way comparisons in the long term would be more favourable to the motorway.

The Leitch report included preliminary results of a simplified comparison of predicted and observed flows on a number of schemes but which included only two motorways, for one of which predicted flows were substantially less than forecast and for the other somewhat greater.

In conclusion the Committee were convinced of the value of before and after studies and expressed surprise that the Department of Transport had not thought it worthwhile to pursue them in the past. It may be remarked that the research in this area at the RRL was undertaken as part of the programme of the Road Research Board of the Department of Scientific and Industrial Research. After 1965, the Ministry of Transport assumed responsibility for the research programme of the Laboratory.

As a result of the Leitch Committee recommendations the Department of Transport in 1981 prepared a manual of recommended practice for traffic fore-casting in scheme appraisal on trunk roads, which included a section on methods of making before and after studies of major road schemes.

Motorways and regional development

The M62, which was originally conceived as the Lancashire–Yorkshire motor-way and later extended to a complete east–west route (Hull–Liverpool), was justified on the basis of a standard cost/benefit analysis. In a study of trans-Pennine movements and the M62, Gwilliam and Judge[4] investigated to what extent there were secondary benefits of increased economic activity generated by the motor-way as distinct from those included in the cost/benefit analysis. They also investi-gated whether there was any evidence to support the proposition that building the M62 had aided the development of economic activity in the region.

The study concentrated on traffic effects and essentially actual changes in traf-fic were compared with what might have been expected if the M62 had not been built. It was concluded that there was a very substantial reassignment of traffic between trans-Pennine routes after the opening of the M62 and that there was some redistribution of trips as evidenced by increases in mean trip length. Evidence of an increase in the total number of trans-Pennine trips was, however, not strong and any increase was not of an order to nullify benefit to "base load" traffic.

The very large reassignment of traffic resulted in reductions, often very large, of traffic on the original network giving substantial benefits to the initial traffic and some substantial environmental benefits to residents on the initial road network.

As for regional development, they saw little strong evidence that the motorway had much influence on inter-regional location of activity.

In another study of the economic impact of the M62 Dodgson[5] concluded that the effect of the motorway on manufacturing production was small. There was some evidence for a relationship between transport costs and employment growth but the effect of the M62 on areal employment was probably not great. The results appeared to support the view that investment in transport had only a limited effect in stimulating regional growth.

Gwilliam and Wilson[1] have discussed the issue of regional policy and motorway investments and, whilst accepting that good transport infrastructure conferred economic benefits, were not persuaded that motorway investment was necessarily a good instrument of regional development policy. They considered that good local and personal access rather than access to the motorway network was more likely to be dominant in local transport decisions.

The Leitch Committee[2] after examining evidence concerning the effects of trunk road construction on economic growth concluded that such construction "does not yield significant economic development gains over and above the direct benefits to road users already measured in the COBA appraisal. The only exception is likely to be where new construction links previously separate regional or national networks giving very large reductions in generalised cost (for example the Channel Tunnel and possibly some estuary crossings)".

Views of industry

In the discussion on the paper by Gwilliam and Wilson[1] at the conference on 20 years of British motorways, C.J. Groome of the National Economic and Development Office (NEDO) said that "if we wait for all the answers to the research into the location of industry which was suggested by Professor Gwilliam we would probably be out of business before we got there." He then instanced research into business investment decisions, mainly concerning factories, which had been carried out by NEDO, in which questions were asked of industrialists about infrastructure. On a three-point rating of infrastructure and its importance to industrialists, roads came out top with 73%, with 24% for rail, 15% for sea ports and 13% for airports. In his view it was what businessmen decide on that counts and if that included their own and their customers' travel arrangements and not just costs, then that had to be taken into account in policy formation.

In a statement on the North Devon link road in December 1978, the South Western Regional Office of the Department of Industry quoted evidence by industrialists in the House of Commons Expenditure Committee Report on regional development incentives in 1973/74 that providing improved transport facilities was a necessary condition for attracting new investment and job creation. The statement referred to the Leitch Committee conclusions that evidence was hard to find that good road communications *per se* engendered industrial development; it went on to say, however, that there was good evidence that the absence of good communications inhibited development.

The statement included information from a national survey by the Board of Trade into location attitudes and experience which showed that access to specific transport facilities was the seventh most important major factor determining the location chosen by mobile firms. The most important factor by far was labour availability, followed by knowledge or expectation of an industrial development certificate and access to markets or suppliers.

Finally that statement concluded that "Improved communications will help make existing firms more competitive by reducing their costs and enabling them to widen their markets and increase output thus providing more jobs. It will also make the area more attractive to companies seeking new sites for their activities."

In a study of the role played by roads in Bradford's industrial development, Thornton and Wheelock[6] concluded that, as far as new industry was concerned, the main criteria determining the selection of a location were personal factors, labour factors, and land and buildings. The secondary considerations were Bradford's position on the motorway network and the central location of the area in relation to national markets.

The most important factors influencing expansion decisions of existing firms were anticipation of future demand and increased demand for existing products; improved communications came seventh in order of importance.

Some anecdotal evidence of the attitude of industry to motorways was collected by the British Road Federation[7] which indicated that individual firms had found benefits from motorways, for example by reducing the number of operating depots, better stock control (a reduced level of stocks was possible), swifter and more reliable delivery service and the opportunity to alter the areas covered by representatives and managers. Some instances of industrial premises located specifically near motorways in Yorkshire are: the Lyons bakery in Barnsley near the M1; the Carlton industrial estate at Barnsley; development near the M62/M621 interchange at Gildersome; and the Wakefield freight interchange near the M1/M62 interchange.

Governments' views on roads and industry

Views of recent Labour and Conservative administrations on the relation of motorways and industrial activity have been expressed in answers to Parliamentary Questions. In December 1977 the Labour Minister of Transport, William Rodgers, stated "Ready access to the motorway network clearly increases the potential of an area for industrial investment. But it is difficult to place an exact value on the benefit of individual motorways to industrial investment or job creation." He went on to say that he would consider this further in the light of the Leitch report.

In response to a later question following the publication of that report he said "Good communications are relevant to industrial investment even if they are not decisive, and investment is relevant to growth." In answer to a supplementary question he went on to say that the House of Commons had generally accepted that "the evidence is strong that good communications are relevant to industrial investment which means jobs and growth."

In December 1979, the Conservative Minister, Norman Fowler, in answer to a question about what research had been done on the impact that development of the motorway and trunk road programme had had on the cost of freight transport, the distribution of industry and on lorry traffic, said "My Department's normal evaluation of trunk road schemes provides estimates of their effects individually on both freight transport costs and lorry movements. While without the roads programme of the last 20 years the costs and volume of freight transport and the pattern of industry's distribution system would be very different, little research has been undertaken by my Department directly on its cumulative effects."

Motorways and property values

There appear to be mixed views and only limited evidence as to the influence motorways have had on property values. Gerald Ely, writing in *The Times* on 3 July 1972, gave as his opinion that "Industrial estates are drawn to motorways these days like pins to a magnet". In the *Yorkshire Post* of 15 March 1973 it was stated that industrial demand for property had been stimulated by the coming of the M1, M62 and M18 to Yorkshire. A little later, on 3 September 1973, in an article on access to motorways in the *Financial Times*, Peter Foster wrote "In terms of benefit to the regions and regional property values, the motorway developments over the past 15 years . . . have succeeded in doing something which no amount of financial aid could achieve; they have removed the question mark which industrialists saw whenever he looked north". He said that industrial estates were springing up near motorways in the East Midlands, Midlands and the North and that there was a trend for developers to take estates nearer to strategic motorway sites rather than near labour supply, thus making the work force travel farther to work.

Schiller[8] made a study of industrial rents in which a comparison was made of rent points of a group near motorways with a group of others. He concluded that rent points near motorways tend to be higher than non-motorway rent points but that there was no evidence that the motorway group experienced a faster overall rental growth between 1965 and 1978. Roughly three times out of four he found that a motorway opening which had significant impact on the accessibility of a town was followed by a 2 year period of growth faster than for the surrounding region but that this was short-lived and followed by 2 years' below-average growth.

The relative effect of the recession on property near motorways and elsewhere in the Midlands was indicated by Robert Golding in the *Birmingham Post* for 12 August 1980. Basing his comments on studies by chartered surveyors Debenham Tewson and Chinnocks he wrote that "confidence in industrial property in the West Midlands is dropping except for the area bounded by the M6, M5 and M42."

Once again there appears to be only limited research material available on which to make an objective assessment of the influence of motorways in a particular area of economic interest.

Commercial traffic

In 1971 Wilson[9] estimated that about one tenth of the gross national product was paid out in freight for inland surface transport, and of this some 90% was accounted for by road transport (the percentage in terms of tons and ton-miles was a little lower). The proportion of freight traffic travelling by road was between 80 and 90% 10 years later and some 15% of all-goods vehicle-kilometrage and 23% of heavy-goods vehicle-kilometrage was travelled on the motorway network. The importance of the motorways to commercial traffic is thus considerable and Wilson argued that the railways could not provide an economic or practical substitute for the motorways. As most merchandise transits are of 100 miles or under he said that "both the tradesman's van and the heavy lorry find that it pays in every sense to use the motorways for relatively short distances." As a consequence of the reduction in running times brought about by use of the motorways then in existence, which had often been 30% or more, charges had been contained at a lower level, productivity of manpower utilisation of both infrastructure and vehicle had been better planned, safety had been increased and service improved.

Some evidence for the savings in journey time by commercial traffic as a result of the development of the motorway network was provided in a study in 1965 of a group of companies in the West Midlands.[10] Details were obtained of journeys by goods vehicles from the companies' factories, and shortest journey times by routes which would have been possible if motorways had not been available were compared with the shortest journey times which could be achieved using motorway networks at various stages of development. The results suggested that savings in journey time of between 15 and 18% could have been achieved by the companies if the 1980 motorway network had been available to them.

In 1972 Pearson[11] gave some views of hauliers on the value to them of the motorways then available. It was claimed that motorways had helped to contain rising costs; time savings meant that drivers could return to base for a load rather than waste time looking for a return load; and unloading could often be fitted into a day's work. One company said that motorway development had improved transit times between ports and their depot in the Midlands. Another had found that the M4 enabled management to make lightning visits to check their depots.

Motorways and agriculture

According to Hughes[12] the 1,300 miles of motorway in 1980 covered some 40,000 acres of land, giving a land-take of some 30 acres per mile, most of which was in agricultural use. A detailed assessment of the land-take of a total of 28 miles of some sections of the M11 and M40 by Hearne et al.[13] suggested that the amount of land taken by new motorways was unlikely to exceed 40 acres per mile and the amount of agricultural land taken was unlikely to be more than 35 acres per mile. These authors reported that as a result of urban development some 40,000 acres were being transferred from agricultural to urban use annually. This means in the light of Hughes' figures that the total loss to agriculture in the course of 20 years as a result of building the motorways had only been about the same as that lost annually to urban use. As a result of their analysis, Hearne et al. concluded that the road building programme, which in 1976/77 included some 100 miles of high class road per annum, should not be halted on land-take grounds alone.

One of the problems arising from the building of motorways in rural areas is that of land severance. This occurs when part of a farm is cut off from the rest by the motorway and the question arises of access across the motorway between the two areas. Such access is provided by bridges over the motorway or by "under-creeps" under the motorway.

The importance of severance has been studied by Boddington et al.[14] with the object of "making available the type of information and analytical framework which will enable both government officials and individual farmers to better in-form the Secretaries of State for the Environment and Transport about the severance on any section of new road." They evolved a methodology in which the cost of severance was equated with the cost of extra movement that men, machines and animals have to make to reach severed lands. These extra travel costs depend on

—the amount of land severed
—the extra return trip distance necessary to gain access to the severed land
—the number of trips per acre needed to perform the tasks of husbandry associated with the enterprises practised upon the severed land
—the speed of travel
—the current costs of labour and machinery in the agricultural industry.

Examples of the use of the methodology were given by Boddington et al. and also by Hearne and van Rest[15] and it was concluded by these authors that

(1) severance costs for arable farmers are unlikely to be high except in extreme circumstances
(2) severance costs for dairy farmers will be much higher for all areas of land severed and all return trip travel distances.

A small sample study of farm disturbance due to the construction of a new road[13] indicated that disturbance during construction was far more upsetting than the nuisance created by the road once in use. (This conclusion evidently con-flicted with other work by Frost et al.[16]) The single most important disturbance was that of inadequate drainage reinstatement. The most important post-construction problem was that of compensation payment, particularly the length of time taken by the administrative procedures involved in reaching settlements, and it has been reported[1] that the cost to the farmer has not always been met by the compensation paid to the farmer.

Factors affecting the degree of economic impact on any individual farm unit have been identified as including the following.[13]

(1) The most vulnerable farms are those with a small area intensively worked near the economic margin.
(2) Motorway junctions can bring extra problems of land-take and severance difficulties.
(3) Land loss becomes critical at the 10% level.
(4) Severe severance problems can be damaging but these are not so frequent.
(5) The need for a change in farm system will very likely push the income of any unit on to a lower level.

A guide for the benefit of county secretaries of the National Farmers' Union was prepared in 1976[17] which explained the various stages of planning and construction of new roads, how farms may be affected and what can be done to minimise the possible adverse effects. The guide was largely based on the practical experiences of farmers who had been faced with road construction across their land.

Environmental and social aspects

Reference has been made in earlier chapters, especially those describing actual motorway schemes, to the increasing concern as the motorway programme progressed with environmental and social issues arising from the building of motorways and, indeed, other new roads. Identification of these issues and the investigation and examination of ways of including them in the assessment of road schemes, particularly motorways, were prominent in the work of both the Urban Motorways Project Team[18] and of the Leitch Committee.[2] Gwilliam and Wilson[1] provided a brief summary of some of the main changes in the first 20 years of British motorways in: concern for the environment; effects on property; noise, vibration and pollution; visual impact and severance; and accessibility. They pointed out for example that householders affected by compulsory purchase of their property are usually unwilling sellers, and before the Land Compensation Act 1973 there was no possibility of offering compensation above the market value received and that at which those householders would become willing sellers; the Act now goes some way to bridging this gap. In introductory remarks on their paper[1] Wilson suggested that probably a little over half of owner-occupiers might be satisfied with the normal market price and compensation for their property, but he thought also that some 15% probably remained uncompensatable.

As has been remarked earlier, it is in urban areas that motorways have given rise particularly to environmental and social problems; the minimising of those problems has involved in some cases substantial extra expenditure on construction. In discussing the evaluation of urban motorway schemes Pearce and Nash[19] have argued that, because motorway schemes are likely to have a substantial environmental impact, a full comparison should be made of such schemes with alternative solutions which are likely to have a lower environmental impact. Included in their argument is the suggestion that urban motorway schemes contain systematic equity biases which should be allowed for. They suggest that: user benefits mainly accrue to out-of-town residents; that the motorway will cause a shift from public to private transport; and that motorways tend to be routed through areas of relatively low value. In consequence they thought that equity effects are likely to be biased against the relatively low income groups.

Pearce and Nash were concerned with estimating possible results of building a motorway in Southampton. The actual effects of building five major road schemes in the London area, including one motorway, which had been studied by a research team from Surrey University, were reported by Judy Hillman in the *Guardian* of 26 September 1974. She observed that although a new road cuts a swathe through the existing neighbourhood, within 5 years people adjust to its arrival. The centre of the neighbourhood moves back from the road allowing people to have as rich a life as before.

The accident record of motorways is discussed in chapter 11 and it is clear that personal injury accident rates are appreciably less on motorways than on all-purpose roads, but that when an accident does occur on a motorway there is a high probability of death occurring.

Accidents involving heavier vehicles are more likely to be serious than those between light vehicles. In the search for economy in use the trends in lorry design are towards vehicles which are larger and which are capable of carrying larger payloads. On the other hand in the interests of fuel-saving the trend in car design is towards smaller vehicles. This tendency towards a polarisation in size between goods vehicles and cars could have serious consequences so far as accidents on motorways are concerned where speeds are high, although a mitigating factor could occur if motorists adjusted their speeds downwards in the interests of fuel economy.

Accessibility

Gwilliam and Wilson[1] used journey time as an indicator of accessibility and gave examples of the change over 20 years that the improved road network had had on journeys from London and from Manchester (the effect of motorways alone could not be isolated from changes to all-purpose roads). Their results suggested for example that, whereas a 4 hour car journey from London in 1959 might have reached as far as Derby, in 1979 it would probably have reached well to the north of Leeds; and a 4 hour journey from Manchester in 1959 which might have reached as far as Gloucester, would in 1979 probably have reached Exeter.

Increased accessibility had been seen as a factor affecting leisure travel for instance by making places like the Lake District much more accessible to travellers from Manchester and the Midlands. Gwilliam and Wilson commented that this increased accessibility had brought problems to areas like the Lake District by putting pressure on their amenities and imposing certain social costs in consequence.

The forecasting of the effects of highway improvement on traffic to holiday and recreational areas has been studied by Gordon and Edwards[20] and by Edwards and Vinden[21] with particular reference to trips to the West Country. Completion of the M5 to Exeter and improvements to the A38 from Exeter to Plymouth were forecast to yield: well over 1 million extra visitors to the South West Region[19]; 7% more day trip visitors to Dartmoor[20]; and between 0.5 million and 0.75 million day visitors to the North Somerset Coast.[20] There do not appear to be any published data to show whether those forecasts have been borne out since completion of the M5.

Some policy issues

There are many questions that can be asked about the policies adopted by Governments towards motorways and some were raised in 1976 in a consultation document on transport policy.[22] Examples of some specific policy issues concerning motorways might include the following.

—Has the motorway programme been justified?
—Has the level of investment in motorways been adequate?
—Have motorways a future in urban areas?
—Would further development of the strategic motorway network be more satisfactory than piecemeal local improvements such as by-passes?

It is very difficult to reach satisfactory answers to questions of this sort, largely because adequate data on which to attempt answers are not available.

Travel demand

There has undoubtedly been a big increase in private motoring over the past 25 years. In 1955 there were some 3.6 million private cars and vans licensed in the UK and by 1979 this number had increased to 14.9 million. The growth in the number of goods vehicles from 1.1 million to 1.8 million was less spectacular but the size of goods vehicles increased appreciably. The capacity of the road system to meet the demand for travel was judged to be inadequate in 1957[23] and so without the improvements to the road system, particularly the addition of high-capacity motorways and other dual carriageways, congestion would have been severe. It is of course possible that traffic would not have increased so much if the extra capacity had not been supplied, but this would have meant that the desire of people to have their own means of transport would have been frustrated to some extent.

The desire for private transport is reflected in the growth in number of driving licences held, in the way ownership of cars in households has increased and by the amount of household income that is devoted to the use and maintenance of vehicles. The number of driving licences increased by over twice between 1960 and 1980 to a total of about 24 million. In 1961, 69% of households did not have regular use of a car but by 1979 this percentage had fallen to 42.[24] Car ownership per head was 0.25 in 1975 and is forecast to increase to between 0.37 and 0.42 by the year 2000[25] so that, although there has been a cut-back in road-building programmes at the present time, demand for private travel is expected to grow appreciably in the next 20 years. Data obtained in Government Family Expenditure Surveys show that whereas in 1959 about 1.6% of household expenditure (net of income tax and insurance) was spent on buying motor vehicles, by 1979 this had risen to about 5.1%. Similarly the expenditure on maintaining and running vehicles increased from some 3.3% of expenditure in 1959 to about 6% in 1979. Furthermore, whereas the proportion spent on buying vehicles fell after the oil crisis of 1973, the proportion spent on using vehicles remained fairly constant.

Assessments

The arguments in the report of the Advisory Committee on Trunk Road Assessment and in reports by that Committee's successor, the Standing Advisory Committee on Trunk Road Assessment, have shown that there is no single criterion which can be applied in assessing the worth of a motorway proposal and that many factors, some of which are highly subjective, have to be taken into account. Judged solely on economic criteria it appears that the motorway programme so far has been worthwhile,[1] but information with which to judge whether the right projects have been selected, even on those criteria, is not available. Furthermore, there has been insufficient research carried out (or at any rate published), e.g. by before and after studies, to attempt to assess directly what effects the motorways have had on the economy and on environmental and social conditions generally.

A similar difficulty arises in any attempt to assess whether there should have been a greater proportion of public funds devoted to motorways at the expense of other public investment. This was a matter to which the Leitch Committee[2] also addressed itself as far as comparability of investment in road and rail was concerned. They recommended that "Where direct alternatives arise between road and rail schemes the competing solutions should be compared using cost benefit within the broader framework we have discussed" and that "Strategic or policy studies conducted to compare the rates of return from investment in road and rail should be conducted on the basis of cost benefit analysis, within the framework, rather than financial appraisal."

It is perhaps worth pointing out that the expenditure on building motorways averaged out over the first 20 years at some £200 million per year at 1980 prices[12] or something under £4 per year per head of population.

Urban areas

The complexity of living and working in large urban areas is well known but satisfactory solutions to those problems are hard to find. Studies of several kinds have been made of these areas and it is clear that resolving transport problems must figure largely in any improvement to city life. Issues such as the introduction of road pricing, more extensive traffic management schemes and investment in public transport, as well as the building of new roads including motorways, have been and continue to be debated. Some cities, e.g. Glasgow, have adopted urban motorways as a basis for solving some of their transport problems; others such as Liverpool have contemplated similar action but then rejected it. It would be a valuable guide to the effectiveness of such policies if studies, some of which have been made in Glasgow, were undertaken on a wider scale. It is clear that environmental and social factors are much more important in relation to urban motorways than to those in rural areas, and attempts to compare investment in rural and urban motorways are bound to be affected by the subjective nature of some of the assessments which have to be made. It is also clear that investment in motorways in urban areas is much more expensive than in rural areas although urban motorways can sometimes be fitted into more comprehensive schemes of urban renewal.

New roads to by-pass urban communities have been successful not only in relieving congestion but also in improving amenity, particularly where heavy lorry traffic has been concerned. Motorways have undoubtedly proved valuable in this respect and the argument as to whether all-purpose by-passes specifically designed to by-pass local areas are a more efficient use of resources than the building of motorways as a system is one which does not seem to have been researched in depth. It is interesting to look at arguments put forward by Governments in relation to these matters.

Strategies

The trunk road programme of the 1960s had as a main objective the establishment of "a much needed basic network of high quality routes—mostly motorways —to provide the vital access between regions and between major cities."[26] The programme also included many smaller schemes to reduce congestion and accidents. In discussing proposals for the 1970s and early 1980s, the Government in 1969 proposed that a substantial part of the roads programme should be concentrated on providing a main system of high class roads to which all important centres of population would or could easily be connected. In addition there would be a sizeable programme of localised improvements in areas with particular problems.

It was argued that benefits derived from isolated improvement schemes were largely confined to the immediate lengths of road concerned and their surroundings, whereas if a route were improved comprehensively along its length, benefits additional to those from drawing traffic away from existing roads arose from concentration of longer-distance traffic on the new route. In support of this it was argued that there was a much higher rate of traffic growth on motorways and comprehensively improved routes than on other inter-urban roads. It was also suggested that the transfer of heavy streams of long-distance traffic facilitated the circulation of local traffic on essential local business.

It was considered that there was "a strong case for basing a future highway strategy on the careful selection of roads for comprehensive improvement rather than upon a series of isolated improvements to the most congested lengths of the trunk road network. It would relieve traffic on these roads but do so as part of a conscious plan to direct the traffic to a more effective network of routes".

During the 1970s Governments and their attitudes towards road programmes changed. Much of the change can be attributed to the economic problems stemming from the oil crisis of 1973, but concern for the environment as it was affected by roads and traffic and for problems in urban areas also played an important part in changing policy. Substantial cuts were made in the level of expenditure on roads and in 1977/78 the Government stated[27] that the strategic network of roads was to be modified and that roads would be improved in phases "dealing with the worst stretches first and varying the standard of a road throughout its length to reflect the different degree of use." It was envisaged that "building to a lower standard on some stretches would save money which could then be spent on more bypasses to relieve hard-pressed towns and villages." The Government at that time also decided to favour investment in bus and rail at the expense of roads and to require that road proposals should be conceived in a wider planning and environmental context.

In *Policy for roads: England 1978*[28] it was stated that "the abandonment of a policy of comprehensive improvement of whole routes means that for a number of schemes improvements more limited than those originally envisaged will be adequate". However, as a result of a review of schemes in progress "it was clear that the current top priorities—the M25 round London, the main industrial routes and routes to the ports—must remain unchanged."

The next Government's *Policy for roads: England 1980*[29] continued the reduced programme of expenditure on roads; "spending will be stabilised at roughly the level reached after the massive cuts of the previous administration." Construction of the M25 and of orbital motorways round Manchester and south of Birmingham was to continue together with a few other important routes, but then emphasis would be placed on fitting in "as many by-passes as possible" with priority being given to removing traffic from historic towns and rural communities at the expense of some major projects.

M25

The M25 orbital motorway round London when completed will form part of the strategic network of motorways in Britain and will also by-pass many small towns and villages. An excellent opportunity thus exists to investigate several of the policy issues which have just been described.

References

1. GWILLIAM K.M. and WILSON R.L. Social and economic effects of motorways. *Proceedings of the conference on 20 years of British motorways.* Institution of Civil Engineers, London, 1980.
2. DEPARTMENT OF TRANSPORT. *Report of the Advisory Committee on Trunk Road Assessment.* HMSO, London, 1977.
3. COBURN T.M. *Rural motorways.* Road Research Laboratory, Harmondsworth, report LN/787/TMC, 1965 (unpublished).
4. GWILLIAM K.M. and JUDGE M.J. The M62 and trans-Pennine movement 1970–77: Implications for regional and transport planning. *Proceedings of the Regional Studies Association conference on transport and the regions.* Regional Studies Association, London, 1978.
5. DODGSON J.S. *Motorway investment, industrial transport costs and sub-regional growth: a case study of the M62.* Regional studies 8. Pergamon Press, Oxford, 1974.
6. THORNTON P. and WHEELOCK V. *Roads: the price of development?* University of Bradford, 1978.
7. BRITISH ROAD FEDERATION. *Better roads for a better economy.* British Road Federation, London, 1978.
8. SCHILLER R. *The effect of motorways on industrial rents.* Hillier Parker Rent Index Research Report no. 2. Investors Chronicle, London, 1979.
9. WILSON SIR R. Commercial views. *Proceedings of the conference on motorways in Britain.* Institution of Civil Engineers, London, 1971.
10. BRITISH ROAD FEDERATION. *Motorways and industry. A report of a study at the University of Newcastle upon Tyne.* British Road Federation, London, 1968.
11. PEARSON G.A. Are hauliers getting value from motorways? *Roadway*, June, 1972.
12. HUGHES T.P. Roads policy at national, regional and local levels and the role of the motorways. *Proceedings of the conference on 20 years of British motorways.* Institution of Civil Engineers, London, 1980.
13. HEARNE A. *et al.* The physical and economic impact of motorways on agriculture. *Int. J. Environ. Studies*, 1977, **11**, No. 1, 29–33.
14. BODDINGTON M.A.B. *et al. Motorways and agriculture: severance.* Rural Planning Services no. 5. Rural Planning Services, Horner, Ipsden, Oxon, 1978.
15. HEARNE A.S. and van REST D.J. Farming considerations in highway assessment. *The Highway Engineer*, 1979, **26**, no. 7.

16. FROST S. *et al.* A survey on the impact of motorways on agriculture. *Int. J. Environ. Studies*, 1976, **9**, No. 3, 169–175.

17. BELL M. *et al. Motorway, trunk road development and the farmer.* Wolfson Study Group, University of Aston/National Farmers' Union, Birmingham, 1977.

18. DEPARTMENT OF THE ENVIRONMENT. *Report of the Urban Motorways Project Team.* HMSO, London, 1973.

19. PEARCE D. and NASH C. The evaluation of urban motorway schemes: a case study —Southampton. *Urban studies*, 1973, **10**, no. 2.

20. GORDON I.R. and EDWARDS S.L. Holiday trip generation. *J. Transp. Economics and Policy*, 1973, **7**, no. 2.

21. EDWARDS S.L. and VINDEN C.A. Recreation trip attraction. *Traffic Engineering and Control*, 1973, **14**, no. 11.

22. DEPARTMENT OF THE ENVIRONMENT. *Transport policy: a consultation document.* Vol. 1. HMSO, London, 1976.

23. INSTITUTION OF CIVIL ENGINEERS. *Proceedings of the conference on the highway needs of Great Britain.* Institution of Civil Engineers, London, 1957.

24. DEPARTMENT OF TRANSPORT, WELSH OFFICE and SCOTTISH DEVELOPMENT DEPARTMENT. *Transport statistics: Great Britain 1969–1979.* HMSO, London, 1980.

25. DEPARTMENT OF TRANSPORT. *National road traffic forecasts.* Department of Transport, London, 1980.

26. MINISTRY OF TRANSPORT. *Roads for the future.* HMSO, London, 1969.

27. DEPARTMENT OF TRANSPORT, SCOTTISH DEVELOPMENT DEPARTMENT and WELSH OFFICE. *Transport policy.* HMSO, London, 1977.

28. DEPARTMENT OF TRANSPORT. *Policy for roads: England, 1978.* HMSO, London, 1978.

29. DEPARTMENT OF TRANSPORT. *Policy for roads: England, 1980.* HMSO, London, 1980.

Index

Printed in the United States
153622LV00005B/11/A

9 780727 701596